VIOLENCE BEHIND BARS

AN EXPLOSIVE REPORT ON PRISON RIOTS IN THE UNITED STATES

VERNON FOX

GREENWOOD PRESS, PUBLISHERS
WESTPORT, CONNECTICUT

Library of Congress Cataloging in Publication Data

Fox, Vernon Brittain, 1916–
   Violence behind bars.

    Reprint of the ed. published by Vantage Press,
New York.
    1. Prison riots--United States. I. Title.
HV9471.F65 1973   365'.641   73-13414
ISBN 0-8371-7131-8

Originally published in 1956 by Vantage Press, New York

Reprinted with the permission of Vernon Fox

Reprinted in 1973 by Greenwood Press,
a division of Williamhouse-Regency Inc.

Library of Congress Catalogue Card Number 73-13414

ISBN 0-8371-7131-8

Printed in the United States of America

To Laura, my wife, and to Haydn, my brother,
who enjoy turbulence considerably less than I

Foreword

I know of no serious social problem about which less clear, constructive thinking has been done than the one dealt with in this book. The story of a prison riot, placed in the hands of our agencies of communication, usually sets off an explosive chain reaction of political scapegoating and public hand-wringing which soon shifts the focus of attention from the drama inside to the one outside the prison walls. This sleight of hand may or may not tell us something worth knowing about the general treatment of our prisoners. It may or may not inform us of the strengths and weaknesses of our political structure. But the confusion which it creates is so complete that the serious student of penology, not to mention the newspaper-reading public, finds it next to impossible to keep his eye on the thing he is trying to observe and study.

There is another reason why prison riots have remained relatively unexplored and unexplained. The emotional overtones of the word and deed, *riot*, too easily drown out the quiet voice of reason. *Riot* speaks of hatreds dammed up beyond the point of human containment and spilling over in mass hysteria, mayhem, murder, and unbelievably wanton destruction. It brings to mind the hours and days of awful suspense when the finger of death is publicly pointed at innocent men by a handful of public prisoners. It tells of the soul-deadening effect of living under watching eyes, and the eternal boredom of a cramped society of men without normal resources for thought and action.

Most of us are dependent upon the press, radio, and grass-roots sources of information and enlightenment. Since none of these is noteworthy for its avoidance of the political or emotional implications of a given subject, we are in danger of foundering in both the political and the semantic sense, when trying to think through our civic responsibilities in this matter. Because of the traditional pattern of riot-reporting, it has become axiomatic for many of us that there is a direct causal relationship between prison riots and too strict or unjust disciplinary practices. A popular corollary to this is that these practices can usually be traced back to the popular whipdogs, political inadequacy and corruption. Many of the readers of this book are due for an experience halfway between surprise and shock at having this dogma dispelled and a common-sense explanation revealed which is not only infinitely simpler but which seems to be administratively practical.

In this rather brief presentation of what I see to be Dr. Vernon Fox's thesis, perhaps I am giving the impression that he has brewed a patent medicine to cure the ills which many conscientious wardens and public servants could not cure; or that clear thinking is peculiar to the scientific-minded. Not so. He has done what I believe to be a particularly diligent job of observing, and using the sharp instruments of his trade, has succeeded in slicing away much of the tissue of emotionally loaded half-truths which usually surround the subject. In so doing, he has achieved a degree of insight for which I am personally grateful, and which I believe should be in the public domain.

I know of no one better qualified to speak on the subject than the author of this book. In the many years since his first arrival as a student at the Starr Commonwealth for Boys, I have watched him rise from disheartening circumstances to adult professional status. He has brought with him a sense of humility and a devotion to his ideal of justice.

I was in close touch with Vernon as he felt his way through the difficult negotiation of terms with prisoners during the notorious Michigan State Prison riot in 1952. He carried the leading role in that terrible event, for three reasons: first, as psychologist for that institution he had established rapport with many of the inmates; second, he knew that the lives of several guards were at stake, and his sense of responsibility pushed him to the fore; third, he is a brave man.

I believe that the reader's appreciation of this book will be enhanced by the image which I have of its author walking alone and unarmed into cell-block fifteen of the State Prison at Jackson, which had been rioting for days. Into a mob of glaring, grumbling, snarling prisoners he carried the thought of his wife and three children, and the very realistic question as to whether he would be alive five minutes hence. Voices were heard in the background, shouting, "Get him! Get him! Get him! Don't let him pull none of that psychology stuff on us! Get him!" But he walked through them to the stronghold of the leaders, offering them concessions and a steak dinner, and set in motion the wheels of orderly system, where chaos had been before.

FLOYD STARR

President, Starr Commonwealth for Boys
Albion, Michigan
August 23, 1955

Preface

This book had to be written. It had to be written to help me comprehend and understand objectively what happened during and after the Michigan riot of 1952. After ten years of conscientious and respected effort, indelibly recorded, toward a better corrections system in Michigan and after contributing to the successful termination of what has been considered to be unquestionably the most dangerous riot in prison history, becoming a political issue without knowing anything about politics was a surprising event to me. This book had to be written to help me understand what happened.

How so many people could draw so complete conclusions on so little basis when they were so far from the tension, and then crusade so intensely for social action so incongruent with good prison management was an intriguing matter. I wanted to survey an area where attitudes, opinions, hatreds, loyalties, political interests, self-interests, grudges, prestige, and fears were facts that became more important than the original overt facts inherent in the violence. I was amazed how so inextricably intertwined could fact and fancy become, and had to examine it further.

To learn of other prison riots and violence, I examined past issues of the *New York Times, London Times, St. Louis Post-Dispatch*, and many other newspapers to a lesser extent. The subject of prison riots and violence is unorganized, and accurate data are difficult to find. The microfilming process as applied to back issues of newspapers saved hours and hours of time. Other materials came from correspondence with friends, acquaintances, and proper officials. Inmates of the prison system of Michigan have been of utmost help in giving general background for my better understanding of the total picture.

A major share of appreciation goes to Joe B. Dellinger and to Miss Joann Volakakis. Joe, now Chief of the Section of Alcohol Studies in Maryland's Department of Health, was group therapist at the State Prison of Southern Michigan at the time of the riot. Joe supported me when support was needed, and stood up to be counted when to do so was to his immediate disadvantage. Joann was supervisor of the Research and Selection office at the prison, and is now Executive Secretary to the Dean of the School of Business at Florida State University. Joann supported me similarly and, not only that, Joann typed much of the first draft of this book. My appreciation also goes to many other loyal friends, many now in other positions, some still at the prison.

Appreciation of a different sort goes to Ray E. Hibbs and Dr. Coyle E. Moore. Ray E. Hibbs of Ray E. Hibbs & Associates, management consultants in Toledo, Ohio, gave me valuable experience in a field of interest different from penology and I prize his friendship. Dr. Coyle E. Moore, Dean of the School of Social Welfare at the Florida State University, assisted me in making the transition from prison to university life, and I hold him and his practicality in highest esteem. So frequently has appreciation been expressed that it comes almost as a matter of course to "Uncle Floyd" Starr, who trained me as a boy in his school, counseled with me in later problems, assisted me in selecting from among employment possibilities after the riot, and wrote the Foreword for this book.

My experience in the riot and after is the only experience of that sort anywhere, and I am fortunate to have been privileged to have it. Any weaknesses in this book can be attributed to my own shortcomings in the ability to perceive and to accurately record the events as they happened and my inability to interpret their meanings. The book stands on its own strength. I cannot add further to it. May God help us see the light as He would have us see it.

                                                        VERNON FOX

Tallahassee, Florida
August 15, 1955

Contents

CHAPTER I

The Pattern of Prison Riots

First came prisons—then came prison riots. They came together, about a century and a half ago. The earliest prison riot I know of was reported from Connecticut in 1774. Connecticut was just beginning in the prison business at that time. The earliest prison disturbance I have discovered in Michigan, where I began learning about prisons, was one in which a deputy warden was "almost killed" on August 16, 1843. The prison had opened behind a wall of tamarack poles in 1837.

There will never be a complete and exhaustive study of prison riots because prison riots are hard to find. Warden Bannan commented in 1952 that some of the disturbances they were having at the State Prison of Southern Michigan would be considered "riots" in normal times, but at that time they were not newsworthy. He added that one time in the Michigan Reformatory at Ionia there was a pretty good riot and "I was picking pea soup out of my ears for a week," but that riot was never reported in the newspapers. I happened to be in the state office of the prison division of the highway department of a Southern state one morning in 1953 when the man behind the desk was on the telephone receiving information and giving orders and policy regarding how to handle an "incident" in one of the road camps, which locally was called a riot. The "incident" never appeared in the newspapers.

It is not to the advantage of a prison administration to let it be known that a riot has occurred. Most prisons are so closely associated with politics that a riot is likely to have some political implications. Frequently, a riot is reported or newspapers are notified only when it is so serious and of such moment that information would leak out anyway. It is reported when the withholding of such information would cause repercussions, political or otherwise. There is no way of telling how many prison riots there have been. There is no way of knowing what proportion of these riots were reported to the public through the newspapers and radio and other means of communication.

There have been errors in judgment in withholding information about riots. For instance, the Sing Sing authorities concealed the existence of rioting for some time prior to the release of a prisoner in 1913, who took the occasion to report the fact that "much fighting" had taken place within the walls for several months. An inquiry into the situation resulted in confirmation of the ex-prisoner's reports, a change of administration, and modification of prison policies. Had the prison been farther away from New York City, where large newspapers and news centers are located, probably the existence of riots would never have been made public information.

The effectiveness of reporting, number of newspapers, contacts with media of communication, and the public interest in big-name criminals may also have had their effect on reporting of riots. It would appear significant that most of the early riots reported to the public were either in New York or in the federal prison system. Any riots from other states were usually relegated to page 26 or thereabouts under the heading, "disturbance." On occasions, also, when a riot has not been directly reported, the political action "as a result of the recent disturbance" has been.

The 1922 outbreak at the Banner mining camp in Alabama, in which $10,000 worth of machinery was dynamited, was called to public attention by the return of the whipping strap to Alabama and consideration of abolishing the system whereby convicts were leased to private operators for labor. It may further be noted that, with the nation-wide improvement of news reporting, media of communication, and wire services, prison riots are now reported from most areas of the country, with New York and the federal prison system being credited with but a proportionate share.

One would think that major riots anywhere in the country would be reported. Whether or not the "pea soup riot" at Ionia to which Warden Bannan referred was "major" is difficult to tell. Certainly, it was not sufficiently "major" to attract newspaper attention. On the other hand, little incidents like escape plots have made headlines all over the country. Leavenworth in 1921, for instance, made headlines when a plot to blow up a section of the wall was discovered. Even Ionia, to which Bannan referred, made such headlines with escape attempts several times. One almost unique plot was discovered at Ionia on June 24, 1929, when an inmate self-styled chemist made nitroglycerine from glycerine stolen from the reformatory's soap factory to blow out a section of wall.

Escape plots are discovered frequently in most prisons throughout the land and cause nothing more exciting than a few choice words in the deputy warden's office. The more minor disturbances either go by unnoticed by the public or are reported as they are interpreted by the prison administration.

Whether a riot is reported, then, appears to be dependent upon a variety of factors, including (1) the magnitude of the group participating, (2) the intensity of the participation, i.e., whether it was a plot or a massacre, (3) the proximity of the prison to metropolitan centers where big newspapers are looking for news, and from which "big-name criminals" are received, (4) the activity of the news reporters, (5) the solidarity or factionalism of the political situation within the state as it manifests itself in the prison, and (6) the policies of the prison administration with regard to reporting to the public.

Disturbances have been reported in the news as (1) plots to riot or escape, (2) strikes, (3) mass escapes, (4) fights among prisoners, and (5) violent defiance of the authority of the prison officials. Plots to riot or escape occur so frequently and are unreported to such an extent that they present a unique problem in gathering information and analyzing it. Mass escapes that do not involve direct aggression against a member of the prison administration present another unique situation. Consequently, in the searching for a pattern in rioting, these plots and nonaggressive mass escapes have not been considered. Our interest in riots concerns mass escapes when guards are attacked, fights among prisoners, and violent defiance of prison authority.

The "patterns" of riots as discussed here are based on some of the riots which have been recorded in the past hundred years. Of the more than 200 prison riots and disturbances easily identified in the past century, only about three dozen were reported between 1850 and 1900. With an increasing number of prisons and prisoners, there is a proportionate increase in the number of prison riots. Further, with better news reporting and media of communication, fewer such disturbances escape public notice. The disturbances and riots which have been examined to learn their patterns are as follows:

Nov.	27, 1855	Sing Sing
Nov.-Dec.	1856	Charlestown, Massachusetts
Jan.	19, 1857	Auburn
Mar.	7, 1857	Auburn
May	10, 1857	Sing Sing
May	13, 1870	Sing Sing
Aug.	15, 1870	Wethersfield, Connecticut
Feb.	16, 1871	Sing Sing
July	12, 1871	Charlestown, Massachusetts
Nov.	1, 1871	Ohio
Nov.	28, 1873	Auburn
Nov.	29, 1873	Clarksville, Arkansas
Sept.	25, 1873	Trenton, New Jersey
June	3, 1874	Missouri
Jan.	15, 1877	Westborough Reform School Riot

Oct.	8, 1877	Blackwell's Island Revolt
May	26, 1880	Passaic County Jail
Nov.	12, 1880	Dartmoor, England
June	25, 1882	Western Pennsylvania Penitentiary Strike
July	6, 1882	New Hampshire State Prison
Feb.	21, 1883	Missouri Penitentiary
Feb.	20, 1883	Sing Sing
July	18, 1885	Kings County Penitentiary
Oct.	6, 1885	Kansas and Gulf Shore
July	16, 1886	Kings County Penitentiary
Sept.	20, 1886	Trenton State Prison, New Jersey
Dec.	10, 1889	Leavenworth (female prisoners)
Mar.	30, 1890	Trenton State Prison, New Jersey
Aug.	8, 1890	Charleston State Prison
Sept.	14, 1891	San Quentin
Feb.	4, 1892	Deer Island (Boston)
Oct.	13, 1892	Huntingdon Reformatory
Dec.	27, 1894	Ohio State Penitentiary
Apr.	21, 1895	Ludlow Street Jail
June	1, 1898	Leavenworth
Nov.	7, 1901	Leavenworth
Mar.	15, 1912	Nebraska State Penitentiary
Apr.	25, 1912	Sing Sing
June	10, 1912	San Quentin
Aug.	22, 1912	Dayton, Ohio
Sept.	1–6, 1912	Michigan
July	23, 1913	Sing Sing
Apr.	22, 1914	Sing Sing
July	8, 1914	Blackwell's Island
Mar.	15, 1915	Hart's Island Reformatory
July	3, 1915	Sing Sing
Sept.	12, 1915	Bronx County Jail
Dec.	29, 1915	Kansas State Penitentiary
Apr.	1, 1916	Bronx County Jail
June	5, 1917	Joliet, Illinois

Feb.	7, 1919	Leavenworth
Apr.	21, 1919	Leavenworth
June	15, 1919	Clinton State Prison, Dannemora
July	22, 1919	Leavenworth
Aug.	4, 1919	Connecticut State Prison
Jan.	2, 1920	Bedford Reformatory for Girls
Oct.	5, 1920	Leavenworth
Sept.	18, 1923	Banner coal mining camp, Alabama
Feb.	18, 1925	San Quentin
Jan.	25, 1926	Portonville Prison, London, England
Apr.	9, 1926	Tennessee State Penitentiary
June	26, 1926	Bucharest, Roumania
July	10, 1926	Kansas State Penitentiary
July	18, 1926	Cook County Jail
Aug.	9, 1926	Michigan Reformatory, Ionia (25 inmates force officers in cells and escape)
June	21, 1927	Kansas State Penitentiary
Sept.	29, 1927	French Naval Prison, Toulon
Nov.	24, 1927	Folsom Prison, California
June	27, 1928	Elmira Reformatory
July	1, 1928	Atlanta Jail, Georgia
Sept.	9, 1928	Louisiana State Penitentiary
Oct.	2, 1928	Wynne State Prison Farm, Texas (Huntsville)
Nov.	4, 1928	Clements State Prison Farm, Brazoria, Texas
Jan.	13, 1929	Philadelphia County Prison, Homsburg
Jan.	19, 1929	Mexico City Prison of Balem
May	1929	Massachusetts
June	20, 1929	Clements State Prison Farm
July	23, 1929	Clinton Prison at Dannemora
July	28, 1929	Auburn
Aug.	1, 1929	Leavenworth

Aug.	5, 1929	Angola Prison Farm, Louisiana
Aug.	6, 1929	Kansas State Penitentiary
Aug.	15, 1929	Lielge Prison, Poland
Oct.	3, 1929	Colorado State Prison
Oct.	13, 1929	Oakalla Jail, Vancouver, B.C.
Nov.	14, 1929	Tammisaaris Prison, Helsingfors, Finland
Dec.	11, 1929	Auburn
Apr.	21, 1930	Ohio State Penitentiary (famous fire in which 335 inmates died)
Apr.	23, 1930	Cuba Prison
Aug.	11, 1930	Tampico City Jail, Mexico
Oct.	25, 1930	Fernando de Noronha Island, Brazil
May	26, 1931	Bilbao Jail, Spain
Aug.	25, 1931	Michigan (physician killed) (Marquette)
Jan.	24, 1932	Dartmoor Prison, England
Jan.	28, 1932	Dartmoor Prison, England
Feb.	20, 1932	Dartmoor Prison, England
Sept.	5, 1932	Buenos Aires Jail, Argentina
Feb.	28, 1933	Canada
May	28, 1933	Manchukuo
Aug.	25, 1934	Pennsylvania
June	20, 1935	Nisek Penitentiary, Yugoslavia
June	27, 1935	Belgrade
June	27, 1935	Sliven Jail, Bulgaria
Aug.	3, 1935	Ploesti Jail, Rumania
Aug.	4, 1935	Palestine
Aug.	13, 1935	Mexico
Dec.	3, 1935	Muskogee Jail, Oklahoma
Jan.	21, 1936	Alcatraz
Mar.	18, 1936	Ocana Prison, Spain
Mar.	28, 1936	Cuba
Apr.	18, 1936	Greece
May	24, 1936	Guantanamo Jail, Cuba
June	18, 1936	Rio de Janeiro Jail

Aug.	29, 1936	Guard killed in DeKalb County, Georgia
Jan.	10, 1937	Manchukuo
Feb.	21, 1937	Mahoning County Jail, Ohio
Apr.	4, 1937	Escape from Cherokee County (Georgia) chain gang
Apr.	22, 1937	Presidio Maria Zelia, Sao Paula
June	4, 1937	Matanzas Jail, Cuba
June	4, 1937	(New York) (sit-down strike)
June	19, 1937	Anderson County Jail (sit-down strike)
July	16, 1937	Texas
Sept.	24, 1937	Alcatraz
Feb.	20, 1938	Nueva Ecija, Philippines
May	23, 1938	Alcatraz
Nov.	20, 1938	Devil's Island
Jan.	13, 1939	Alcatraz
Aug.	1, 1939	Brazil (escape after killing guard)
Aug.	19, 1939	Elmira Reformatory, New York
Sept.	26, 1939	Michigan (40 escape and take 4 officials as hostages) (Marquette)
Nov.	5, 1939	Michigan (6 escape, kill guard) (Jackson)
Nov.	26, 1939	Georgia (7 escape Dougherty County Prison Farm)
Mar.	21, 1940	(New York) (guard killed)
Mar.	25, 1940	Dallas Prison Camp (4 inmates break legs to escape quarry work)
July	21, 1940	Alcatraz
Aug.	28, 1940	Sing Sing
Sept.	2, 1940	Arkansas
Feb.	26, 1941	Chartres Reform School, France
July	20, 1941	Guayaquil, Ecuador
Oct.	20, 1941	Mantinglupa, Philippines
Feb.	16, 1942	San Juan, Puerto Rico
Nov.	8, 1943	Georgia (mass escape)
Nov.	21, 1943	Santo Stefano Island, Italy

Aug.	25, 1944	Duval County, Florida
Nov.	23, 1944	Rome Jail, Italy
Dec.	5, 1944	Federal Penitentiary, Atlanta, Georgia
Mar.	1, 1946	Tennessee Jail
Apr.	22, 1946	San Vittore Jail, Milan, Italy
May	2, 1946	Alcatraz
Sept.	29, 1946	Coiba Island, Panama
Mar.	3, 1947	Acre Prison, Palestine
May	6, 1947	(Federal)
May	13, 1947	Mercedes, Argentina
June	20, 1947	Central Prison, Palestine
July	2, 1947	Calapan, Mindoro, Philippines
July	11, 1947	Georgia, Escape Attempt
Nov.	24, 1947	Wisconsin
Nov.	30, 1947	Acre Prison, Palestine
Jan.	4, 1948	Palestine
Feb.	23, 1948	Mexico City Penitentiary
Mar.	1, 1949	Colombia
May	13, 1949	Tehachapi (women), California
Aug.	3, 1949	Michoacan, Mexico
Oct.	21, 1949	Havana, Cuba
Oct.	22, 1949	Arizona
Nov.	23, 1949	Hakari, Turkey (149 escape)
Feb.	11, 1950	Salem Prison, India
May	28, 1950	Muntinglupa Prison, Philippines
June	9, 1950	Patiala Prison, India
June	21, 1950	Madura Prison, India
July	8, 1950	Michigan (try to use Governor Williams in escape from Marquette)
Oct.	28, 1950	Puerto Rico
Nov.	1, 1950	New Jersey
Nov.	21, 1950	New Mexico State Prison
Jan.	27, 1951	Rio Piedras, Puerto Rico
Feb.	25, 1951	Louisiana (16 inmates cut tendons)
Mar.	24, 1951	Mobile County Jail, Alabama

May	18, 1951	Utah State Prison
May	20, 1951	Utah State Prison
June	26, 1951	Passaic County Jail, New Jersey
July	16, 1951	Colorado State Prison
Aug.	14, 1951	Utah State Prison
Aug.	15, 1951	Oregon
Aug.	18, 1951	(Illinois) Jail
Sept.	16, 1951	Alabama (30 escape after seizing guards)
Oct.	16, 1951	West Virginia
Nov.	22, 1951	Alabama, Kilby Prison
Dec.	26, 1951	Buford Prison, Georgia (30 inmates slash tendons)
Feb.	1, 1952	Muncie Jail, Indiana
Feb.	18, 1952	Koje Island POW Camp
Mar.	10, 1952	South Dakota
Mar.	13, 1952	Koje Island POW Camp
Mar.	29, 1952	Trenton State Prison, New Jersey
Apr.	6-7, 1952	Trenton, New Jersey
Apr.	15, 1952	Trenton State Prison, New Jersey
Apr.	17, 1952	Rahway Prison Farm, New Jersey
Apr.	20, 1952	Michigan
May	4, 1952	Bordeaux Jail, Montreal
May	5, 1952	San Francisco County Jail
May	9, 1952	Koje Island POW Camp
May	12, 1952	Louisiana
May	22, 1952	Australia
May	24, 1952	Idaho State Prison
May	30, 1952	North Carolina
May	30, 1952	Trenton, New Jersey (sit-down)
June	26, 1952	Kentucky
June	27, 1952	Kentucky
July	1, 1952	Soledad Prison, California
July	1, 1952	Concord State Reformatory, Massachusetts
July	6, 1952	Michigan
July	7, 1952	Ontario Reformatory

July	19, 1952	Denver County Jail
July	23, 1952	Charleston State Prison
Aug.	5, 1952	Bordeaux Jail, Montreal
Aug.	30, 1952	Tunis Jail, Africa
Sept.	1952	Chilicothe, Ohio
Sept.	1952	El Reno, Oklahoma
Sept.	22, 1952	Menard State Prison, Illinois
Oct.	2, 1952	Oakalla Prison, British Columbia
Oct.	12, 1952	Trenton, New Jersey
Oct.	24, 1952	Menard State Prison, Illinois
Oct.	28, 1952	Puerto Rico
Nov.	1, 1952	Ohio State Penitentiary
Nov.	1, 1952	Oregon
Nov.	3, 1952	Ohio State Penitentiary
Nov.	18, 1952	Michigan
Dec.	29, 1952	Olmos Prison, La Plata, Argentina
Jan.	16, 1953	Mahara Prison, Ceylon
Jan.	18, 1953	Western State Penitentiary, Pennsylvania
Jan.	19, 1953	Rockview Penitentiary, Pennsylvania
Jan.	19, 1953	Allegheny County, Pennsylvania
Jan.	21, 1953	New Mexico (gang fight)
Feb.	6, 1953	Arizona (strike)
Feb.	9, 1953	Oregon
Feb.	15, 1953	La Princesca Prison, Puerto Rico
Mar.	14, 1953	Uskudar Prison, Turkey
Apr.	11, 1953	Minnesota
May	3, 1953	Eastern State Penitentiary, Pennsylvania
May	9, 1953	Austria
June	15, 1953	New Mexico
July	10, 1953	Oregon
July	13, 1953	Himeji Juvenile Penitentiary, Japan
Aug.	20, 1953	Washington State Penitentiary
Sept.	28, 1953	Charleston State Prison, Massachusetts (escape)

Oct.	2, 1953	Charleston State Prison, Massachusetts (sit-down)
Nov.	14, 1953	Louisiana (17 inmates slash arms)
Jan.	29, 1954	Lincoln, Nebraska
Mar.	2, 1954	Avigliano Reform School, Italy
Mar.	13, 1954	San Marcos Prison, Guatemala
May	3, 1954	Cali Prison, Colombia
May	26, 1954	Wandsworth Prison, England
June	17, 1954	Puerto Boniato Jail, Havana, Cuba
June	23, 1954	Pontiac, Illinois
July	28, 1954	Rome, Italy
Aug.	15, 1954	Kingston, Ontario, Canada
Aug.	21, 1954	Women's Jail, Raleigh, North Carolina
Sept.	22, 1954	Jefferson City, Missouri
Sept.	24, 1954	Women's House of Detention, New York City
Sept.	25, 1954	Chicago, Illinois (jail)
Oct.	11, 1954	South Dakota
Oct.	22, 1954	Jefferson City, Missouri
Nov.	5, 1954	Hippodrome Prison, Sao Paulo, Brazil
Nov.	29, 1954	State Institution for Insane, Trenton, New Jersey
Jan.	8, 1955	Olmos Prison, Eva Peron, Argentina
Jan.	18, 1955	Massachusetts (waiting technique used)
Jan.	22, 1955	Dartmoor, England (hunger strike)
Mar.	27, 1955	Lincoln, Nebraska
Apr.	6, 1955	Raiford, Florida (assistant superintendent killed—not a mass riot)
Apr.	12, 1955	Texas State Prison (sit-down)
Apr.	16, 1955	Rusk State Hospital, Texas
May	6, 1955	Michigan (sit-down)
June	3, 1955	Massachusetts (escape attempt)
July	5, 1955	Walla Walla, Washington

July	11, 1955	Rhode Island (sit-down)
July	12, 1955	Saskatchewan Penitentiary, Canada
July	16, 1955	Wyoming State Penitentiary
July	19, 1955	Nevada State Prison
July	26, 1955	Bexar County Jail, San Antonio, Texas
Aug.	2, 1955	Bexar County Jail, San Antonio, Texas
Aug.	14, 1955	Walla Walla, Washington
Aug.	16, 1955	Nebraska
Aug.	17–18, 1955	Great Meadows, New York
Aug.	18, 1955	Women's Reformatory, Framingham, Massachusetts
Aug.	21–22, 1955	Nebraska
Sept.	9, 1955	Nebraska
Sept.	16, 1955	New Mexico
Sept.	26, 1955	Decatur Camp, Georgia
Oct.	1, 1955	Deer Island Jail, Boston, Massachusetts

The series of prison riots that swept the country in 1912, 1913, 1914, and 1915 were, like those in 1928, 1929, 1930, and 1931, reported most widely in New York and in the federal system. The Michigan riot in 1912 received some note, partially because of the famous Detective Burns entering the prison in disguise and identifying the ringleaders by conversing with the prisoners. While there are very few years in which a prison riot is not reported from some prison, there is a tendency for them to group into definite periods of time. Reasons for this may be a combination of encouragement for aggressive inmates ready to riot to translate their resentment into action just as the others did, and a tendency on the part of prison administrators and newsmen to feature the riots as long as they are occurring elsewhere, too. Riots have occurred in series in 1856–7, 1870–1, 1873–4, 1882–3, 1885–6, 1890–2, 1912–15, 1919–20, 1928–30, 1939–40, 1946–7, and 1949–53.

Examination of these disturbances reveals that the expression of aggression has assumed four rather definite directions. First, the rather harmless strike appears to be a compromise between aggression against the prison administration and the desire to remain in a relatively safe position. The hunger strike appears much more frequently in foreign countries, such as Spain's Bilbao Jail difficulty in 1931, the 1935 difficulties in Palestine and Yugoslavia, and Puerto Rico in 1942. The hunger strike has appeared in America in 1937 in a federal institution and in Wisconsin, and in 1953 in the Essex County (New Jersey) Jail. The sit-down strike appears to be an American form, having occurred in 1937, along with the famous C.I.O. sit-down strikes in industry at that time, in Alcatraz, South Carolina, and New York. Alcatraz also experienced one the year before. New Jersey in 1950 and 1952 and Oregon in 1951 reported sit-down strikes.

The second method which emerges is self-slashing which appears to be the expression of hostility inward in a situation so oppressive that the men do not dare to express hostility outwardly. By such inward expression of hostility, however, the person is able to thwart his captors' attempts to exploit him. Such were the patterns reported from the Buenos Aires jails in 1932, when 53 inmates broke their legs to escape rock quarry work; from Georgia in 1951 when 30 Buford Prison inmates cut their heel tendons to protest isolation; and from Louisiana in 1951 when 16 inmates slit their tendons to protest against brutality.

Escape is the third method which emerges. This appears to be an attempt to avoid the frustrating situation with as little conflict with authority as possible, but enough to effect the escape. Examples may be the mass escape reported from Ionia, Michigan, in 1926, when 25 inmates locked guards in cells and escaped; the series of mass escapes from Texas prison farms in 1928; the escape from Cayenne (Devil's Island) in 1938; the escape of eight men from the Cherokee (Georgia) County Jail and the subsequent investigation into the deaths of inmates; the 1939 escape from the Dougherty (Georgia)

County Prison Camp; the escape of six men from the State Prison of Southern Michigan in 1939, killing a custodial captain; the escape of 40 men from Michigan's Marquette Prison in 1939, holding four officials as hostages; the 1940 escape of 36 men from Arkansas Prison, killing a guard; Puerto Rico's escape of 112 with two guards killed in 1950; the 1949 escape of 149 from Turkey's Hakari Prison; and Alabama's escape of 30 men after seizing a guard in 1951.

The fourth method which emerges is that of direct and violent aggression, which is recognized as the full-fledged riot or mutiny, and in which weapons and threats are used by inmates in conflict with prison personnel. It is this form of disturbance, the riot or mutiny, which concerns us primarily.

The beginnings of riots have been varied. Most seem to have been preceded by a period of mounting tension in a small group, not necessarily in the entire prison. For instance, the riot immediately after Christmas, 1894, at Columbus, Ohio, began when officers tried to tighten discipline in the mounting room in the foundry. The inmates had progressively gained more and more control of that room until it was conceded by everyone that the inmates ran the mounting room. Officer Temple was selected to enforce the rules. After a few days, officials were "tipped" that the prisoners were going to kill Temple. The officer armed himself with a pistol. On the morning of December 26, the prisoners attacked Temple after they were inside the foundry, prevented Temple from pulling the pistol, and beat him about the head. After other guards came, Temple deliberately shot and killed inmate O'Day. The other prisoners ran in all directions in the yard, but the disturbance was quelled in a few hours with additional armed guards.

The early prison riots were smaller and more directly to the point than the larger and diffuse modern riots. Prisons were smaller. The report of the Agent of the Prison Association of New York of October 11, 1852, for instance, gave the population of Brooklyn Prison as 78, including 20 men, 13 women, 36 boys, and nine girls. Protest against treatment and attempts to escape were the apparent motivations behind the early riots. On November 27, 1855, at Sing Sing, protest against treatment found its expression in the attacking of the relief officer as he entered the prison foundry, but other guards in the prison were able to contain the disturbance. On the following day, however, the disturbance broke into a riot, one inmate was shot with a carbine, and the guards (they were called "keepers" during this period) were able to contain the riot again.

Typical of early disturbances was the incident at Auburn which was reported after it "came to the attention" of the newspapers through a person who was at Auburn. On Saturday, January 17, 1857, Mr. Curtis, the contractor in the machine shop, ordered an inmate to perform a task, the inmate refused and was placed in solitary confinement. On Monday, January 19, 60 inmates in the shop picked up hammers and other tools for the fight. They demanded the instant release of the inmate. The inmate was released immediately, and the men went back to work.

An example of an early attempt at mass escape was reported from Sing Sing when, on Sunday, May 10, 1857, the men marching from the mess room to the chapel broke from formation. Armed with slingshots, knives, hammers, and other tools, it was a somewhat disorganized fray, with every man for himself. Two groups of inmates tried to join, but were prevented from doing it by the keepers, armed with pistols, who were able to prevent the escape.

As prisons grew bigger, their riots grew bigger, too. One of the early big riots occurred at Sing Sing in 1913 after a change of wardens with some political connotation. On Tuesday, July 22, the mat factory was set afire. The north gate of the prison was burned down and the men became uncontrollable in their cells, shouting and banging and expressing resentment against the whole system.

The following day at breakfast, 1,447 inmates complained that the food was not good. One hundred and fifty second- and third-term men started to mutiny when Warden James H.

Clancy ordered the unemployed men to their cells. They refused to go at first, but with promises of improvement, they returned to their cells. After being released at noon for dinner, however, they refused to return to their cells. They stormed the burned north gate, but a heavy guard stationed outside prevented a break. That evening, the men went to their cells after the warden withdrew the order that the unemployed men go to their cells. Warden Clancy had been in office eleven days, having replaced Warden Kennedy, who had been indicted by a grand jury. The state superintendent of prisons had been replaced, the warden had been replaced, and key personnel in the prison were being replaced. This unstable administrative condition furnished background for the mutiny.

The following spring, on April 22, 1914, a fire in the enamaline shop was set. A strike in the knitting shop involved 180 men. This action was interpreted as protest against Governor Glynn's refusal to sign a bill which would permit all prisoners to make application for parole at the end of one calendar year of service in prison. It was also interpreted as a protest among some prisoners against the pending departure of Warden Clancy. Rumor was that the charges against ex-Warden Kennedy would be quashed and he would be appointed warden again.

One of the most unusual means of settling a prison riot and restoring morale occurred at Blackwell's Island, New York, in 1914, when a religious approach was used. On Wednesday, July 8, 40 men of the 600 in the dining hall started throwing dishes. They wanted Warden Hayes fired. Warden Hayes stepped into the hall and shouted, "Fall in!" The 560 nonrioting prisoners fell in, and they were then followed by the 40 rioters. The rioting ringleaders were then placed in disciplinary status. The following day, 700 other men mutinied, demanding that the ringleaders be given normal liberty. Machinery was broken in the shops, but finally the men were forced back into their cells by guards armed with pistols. On Friday, a new mutiny developed, 44 men joining in the new fight. Miss Davis, Commissioner of Corrections, arrived and talked with the men to get them back in their cells. On Sunday, Miss Davis preached the sermon in fervent religious style. The camp-meeting spirit prevailed, and the men promised in their utterances during the fervent service, "We'll be good!"

At the Portonville Prison in England, the religious service of Sunday, January 25, 1926, must not have been quite so inspiring. It was after chapel that day that the prisoners attempted to mob Major A. C. H. Benke, acting governor of Portonville Prison. Benke had introduced harsh regulations and unrest had resulted. When inmate Thornton committed suicide after a period of time subjected fo Benke's new rigid regulations, the inmate body was incensed. Benke was protected by guards long enough to escape to safety.

The Kansas State Penitentiary was the scene of the only negotiation by a university professor of a riot in which prisoners held guards as hostages. On December 29, 1915, 300 prisoners in a coal mine struck and held a score of guards. Professor Grider from the School of Mining and Engineering of the University of Kansas was taking a small group of students on a field trip that day. When they went down the shaft, they were captured by the prisoners. Professor Grider convinced the prisoners that they should permit him to act as negotiator between them and the warden. The subsequent negotiations resulted in Warden Codding's promise for better food and for personal talks with the inmates about working conditions.

Riots continued to grow bigger as prisons continued to grow bigger. On June 5, 1917, at Joliet, Illinois, National Guardsmen had to be called to quiet 1,000 rioting inmates who set fire to buildings. There were three separate culminations of action through the continuous riots, then called by some three separate riots during the same continuum. The riot started at breakfast because Warden Bowen refused to permit visits and correspondence with anyone but close relatives. Falling rain dampened the ardor of some of the rioters and quenched some of the fires. The National Guardsmen had to fix bayonets and drive to their cells the last 200 men who had stood their ground in the face of the rifles.

Military prisoners at Leavenworth in 1919 maintained a continuing unrest. With 3,000 men, Leavenworth had the largest prison population in the country. When the prisoners went on strike and the quartermaster's section was set afire, the prisoners and the warden, Colonel Sedgwick Rice, came to an armistice while Colonel Rice went to Washington to negotiate with his superiors. There were three strikes in six months. In the riot of July 22, 1919, no attempt was made to compel the men to return to work or to their cells, and the affair quieted down without force. An effort for an improved program on the part of Colonel Rice met resistance in Washington, and Secretary of the Army Baker signed courts-martial orders against the strikers.

Two race riots in institutions gained national publicity in 1920. The Bedford Reformatory for Girls in New York had been the scene of some unrest and "noise riot" activity. On July 24, 1920, 150 white and Negro women began fighting. It started in the laundry when a white woman and a Negro began fighting, and the Negro threw a flatiron at the white woman. Institution officials did not want force used, but police who were called ignored their protests and broke up the riot by force. On October 5, 1920, 200 white and Negro men engaged in a similar fight at Leavenworth, but the arrival of the provost marshal quieted that one. San Quentin experienced rioting between native white and Mexican prisoners on Wednesday, February 18, 1925, resulting in the death of a Mexican prisoner.

Michigan was making the national news for its escapes in the roaring twenties. On Sunday afternoon, November 26, 1922, fifteen men escaped from the State House of Correction and Branch Prison at Marquette, and prison guards were hampered by a snowstorm. A brazen mass escape occurred from the Michigan Reformatory at Ionia on August 8, 1926, when twenty-five inmates forced officers into cells and escaped. A similar incident had occurred on April 9, 1926, when sixteen men overpowered guards and escaped from the Tennessee State Penitentiary.

Perhaps the most unusual prison riot occurred on Saturday, June 26, 1926, at Bucharest, Rumania. Forty lifers bribed prison guards and obtained their rifles. The inmates then dug trenches and fought a World War I style battle with the remaining guards. They retired fighting and escaped to the surrounding mountains. Some of the officers who had been bribed were subsequently placed in the cells left empty. Their enthusiasm for fighting must not have been very intense. No casualties were reported on either side.

A similar but less dramatic incident occurred at the Louisiana State Penitentiary on September 9, 1928, when a group of inmates covered the foreman of a camp enclosure with an automatic, went out the gate, obtained shotguns and ammunition from a locker, and headed for the Mississippi River. Guards and inmates carried on a running battle, resulting in six inmates killed and one fatally wounded. Casualties on the guards' side were a trusty, fighting alongside the guards, killed and Captain Singleton wounded about the head with shotgun pellets. Officials said that four men probably got away.

A few of the prison riots stand out in their magnitude. These riots have more men involved, more inmates or guards killed, more hostages held, more property damage done, and greater intensity of public furor following them. The following large and serious riots were selected from those of lesser magnitude for special examination:

June	5, 1917	Joliet, Illinois
Apr.	21, 1919	Leavenworth
June	21, 1927	Kansas State Penitentiary
Nov.	24, 1927	Folsom Prison
June	23, 1929	Clinton Prison at Dannemora
June	28, 1929	Auburn
Aug.	1, 1929	Leavenworth
Oct.	3, 1929	Colorado State Prison
Dec.	11, 1929	Auburn
Apr.	21, 1930	Ohio State Penitentiary
Jan.	26, 1932	Dartmoor, England

Dec.   5, 1944   Federal Penitentiary, Atlanta
May   2, 1946   Alcatraz
Feb.   11, 1950   Salem Prison, India
May   20, 1951   Utah State Prison
Apr.   15, 1952   Trenton, New Jersey
Apr.   17, 1952   Rahway, New Jersey
Apr.   20, 1952   Michigan
Nov. 1-3, 1952   Ohio State Penitentiary
Oct.   28, 1952   Menard State Prison, Illinois

Several of these riots have special implications and importance. The Illinois riot of June, 1917, was the biggest riot up to that time when 1,000 men took part in the rioting in the prison yard; the last 200 men made a stand against the advancing National Guard and they had to be driven to their cells. In 1919 at Ft. Leavenworth, 2,300 military prisoners went on strike, but "the success of democratic, non-military methods" prevented a riot. The three uprisings at Leavenworth in 1919 were strikes, and nobody was hurt, even though troops from Camp Grant were moved in. The first major request that the inmates' demands be published in the newspapers occurred in the Kansas State Penitentiary's mine mutiny in July, 1926. The demand was that copies of the newspapers be thrown down the shaft so they could not be double-crossed by prison officials. The demands were refused and they were starved out.

Riots continued to grow bigger. At California's Folsom Prison on Monday, November 24, 1927, 1,200 to 2,000 inmates fought National Guardsmen. Seven hostages were held. Police circled the prison, 400 National Guardsmen surrounded the building which the prisoners defended, tanks were brought in, National Guard airplanes were in action over the scene, one-pound artillery was set up, and a Southern Pacific Railway switch engine trained floodlights on the building. The troops fired round after round. By the time Governor Young arrived and ordered the attacks to cease, nine inmates had been killed, with 31 wounded, three of whom were expected to die; two guards had been killed outright, three were wounded, one of whom was expected to die. An aged officer died from excitement. Governor Young's action prevented what could have gone down in history as an infamous and wanton massacre. The inmates were prevented from getting to the kitchen and their lack of food placed time on the side of the prison officials. The inmates were starved out.

Thirteen hundred men rioted for five hours on Monday, July 23, 1929, at Clinton Prison at Dannemora, New York. Three inmates were killed, buildings and lumber were fired, and the power plant was sabotaged. Armed townspeople and units of the United States Army repelled the convicts as they rushed the walls. A new record for property damage in prison riots was set at Dannemora at $200,000.

On June 28, 1929, 1,700 inmates battled guards for five hours at Auburn Prison, New York, generally called at that time, "Copper John's domain," referring to a former warden. Inmates surprised a guard, threw acid in his face, and entered the warden's office and arsenal, which were inside the walls. Riot guns were seized and the walls were stormed. Six guards were wounded and two inmates were killed. Guards and police were able to bring the riot under control by segregating little groups on the fringe of the riot and gradually working into the center.

The greatest loss of life reported from a prison uprising was the Ohio Penitentiary fire on Monday, April 21, 1930. The fire began at 6:00 in the evening, set by inmates apparently with a view toward creating confusion and then escaping. Two thousand prisoners were loose in the yard and were threatening violence, which did not materialize. Guards would not open the cells in and near burning buildings. Guard Watkinson held the keys, insisting that he did it on orders of Deputy Warden J. O. Woodward, who later denied any such orders. By the time other officers wrested the keys from Watkinson and opened the cells, 317 inmates were reported to have died. It is surprising that the property damage amounted to but $11,000.

The Dartmoor riots in England on January 24, 1932, began a series of disturbances which caused an administrative change. The main building was burned and troops had to be called to quell the riot. A second small riot occurred on January 29 and a third on February 20.

A series of minor riots occurred in America and elsewhere throughout the 1930s and early 1940s. A physician was killed in Michigan's Marquette Prison, Pennsylvania had a riot, Alcatraz, a county prison camp in Georgia, New York, Texas, Michigan's Marquette and Jackson, Sing Sing, Arkansas, and Duval County, Florida, contributed to the prison disturbance news during this period.

The Federal Penitentiary at Atlanta broke into the news on December 4, 1944, when 25 long-term inmates seized four guards and held them in a five-story segregation unit. They threatened to kill their hostages if tear gas were used. Water, heat, and food were cut off. They protested against quartering "regular" inmates with men convicted as Axis spies or saboteurs. On December 6, Warden Sanford sent food to them after they had agreed to surrender provided the *Atlanta Journal* printed their grievances. On December 7, inmate George Hollingsworth said, "This is Pearl Harbor Day. It is a good day to surrender." The inmates gave up their hostages and surrendered when a special edition of the *Atlanta Journal* printed their story. United States Attorney General Biddle ordered them placed in solitary confinement immediately and promised a quick trial.

The riot at Alcatraz, May 2 to 4, 1946, drew national publicity. Warden Johnston in a book on Alcatraz drew the battle lines. Inmates held officers hostage and a pitched battle was fought. Selected marksmen from the San Francisco Police Department, experienced guards from San Quentin, and United States Bureau of Prisons Director James V. Bennett appeared at Alcatraz. The arrival of General "Vinegar Joe" Stilwell began rumors of a large-scale operation. Coast Guard boats and planes circled the island, the Marines landed, and the situation was precarious for a long time, according to

Warden James A. Johnston. Two guards and three inmates died, while about fifteen inmates were wounded. In the end, it turned out that six inmates, armed with a rifle and a pistol taken from the gun gallery had caused all the commotion and constituted the extent of inmate resistance.

Several riots in 1950 and 1952 contributed to the rising crescendo that culminated in the big riots like Michigan and the Koje prisoner of war camp in Korea. One hundred inmates rioted in New Mexico on November 20, 1950, but it was quelled by State Police. In Utah, 400 men rioted on May 20, 1951, to protest unfair treatment on the part of four officials. Upon promise to probe, they ended their riot. A new riot the following day resulted in the resignation of the steward. Another riot on August 15 ended when convicts dropped their demands and released their two hostages. Oregon, West Virginia, Colorado, Georgia, Louisiana, and Alabama experienced minor incidents in 1951. Early in 1952, minor incidents were experienced by Oregon and South Dakota.

New Jersey had a series of disturbances at Trenton State Prison and Rahway Prison Farm. Three riots occurred at the Trenton State Prison within a few weeks. On March 30, 1952, a four-hour riot by 50 inmates was in protest over failure of a prison orderly to provide medical attention to an inmate. A second disturbance on April 6–7 was followed by another minor one a week later. The most serious of the Trenton riots began on April 15, 1952, when 58 prisoners barricaded themselves in the print shop, holding two instructors and two officers hostage. Their demands concerned food, sanitation, beds, rehabilitation program, parole procedure, replacement of Warden McCarty, and investigation of the prison by an impartial body, specifically the Osborne Association. The men were cut off from food, and force was not used because of their threats to kill the hostages. The men surrendered on April 18, having won their demand for an investigation by the Osborne Association.

At the New Jersey Prison Farm at Rahway, 250 "nondangerous" inmates held nine guards in their dormitory on April 18 in a sympathy insurrection aimed at the same objectives as those of Trenton. In addition, they asked for the ousting of Sanford Bates, New Jersey's Commissioner of Institutions and Agencies. Starvation was the technique used against this insurrection, and tear gas was thrown into the dormitory, leading to the surrender of the inmates on April 22, 1952.

Koje Island, the United Nations prisoner-of-war camp off the coast of Korea, provided world-wide collateral interest in prison riots by a series of disturbances. The United Nations had decided to separate Communists from non-Communists. The interviews began. On February 18, 1952, 1,500 Communist-led civilian internees battled security troops until 69 internees and one American soldier died. The Communists charged brutality and massacre. Three investigations began simultaneously. General Colson and General Dodd were given command of Koje. On March 13, a new riot occurred and 12 internees were killed. Lieutenant General Nam Li of North Korea continued the charges of massacre. By April 17, the United Nations announced plans to make smaller stockades to break up the approximately 80,000-man camp to manipulatable proportions. On May 9, General Dodd was dragged through the gates of the stockade during a conference and was held hostage. He tried to negotiate his own release. General Colson, now commandant, negotiated, though tanks and other weapons were prepared to attack. "Some minor concessions" were granted and General Dodd was released. General Mark Clark, Far Eastern Supreme Commander, repudiated the agreement as having been made under duress. Senators and other politicians heatedly announced that Generals Colson and Dodd had caused the riot. By May 24, Generals Colson and Dodd had been demoted to the rank of colonel, and were relieved of command.

On October 23, 1952, a brief riot occurred at the Menard State Prison in Illinois. On October 28, the riot was renewed when 363 inmates held seven officers hostage. The following day, 37 men in the psychiatric division held three officers, but agreed to free them on October 29 after conference with prison officials. The 363 men in the cell-house had seized a lieutenant and six guards. Warden Munie called off plans to storm the building when the inmates threatened to throw the guards off the 50-foot tier. No food was available to the inmates from Monday, October 27, until their surrender on Friday, October 31. There were no demands at first, but by Wednesday, the inmates had three pages of demands. Governor Stevenson responded to their demands to see the governor and had intended to negotiate, according to reports. When he arrived, however, he wrote an ultimatum to free the hostages and then confer. Three hundred and twenty-one State Troopers and prison guards entered the cell-house on Friday, the hostage guards fought inmates to keep from being thrown off the tier, and the riot ended.

The Ohio State Penitentiary riot of October 31, 1952, when 1,200 men rioted, caused a million dollars' worth of property damage. Eight buildings were burned. National Guardsmen moved in and as 600 prepared to attack, the inmates returned to their cells. On November 1,200 men wrecked cell-blocks. On Monday, November 2, 1,600 men renewed the riot, going out from control in cell-blocks G, H, I, and K. National Guardsmen moved in and ringed the buildings with machine guns. There was no food available to the inmates and the cold water had been turned off. There were no hostages. By Tuesday night, the warden was able to issue a "surrender or starve" ultimatum, after which the inmates gave up.

From this mass of riot data, three prison riots emerge above the others secondarily in their magnitude and gravity, but primarily because they portray most vividly the pattern which seems to underlie most riots. The Colorado State Prison riot of October, 1929; the Auburn Prison riot of December, 1929; and the riot at the State Prison of Southern Michigan of April, 1952, most vividly portray this pattern and their impact still affects corrections in their respective jurisdictions.

In Colorado, on Friday, October 3, 1929, 150 inmates, three of whom were murderers, obtained four guns and barricaded themselves in cell-house No. 3, holding seven guards hostages. Prison officers attacked the cell-house, and the inmates felled three officers in the first rush, killing them immediately. They demanded that the prison gates be swung open and that they be allowed to escape. If their demands were not met, they threatened to kill a hostage each hour on the hour as long as their demands were ignored. The administration demanded unconditional surrender.

The body of Guard J. J. Elles, the hangman, was the first to be thrown from the cell-house. Austin MacCormick was quoted in 1952 as having said that their heads were sent out on platters, but I was unable to substantiate it. Armed guards had been able to isolate the riot to the cell-house. National Guardsmen were called, bringing in one airplane and several 3-inch field pieces. Warden Francis E. Crawford was shot seriously, but recovered. The Catholic chaplain, Father O'Neil, set the charge of dynamite at the cell-house and exploded it, after which the cell-house was sprayed with machine-gun fire. The prisoners retreated to the undamaged part of the cell-house and continued their fight. The militia advanced, but the prisoners drove them back. Governor Adams endorsed the manner in which the riot was being handled. As their ammunition ran out, inmate leader Danny Daniels shot his lieutenants and then shot himself. The toll was seven guards killed, five inmates killed, $500,000 in property damage—a new record, and an escape prevented.

A similar original situation, handled differently, occurred in Michigan on September 25, 1939. Inmates at the State House of Corrections and Branch Prison at Marquette captured four officials and demanded that they be permitted passage through the gates. Forty prisoners were permitted to escape with their hostages. A few miles from the prison, the hostages were released, all escapees were subsequently captured. The toll was no guards killed, no inmates killed, no property damage, and no successful escape.

The riot of December 11, 1929, at Auburn was staged by 50 men from solitary confinement where they had been placed after the July 28 outbreak. "Copper John's domain" had been rocked on July 28 when 1,700 inmates had battled guards for five hours. The 50 men in solitary as a result of that riot were being marched in the yard for their one-hour exercise when an inmate grabbed Warden Jennings, who happened to be passing. Chief Keeper Durnford started to help the warden, and was killed by a bullet from a pistol in possession of an inmate. The warden and five guards were held hostage. Inmates refused to talk with Father Cleary, the chaplain. Warden Jennings sent messages to let the inmates have what they wanted, but Acting Governor Lehman said, "No compromise." Troopers stormed the building with tear gas and rescued the warden and the hostages. Eight inmates were slain.

A series of investigations, trials for murder, and political charges and countercharges followed the Auburn riot of December 11, 1929, and the aftermath lasted for years. It was in the news as late as 1949 when an inmate's life sentence for his participation in that riot was reduced.

The riot at the State Prison of Southern Michigan in April, 1952, emerges as the largest, most costly, and most dangerous riot thus far recorded. The 179 inmates in 15-block, the disciplinary cell-block, captured four guards on Sunday evening, April 20, and demanded to see Assistant Deputy Warden in Charge of Custody George L. Bacon and some newsmen. When Bacon and the newsmen arrived, the inmate leaders showed them some unusual hand weapons found in 15-block and charged custody with brutality. Through the night, conversations continued between the inmates on the one hand and Deputy Bacon, Warden Frisbie, and the newsmen on the other, sometimes at a distance of thirty feet, sometimes over the telephone. On Monday morning, when the administration attempted to feed the men in the dining hall, 1,600 to 2,600 (the exact number was never agreed upon) men began rioting in the yard. They wrecked the kitchen and butcher shop, where they obtained weapons. They began destroying property, capturing guards, and having a good time. Eight more guards were placed in 15-block.

Before the State Police were able to clear the yard and

isolate the riot to 15-block again, an estimated $2,500,000 worth of property damage had been done, only half subsequently replaced by the legislature. Because of the mental status of the men who held twelve hostages, their homicidal and assaultive backgrounds, their long terms and nothing-to-lose setting in 15-block, the Michigan riot has been called by penal experts, including Austin MacCormick, the most dangerous prison riot in history. By not using force and by manipulating the emotions of the riot leaders, the administration was able to write its own terms, and bring the insurrection to a close on Thursday, April 24, with the loss of but one prisoner's life. The aftermath of the Michigan riot, however—including freedom of news coverage that gave confidence beyond its accuracy—resulted in a series of investigations, confused public opinion, political charges and countercharges, and a loss of progress made in correctional treatment in Michigan.

Observation of the riots over the past hundred years suggests a pattern which all riots tend to approach in various degrees and to various stages. The first phase is one of disorganized confusion during which the patterns of mutinous groupings and leadership among inmates emerges and during which administrative leadership emerges from a group of men engaged in a series of trial-and-error efforts to re-establish custodial control. The second phase consists of a period of tense talking and parrying of ideas between inmate leaders and administrative leaders, during which issues are found or built up for use in bringing the mutiny to a close. The third phase is the surrender of the inmates, actual dislodging them from their position, and restoration of custodial control. The fourth phase is the aftermath in which rival political factions interpret the riot and attendant conditions to the voting public according to their best interests and the group responsible for prison administration becomes engaged in a public relations project. This pattern seems to fit in varying degrees and manners all of the prison riots on which enough data has been accumulated to observe.

The riots at Colorado State Prison in 1929, Auburn in

December, 1929, and at the State Prison of Southern Michigan in April, 1952, stand out above the others because they exemplify most vividly this pattern. Colorado's riot was a bloody one, with seven guards and five inmates killed, but the pattern was followed. Auburn's riot was relatively small, as riots go, while eight inmates were killed, but the pattern was followed. Auburn's riot most vividly emphasizes the fourth phase, that of a long aftermath with political implications in the framing of correctional policy. The Michigan riot most vividly portrayed all phases. For this reason, and because the writer was inextricably involved in it, the Michigan riot later in this volume will be treated in detail.

CHAPTER II

Prisoner Demands

The demands made by prisoners during rioting may or may not have sound bases. Nevertheless, they are generally sufficiently foremost in the prisoners' minds to be verbalized. It is seldom that these demands can be completely ignored with impunity. Their presence may be symptomatic of difficulties more basic. As pointed out by the American Prison Association's Committee on Riots in 1953, complaints about food may be a reflection of an inadequate budget made necessary by an economy-minded legislature. On the other hand, when complaints about food are made, they may be made even where there is an excellent feeding program with adequate budgets and plentiful foods of good quality. Complaints about food in such instances may be interpreted as an attempt to place a generalized hostility on something tangible.

In many riots the hostility is so generalized that it is never committed to specific demands. Riots of protest against consistently harsh rules and regulations are frequent, without identifying a specific objectionable rule. The 1914 riot at Blackwell's Island exemplifies this situation. There were no demands during the first day. After considerable rioting and talking, it became obvious that the rioters were protesting against Warden Hayes.

When a conservative and tyrannical administration exists over a period of time, it has always to watch for aggression. Force begets force, particularly when it is interpreted as unreasonable. Hayes was an elderly man, a veteran of the Civil War, unenlightened in the dynamics of human behavior. When men complained of lack of food, his characteristic reply was,

31

"The expressman hasn't arrived, yet." When the men asked for new shoes or repair of the old and showed him their worn shoes, his characteristic reply was, "Cut a hole in the other side and the water will run out." When the inmates hissed at him on July 4, Warden Hayes decreed that there should be no visitors nor mail for anybody for two weeks. This was the straw that broke the camel's back as far as the inmates were concerned, and the Blackwell's Island riot broke out on July 8.

Toward the end of the second day, they were able to ask for Warden Hayes' dismissal. Then they asked for the release from solitary confinement of the 40 ringleaders who participated in the riot on the first day. These 40 men never issued any demands. The reverse situation occurred in Sing Sing on November 18, 1914, when inmates struck because some "keepers" or guards were to be transferred from one work squad to another, and the men wanted to keep their guards.

Demands by the military prisoners in Leavenworth in 1919 and 1920 involved equality of sentencing for similar offenses and for general amnesty after the war had ended.

Demands made by prisoners in the early riots were recorded as either quite direct and specific or entirely unverbalized. There were many attempts to kill certain persons, such as Colonel Lewis, the agent and warden of Auburn Prison in March, 1857. Several riots had obviously the single objective of escape. There have been many riots, too, in which the demand was a single, specific, direct request, such as the instant release of men held in solitary as at Auburn in January, 1857, and in Ludlow Street Jail (New York) in April, 1895.

Many riots during the earlier periods, and some after 1912, presented no prisoner demands at all. In many of these, reasons were attributed to the prisoners by the administration, generally in terms of escape. Since escape was a logical objective, the prisoners' containment inside the prison walls could be interpreted as an administrative victory. A riot of protest, however, could be embarrassing whether or not the violence was contained. Consequently, journalists have written often that a "curtain of silence" fell over the situation, to be broken by an official announcement involving escape attempts on the part of the prisoners.

General restriction of the rules have produced many riots. Ohio in the 1890s, Mexico City in 1929, and Illinois in 1917 are a few obvious examples.

Beginning in 1912, a new era of rioting appeared to arise. Prisons were growing bigger, communication was getting better, and penal standards were being raised. Nebraska inmates killed a warden and Michigan gave impetus to a new series of prison riots in 1912 in which bad food was the primary complaint, with demands for more and better nutrition. Sing Sing in 1913 added to the food complaint demands that the new warden be removed. The effects of improved mass communication were manifest in the inmates' demands for publicizing their complaints in the Kansas riot of December 29, 1915.

Reaction to these demands varied. Prison officials close to the scene frequently reported that the complaints were "not without foundation," as at Sing Sing in 1913, but the political commissioners in state capitols invariably denied all charges. The only exceptions I have been able to find have been when reports of investigating committees have found abuses which were then blamed on the local prison officials.

Dismiss the warden and let inmates out of solitary confinement have been fairly frequent demands, as at Blackwell's Island, New York, in 1914. Generally, these demands have been accompanied by collateral demands involving specific protests, such as in Illinois in 1917, when inmates wanted to have visitors other than immediate relatives, specifically, girl friends. Some such demands were accompanied by protests against loss of privileges, such as shows.

Demands became more complex in the roaring twenties. Kansas inmates in 1927 demanded (1) more liberties, (2) more liberal parole policies, (3) better and more food, (4) more good times, (5) let the inmates have the good-time consideration allowed them by law rather than the board members' rulings as in the past, and (6) no retaliation by the administration against participants in the riot.

The demands of the inmates in the segregation unit at Atlanta in 1944 were (1) that the *Atlanta Journal* must publicize the grievances, (2) complaint of medical care, (3) complaint that there had been no religious services for six months, (4) complaint that segregated men were paid a lower wage for work than nonsegregated men, (5) complaint that they were housed with Nazi spies and saboteurs, (6) complaint that they had been denied the privilege of communicating with outside persons on legal matters and (7) complaint of lack of recreation.

The protests at Trenton State Prison in New Jersey in 1952 were rather complex, and included demands for (1) better food, (2) suspension of Warden Carty, (3) better sanitation, (4) better beds, (5) improved rehabilitation program, (6) revision of parole procedure, and (7) an impartial investigation of the prison by the Osborne Association. The inmates at Rahway added a demand for the ouster of Sanford Bates, Commissioner of Institutions and Agencies.

Robert R. Hannum of the Osborne Association attempted to find out what the grievances actually were in New Jersey, and spent considerable time interviewing inmates and having them put their grievances in writing. He reported that the hundreds of individual grievances could not be listed, but that they included criticism of sentencing, physical plant, treatment, discipline, and parole. The official report of Governor Driscoll's investigating committee outlined the grievances as follows:

1. Conditions and practices in the institutions themselves:
   a. Inadequacies in institution plants.
   b. Heterogeneous inmate population at Trenton Prison.
   c. Idleness and inadequacies of rehabilitation programs.
   d. Personnel problems, including heavy turnover in custodial force.

  e. Disciplinary practices.
  f. Miscellaneous factors: shortage of necessities, visiting
     arrangements, food, etc.
2. The parole system, with special reference to the parole
   law and the policies and practices of the Parole Board.

The terms presented by the inmates of the State Prison of
Southern Michigan in April, 1952, differed from their original
demands. The terms on which the riot was settled were: (1)
remodel the disciplinary cell-block to improve sanitation and
light, (2) permit the counselors free access to the disciplinary
cells, (3) have a representative of the Individual Treatment
Division on the segregation board, (4) eliminate inhumane
restraint equipment in the disciplinary cell-block and provide
everyone in the prison with full rations, (5) register protest
with the parole board about their conservative policies, (6)
have dental work done on the basis of an orderly listing of
priorities rather than permitting purchase of priorities by some
inmates, (7) elect an inmate advisory council to meet with
the assistant deputy warden in charge of individual treatment
each month, and (8) no reprisals shall be taken by Department
of Corrections officials against the ringleaders in the riot.

These terms did not mention the original complaints of the
inmates, and were not damaging to the administration. As
reported in the newspapers, they were not representative of
the complaints of the inmates in the prison, since they were
actually prepared by an administrative representative and
were related only indirectly to the original inmate complaints.
Complaints heard from the inmates concerned (1) brutality
on the part of a few custodial officers, (2) preparation of food,
(3) brutality on the part of the inmate nurses in the mental
ward, (4) parole board practices, (5) inadequate medical care,
particularly post-operative procedures, and (6) lack of dental
care. For our purposes at this time, then, the latter set of complaints will be considered.

In none of these instances does there appear to be sound
basis for complaint. Prisons in New Jersey, New York, Michi-

gan, and the Federal Bureau of Prisons, of which Atlanta is a part, feed prisoners much better and in greater quantity than many prisons which have never experienced a major riot. The same is true of medical services, enlightenment of the administration, and parole board policies and practices.

The connection between the demands of prisoners and the actual situation in prisons appears to be fairly tenuous where a series of demands are presented. Single demands and attempts at mass escape appear to have more direct and logical connection. Prisons in which rioters have presented a series of complex demands however, have consistently been among those generally conceded to have the highest standards of food preparation and service, more enlightened administration, the better medical services, and respected parole boards and practices. This leads us to believe that, with the exception of single and direct demands of specific nature, most prisoner demands represent not the basic causes of the riot but, rather, a generalized hostility that is best expressed by attaching it to tangible items like food and medical service.

There has been little effort to link prisoner demands with riot causes. Part of the reason may be that prison administrations have denied the complaints and repudiated the demands vehemently, thereby rejecting any taxpayer support that might have been forthcoming. The more important reason appears to be that prisoner demands represent intellectual rationalizations for rioting in many cases and are only sketchily connected with basic issues.

CHAPTER III

Administrative Conditions Prior to Riots

Evaluating administrative conditions immediately prior to riots is an impossible task. Upon reviewing several such "investigations" in which conflicting information is finally reconciled or one viewpoint prevails by sheer weight of numbers of people with that viewpoint or by the political fortunes, the observer is convinced that following a riot the truth of the situation does not much matter. The findings of Blake's prison inquiry in New York just before World War I were disputed and debated until a change of political fortunes brought in new political leaders and a new set of issues without ever settling the old one.

In Alabama, during the early twenties, Circuit Court Commissioner James Davis investigated brutality at the Banner mining camp and became involved in a political dispute which resulted in his attempting to call Governor W. W. Brandon as a witness before the grand jury. When such influencing of statements regarding pre-riot prison administration occurs according to the personal and political interests of the persons making the statements, it becomes obvious that post-riot reports have little value in reflecting accurately the pre-riot administrative conditions.

In order to obtain a clue as to administrative conditions, the only factors which can be relied upon with some degree of confidence are the factual reports of replacement of personnel and the statements made *during* the riot, before there has been an opportunity for modification of these statements according to viewpoint and political fortune. These are not overly

38 *Violence Behind Bars*

reliable, either, because of personal viewpoints in the heat of emotion during the violence, but they seem to be a better index of the actual situation than the carefully prepared and "interpreted" official report. Consequently, in attempting to evaluate to some extent the administrative conditions prior to riots, emphasis was placed on factual reporting of personnel changes, statements of protest during the riots, and factual changes of policy before and during riots, and less emphasis upon the "official" post-riot reports.

Prior to some riots, the administration has been liberal, and the introduction of more conservative rules and regulations creates tension among the inmates and sets the stage for rioting. Whether or not the change is the result of a change of administrations seems to make little difference. The riot at Joliet in 1917 was said to have been the result of tightening of the rules regarding visiting and correspondence by a single administration. The riot in 1926 at Portonville Prison in England was the direct result of dissatisfaction with restrictive regulations introduced by Acting Governor Benke after a change in administration. The riot had followed closely two rather spectacular escapes from Portonville.

Prior to several riots, also, there has been a shift in laxity of administration to greater rigidity, a situation considerably dissimilar to a shift from liberality to conservatism. While some prison personnel regard liberality and laxity as synonymous, it is obvious to most that a strong administration can be liberal, conservative, or "a little to the left of center," just as can a weak administration. The philosophy of an administration has little relationship to its ability to implement that philosophy. In Columbus, Ohio, in 1894, the conservative administration became alarmed that the inmates in the foundry's mounting room were holding full sway, and they decided to put a stop to it. The riot resulted when Officer Temple attempted to enforce the rules which had not been enforced for a long time. One prisoner was killed and Officer Temple was injured.

One of the most complicated administrative situations preceding violence that has been revealed was that at Sing Sing prior to the riots of July 22, 23, and 24, 1913. A change of state administrations resulted in the appointment of John B. Riley as superintendent of prisons. Warden Kennedy had been indicted by a grand jury and Warden James N. Clancy had been appointed warden of Sing Sing. Storekeeper and Buyer Hyman S. Gibbs and Kitchen Supervisor Frederick Haber, each with twenty years' service, had been suspended and new personnel appointed by the warden. The result of this move was that the quality and quantity of food prepared and served the inmates had suffered considerably. In addition, there was a political fight between the governor and the legislature. State Comptroller Michael J. Walsh had refused to honor all state requisitions pertaining to the prisons on grounds that Riley's tenure was of doubtful legality and, further, a decision was being awaited from the attorney general's office as to whether the statutory reference to the "next" session of the legislature could refer to the "special" session Governor Sulzer had called for confirmation of his appointments. As a result, the guards had not been paid since June 1. Morale was so bad that it was facetiously stated that had the prisoners not revolted, the guards would have. Warden Clancy had been in office eleven days when the riot broke.

In the immediate background of many riots and in the remote background of them all, there has been a conflict in basic penal philosophy. The most obvious differences present in the riots early in the twentieth century were those between Warden Thomas Mott Osborne and his superiors in Albany as well as his own custodial personnel. Osborne was a progressive and enlightened man sandwiched between unsympathetic and unenlightened superiors and subordinates. New York State's Superintendent of Prisons John B. Riley called Osborne's methods "pink tea." This situation constituted part of the background of the riot at Sing Sing on July 2, 1915. Immediate center of the conflict between Riley and Osborne was the decision as to who should select men for transfer from Sing Sing to other prisons. Osborne wanted to make up a tentative list and send it to Riley in Albany for approval or further administrative screening. Superintendent Riley insisted on making the selections in Albany without consulting Osborne. Osborne argued that transfers from Sing Sing were considered punishment, and that their selection in Albany without respect to behavior within the institution weakened the prison administration and hampered the operation of Osborne's honor system. The riot of July 2, 1915, followed the transfer of seventy-nine inmates to Auburn Prison.

A "stringing up" incident occurred prior to the 1920 riot at the Bedford Reformatory for Girls. A result of the subsequent investigation was the abolition of handcuffs from the reformatory. Officials had found it advisable to come into the reformatory and modify disciplinary methods. Miss Clark Jones resigned as superintendent because she said that she did not feel equal to the job in view of the restrictions placed on her discipline. Superintendent of Prisons Kennedy announced that nobody would say that an institution can be operated without discipline, but that Bedford is not without discipline. They had to classify inmates and segregate them. He continued that he wanted to find a superintendent who could keep the peace without handcuffs. Superintendent Jones left and a new superintendent was appointed. No further riots were reported from Bedford.

Most of the prisons were overcrowded. Sing Sing in 1926 used the term "jammed" in preference to merely "overcrowded." In addition, most prisons complained of understaffing, limited budgets, and political interference by persons unfamiliar with prison problems.

Problems of interpretation becloud conditions as they exist in prisons. It was in February, 1927, when New York Police Commissioner McLaughlin read a letter purported to have been written by an inmate saying that the service at Sing Sing was good. Sing Sing had records of all letters that went out through its mail office where they were censored, and indicated that the letter was faked, since none had been sent to the Commissioner McLaughlin or his associates. Commissioner McLaughlin launched a bitter attack on Sing Sing for "coddling" its prisoners in luxury. Simultaneously and independently, Jane M. Hoey of the New York State Crime Commission severely criticized conditions at Sing Sing as unsanitary and detrimental to rehabilitation, and asked for better prison equipment and the treatment of defective delinquents. The newspapers in reporting the situation emphasized the coddling, both in headlines and the slant of the stories.

Conditions in the prisons of New Jersey, California, Utah, Michigan, Illinois, Ohio, Pennsylvania, and several other states in which riots occurred in 1952 seem to have been satisfactory. At least, their programs were considered by individual members of the American Prison Association to be good in comparison with many other prison systems.

Discipline in most, but not all, prisons with riots appears to have been on the side of rigidity and sternness, rather than on the side of laxity. This was notably true in Kansas in 1927, New Mexico in 1952, Clinton in 1929, and many others. It seemed not to be true in Michigan and New Jersey in 1952. In Michigan, however, discipline was stern—I think unreasonably so—in 15-block which was the custodial disciplinary block in which the riot originated. In New Jersey, it was noted that the insurrection took place in the "segregation unit" at Trenton. Apparently force in administration is met with force among men who are the inmates. The ramifications of that theme through many phases of human history and relations are obvious.

As has been noted, it is difficult to learn anything for sure about administrative conditions in prisons prior to riots. Unsanitary conditions, overcrowding, obsolete physical plant, harsh or stern discipline, idleness, and poor food have been reported from most prisons with riots. They have also been observed, however, in many prisons without riots. The most important factor contributing to the difficulty in learning about administrative conditions in prisons prior to riots, however, appears to be the "interpreted" reports given by officials during and after riots.

CHAPTER IV

Public Explanations and Aftermaths

The most important phase of prison riots appears to be in the public relations. Explanations to the public as to the reasons for the riot and assurance of action to correct or punish according to public demand are most essential as far as political leadership is concerned. In terms of social action, penal progress, and political security, this public relations phase is without question the most important phase of a prison riot. Over a long period of time, the monetary losses and the dead and injured in prison riots seem less to be considered than the effects of the losses and gains in public support of progressive penal policy or of a political group. Even though prisons and corrections are but a small part of total state government, usually low man on the budgetary totem pole, and certainly less obvious to the taxpaying public than are chuck holes in the highways, the existence of a riot brings the prisons into public focus and their slight influence may be felt in the winning or losing of an election. Consequently, public explanation and assurance has political value.

Patterns of explanation and assurance take on many forms. The size of the riot, the humanitarian or vengeful attitudes of the public, the political situation, and many other factors enter into the formulation of the explanation and assurance and the reconstruction of attitudes that follow.

Sheriff Tamsen explained after the riot at the Ludlow Street Jail in New York in April, 1895, that the Horse Market Gang had initiated the riot, that he had locked the ringleaders in cells to preserve discipline, and the inmates rioted in their cells. "What more can I do?" asked the sheriff, thereby throwing himself on the mercy of the public. In a few days, Sheriff Tamsen published the statutory bases for each of the rules he was enforcing and said he would accept modification from the United States attorney general. In addition, he said that the newspapers had exaggerated the seriousness of the riot. Sheriff Tamsen, who had handled his public relations well, remained as sheriff and maintained his jail.

When the big riot at Sing Sing in July, 1913, was over, Warden Clancy surveyed the $150,000 damage and announced that it was "a trivial affair." Superintendent of Prisons Riley assured the public through the press that the concessions Warden Clancy made to the convicts had averted bloodshed. Bloodshed was prevented at the sacrifice of prison discipline, it was admitted. Guards reported that they could not order the men to do something they could not enforce, anyway, so it made little difference. In order to satisfy the demand for aggression, a grand jury investigation was made to prepare indictments on all inmates guilty of arson. Warden Clancy announced that he would summon all "runners" or inmate spokesmen periodically and ask for their grievances. With this new program, the prison administration was ready to forgive and forget, and start with a clean slate. This approach accomplished its purpose at the time of satisfying the feelings of the public and of the inmates so that the prison could be brought back to normal.

In the spring of 1914, another riot of smaller proportions occurred when Warden Clancy was scheduled to leave and ex-Warden Kennedy, who had been indicted by a grand jury, was scheduled to be reappointed. Twenty-two of the ringleaders were sent to Clinton Prison and 150 others were locked up. Thomas Mott Osborne followed, subjected himself to Superintendent Riley's taunts of "pink tea" methods, and introduced self-government through the Mutual Welfare League made up of elected inmates. The "pink tea" interpretation followed the riot of July 2, 1915, when Riley had transferred 79 inmates to Auburn.

Miss Davis, Commissioner of Corrections for New York City, supported Warden Hayes during the Blackwell's Island uprising in 1914 by reporting that the riot may have been caused by loss of drugs, in which there was considerable traffic before Warden Hayes took over. She was reported to "lay down the law" to the inmates, a procedure which is always popular with the tax-paying public. Warden Hayes was described as a veteran of the Civil War, which was also a popular revelation. At any rate, the aftermath of the riot found the elimination of striped clothing at Blackwell's Island and a self-government program. The *New York Times*, July 11, 1914, carried an editorial concerning Miss Davis as commissioner of corrections in which it questioned whether or not the job was "woman's work."

Tightening of the rules was given to the public as the reason for the riot at Joliet in 1917, and it appears quite probable that the interpretation was accurate. The inmates had wanted visitors other than just close relatives. Congressman William A. Rodenberg of Illinois subsequently in Washington proposed investigation of the Oriental Esoteric Library League, with offices in Washington, and other organizations which encouraged correspondence between prisoners and "young girls." He verbally attacked Dr. D. N. Stokes who was president of the Oriental Esoteric Library League as heading a sentimental movement.

When the military prisoners struck at Leavenworth in 1919, Colonel Rice saw the possibility of building out of the situation a model system for the humane treatment of prisoners. A military investigation team told a "dramatic story of 2,300 prisoners, the spread of the strike, and the success of democratic, non-military methods in preventing a bloody revolt." Secretary Baker of the Army announced sixteen recommendations of the study, including (1) psychiatric units to be placed in conjunction with all Army recruiting stations to screen out undesirable personnel, (2) special training units in the Army for training doubtful men, (3) vocational edu-

cation, (4) correspondence courses, and (5) a classification
of the prisoners at Leavenworth.

The classifications of prisoners included those with (1)
excessively eccentric personality, which included two-thirds
of the group of prisoners, (2) extreme emotional instability,
and (3) inadequate intelligence. When about 1,800 men struck
a few months later, however, Secretary Baker signed courts-
martial orders for them and put them on bread-and-water
diet. The reforms had not come to the institution yet, but had
created a considerable flurry on typing paper in Washington
and in the newspapers. When a new strike occurred in the
face of this flurry of publicity, a change of tactics to direct
aggression became popular.

During a disturbance in the shirt factory in Connecticut
in 1919, an inmate was killed. The public was told that the
shooting was on orders of Deputy Warden C. J. Parker in
order to maintain discipline. "Discipline must be maintained
at all costs" has been a frequent justification for violence in
prisons on the part of the administration. The idea that
concessions to rioting inmates will undermine discipline, that
concessions cannot safely be granted even to save lives, is easily
accepted by an aroused public. In Michigan, in 1952, women
wrote letters to the editor explaining that those guards knew
the risks when they accepted their jobs, so saving the lives of
hostages was no excuse for negotiating with prisoners. At
Auburn, after the riot of January 19, 1857, was settled blood-
lessly by acceding to the inmates' demands, public officials
declared, "This yielding by the prison officers will give the
convicts new courage, and we may expect to hear of further
trouble."

In Kansas, in June, 1927, the riot in the mine began when
the warden refused to let the inmates have cigarettes. The
warden said he feared that drugs would be smuggled in via
the cigarettes. During the riot, newspapers reported that Deputy Warden Hudspeth was "pitting 15 years experience as a
prison official against the second attempt within a year to

nullify prison discipline." Warden Mackay, in Texas at the time, telegraphed Hudspeth, "Glad you are dealing with an iron hand, making no concessions to their childish demands for cigarettes. This may require some hot shot: accommodate them. It is unfortunate the better classes of inmates should suffer the stigma of those brainless idiots."

The same general approach was taken at Folsom in November, 1927, when California's Governor Young said, "I am confident that the prisoners will be subdued in the cell houses. But should they make their way to the yard, I propose to have enough armed men on guard to see that not a convict gets over the prison walls." He did, too, with tanks and National Guardsmen. This statement was made while he was in Sacramento. After he arrived on the scene, however, and found nine inmates and two guards dead and 31 inmates and three guards seriously wounded, Governor Young ordered the attacks to cease.

District Attorney McAllister led the public's aggression and bid for a few votes when he asked for the death penalty and the earliest possible execution of convicted inmates. The State Prison Board investigated causes of the riot, and denied the persistent rumors that parole policies contributed to them. Their statement said that the riot "could not have been caused by failure of the board to keep up the parole calendar. It's true, we're behind, but that makes no difference to inmates, since no second-timer can be paroled until he has served two calendar years."

After escapes in Georgia, the papers reported that six men "sweltered in the depths of solitary confinement." In Texas, after several escapes, an investigation was begun to put a stop to "such wholesale outbreaks as have occurred at frequent intervals in recent years." The Texas legislature was promised that it would be asked to act.

Investigations are a common medium of the expression of aggression. Typical are the threats of District Attorney John Monaghan of Philadelphia who, after the riot at Holmsburg in

1929, reported that if he were notified officially, he would launch an investigation to determine any evidence of mistreatment or brutalizing of prisoners. Simultaneously, Judge Frank Smith "considered" charging a grand jury to investigate conditions. It seems not to matter much whether public aggression is directed toward "convicts" or "corrupt prison administrations," just so long as hostility is expressed, and thereby released.

At Clinton Prison, New York, in July, 1929, District Attorney O'Connell started an inquiry, but Governor Franklin D. Roosevelt saw no call for executive action. When Auburn was rocked with riot a few days later, Governor Roosevelt blamed the rigor of the Baumes Laws (habitual criminal code), strengthened the guard, ordered overcrowding to end, and started a study of the penal law. Dr. Kieb, corrections commissioner, said that riots could not be prevented and that cutting down on privileges would precipitate trouble rather than eliminate it. He blamed the "mental atmosphere" caused by the Baumes Laws.

The 1929 riot in Leavenworth resulted in President Hoover's asking for $5,000,000 with which to end prison crowding, revise the penal system, and increase probation services. The reasons given for the rioting were (1) food, (2) suggestion by the New York riots, and (3) heat-crazed narcotics addicts under a temperature of 100.3 degrees. Sanford Bates' report to the Department of Justice blamed overcrowding, idleness, excessive heat, and information about the riots in the East.

The investigations following the riot at Dartmoor, England, in 1932, resulted in the banning of American crime films. The government's investigator, Herbert du Parcq, reported that the rioters were "modern criminals of gangster class, like Americans." He said that Governor (warden) S. N. Roberts was "most zealous and conscientious" but lacked an "exceptionally strong personality which might have fueled the disorder." He criticized Roberts for telling the inmates, "I am sorry the porridge at yesterday's breakfast was not up to standard," and referred to the speech as "a serious mistake," likely to be interpreted as a sign of timidity or weakness. He recommended Roberts' dismissal. He also said that eighty or ninety inmates will be brought to trial for "murder, arson, and other offenses." The new governor (warden) insisted on "strict discipline" and rifle practice for the guards.

The Board of Inquiry following the Ohio fire in 1930 sagaciously reported that the enormous loss of lives during the fire was due to failure to open the cells and let the men out. Penologists and civic leaders denounced the Ohio legislature for permitting the fire hazard to exist. County Prosecutor John Chester demanded the warden's suspension.

After the riot at Atlanta in 1944, Attorney General Biddle ordered the inmates put in solitary confinement, and promised a quick trial, indicating that he thought the inmates were trying to bring about a general insurrection of 2,000 inmates. The rioters were called "constitutional psychopathic cases." After the riot at Alcatraz in 1946, there were trials in which two men were sentenced to death, and afterward, inmate M. E. Thompson offered his eyes to a blind person, since he would not be needing them any more. James V. Bennett, Director of the United States Bureau of Prisons, announced that the Alcatraz gun gallery would be "completely replanned and rebuilt."

In New Jersey in 1952, a state senate investigating committee and a governor's investigating committee culled over the same material, as did Austin MacCormick of the Osborne Association. Overcrowding, obsolete and bad physical plant, and lack of funds were reported as causes of the riot. Governor Driscoll requested eight to ten millions to replace the antiquated penitentiary.

A "curtain of official silence" was reported from Illinois' Menard State Prison in 1952 when the warden reported merely that "they planned to grab the guards and the keys and go over the wall, but we moved too fast for them." Warden Munie referred frequently to the "psychriatic" (sic) division, but made no startling revelations. A "full" investigation was promised, and a legislative committee moved in. That apparently dissipated public aggression.

Another "curtain of official silence" fell in Ohio in 1952. Warden Alvis gave a "surrender or starve" ultimatum. Alvis promised to take up complaints after surrender. The newspapers reported, "Ohio Warden Wins Full Surrender. Investigations to Follow."

The aftermaths of the riots at Auburn in 1929, Colorado in 1929, and Michigan in 1952 followed the general pattern. Though handled in three different ways, the handling of the riots in each case was criticized. In Colorado, Governor Adams endorsed the rough handling of the riot, but his committee did not. The Colorado governor's committee reported after the riot that cost the lives of seven guards and five inmates, that "There was no one in authority at any stage of the proceedings who was capable of analyzing the problem and reaching a sound conclusion." The immediate cause of the riot was considered to be two desperate criminals who decided to escape or die in the attempt. Underlying causes were reported to be (1) misplacement of the penitentiary—should never be near a city, (2) inadequate housing, (3) failure to segregate different classes of prisoners, (4) two-man cells, (5) "death-trap" towers and, (6) underpaid, inefficient, and disloyal guards, no systematic training of guards, and jealousy and suspicion among the guards.

The aftermath of the riot at Auburn in December, 1929, continued for years after the quelling of it. In July, 1949, inmate Bravata obtained a reduction of the life sentence he received from charges growing out of that riot. After a series of investigations, political charges and countercharges, Warden Jennings resigned in January, 1930. A grand jury opened investigations at which Jennings had to testify. Conditions were inspected by the Corrections Commission and many other committees.

Dr. Raymond F. C. Kieb, commissioner of corrections, pointed out that several factors made the New York prison situation dangerous. The new crime laws (Baumes Laws and others in the same harsh temper), new long sentences, the new type of hardened criminal, and old physical plant and facilities combined to make a bad situation dangerous. He blamed the precipitation of rioting at Auburn on (1) lax administration under ex-Warden Edgar S. Jennings and (2) meddling of Mayor Charles E. Osborne of Auburn, and the community welfare work of Lithgow Osborne, both sons of the late Thomas Mott Osborne, which combined to break the discipline at Auburn.

Charges of mismanagement, corruption in the Mutual Welfare League, lax discipline, smuggling, and incompetence were punctuated in March, 1930, by the killing of the new keeper by an inmate, which started a new series of inquiries. Three inmates were executed and others were sentenced for charges growing out of the December 11, 1929, riot. The state commissioners reported restrictive changes to prevent future riots.

The aftermath of the Michigan riot was even more intense than the Auburn affair. As the representative of the prison administration dealing with the rioters, I was lauded highly during the riot, with a resolution being prepared for the state senate to commend me. Immediately after the riot ended, however, I became the symbol of "kid-glove" handling of convicts and the recipient of considerable editorial criticism. Small-time politicians began calling for my dismissal. A "get-tough" policy was introduced and the guts were torn from the Treatment program. I resigned as of June 28, 1952. The warden was subsequently dismissed as an incompetent. Top management inside the prison was replaced. The law was changed to eliminate the single commissioner of corrections appointed by the governor. No competent man with a national reputation would take the newly created director of corrections job in Michigan, so a smiling and suave employee without a reputation for new ideas was placed in charge. The aftermath in Michigan is explained in greater detail later in this volume.

Gains and losses in progressive prison programs as a result of riots appear to vary widely with the political situations.

It is suggested that when the political situation is fairly secure for the administration in office, there is less need for "get-tough" policies and other drastic defensive action. In such a situation, the riot situation can be used to call public attention to deficiencies in the penal program and the needs for improvement. Legislators in these more secure situations seem to be more willing to grant funds for the improvements. As a consequence of the riot in Ohio in 1952, Director of Corrections Arthur Glattke was able to obtain approval for sweeping improvements in Ohio's correctional program.

When the political situation in a state is so precarious that the administration is insecure, the need for "get-tough" policies and harsh and drastic measures tends to strangle penal progress. Retrenchment to rigidity in custody is more traditional in prisons, and hence more safe politically than venturing in the direction of modern treatment programs which the public opinion may reject as "coddling." Such rigidity simply constitutes a regression to former, better known, and more secure penal policy for the political leadership. In Michigan in 1952, Governor Williams was the only Democrat in the state administration, with his cabinet being elected Republicans and the legislature being predominantly Republican. The Democratic-appointed commissioner of corrections and Democratic governor were blamed by the Republicans for lax discipline.

Governor Williams surveyed the political horizon, introduced a "get-tough" policy, asked for gun turrets in the cellhouses, increased the guard force and, for all practical purposes, tore the guts out of the Treatment program by undermining the morale of Treatment personnel. Because of the insecure political situation, the aftermath of the riot in Michigan negated several years of progress in building up a well-accepted and mature Treatment program integrated with the rest of the prison program.

When administrations can be considered neither secure or insecure, or where enlightenment and pressure for progressive penology is about equal to pressure for rigidity in prison program, a different situation seems to have developed. In the New York system and the United States Bureau of Prisons, many of the policies have been worked out as compromises between the two (or more) points of view. These compromises have been set down in manuals of procedures or personnel manuals. Because Custody is always a safe point of view, over the years, these compromises have tended toward custodial rigidity with the Treatment aspects of the programs carefully delineated or "interpreted."

The aftermath appears to be the most important phase of the prison riot in terms of subsequent penal policy. The direction and form taken by the aftermath appears to be determined by many factors, probably most important of which is the enlightenment and political security of the state administration in office. In any case, the causes of the riot must be interpreted to the public and the measures explained by which a recurrence of violence may be prevented. Such explanation is easier in the absence of political adversaries who complicate the situation by broadcasting their own explanations.

CHAPTER V

Prison Conditions in America

It may be true of all public and private institutions, but it is particularly true of prisons that valid and reliable information beyond a superficial level is difficult to obtain. The size of the yard, the height of the wall, the number of custodial personnel, the annual budget, and similar nonthreatening facts are easily found. A reliable and valid evaluation of the school program, recreation program, classification and the effectiveness with which it actually works, and such programs are very difficult to obtain. Reasons for it are sometimes, but not always, that personnel prefer to conceal uncomplimentary facts.

I have heard the story repeatedly of the Michigan contingent that visited Sing Sing just prior to World War II on the way to an American Prison Association meeting in the East. G. I. Francis was then Director of Education at the State Prison of Southern Michigan. As the group entered the school facilities at Sing Sing, G. I. wandered toward a schoolroom, ignoring the shouts of a guard telling him to stay with the group. Walking up to a big man sitting before his books, G. I. asked, "What are you studying?"

"I ain't studyin' nothin'," came the reply, "they told me to sit here while youse guys went through."

During my years in the Michigan Department of Correction, I was convinced that many personnel, some of whom had been there longer than I, were unaware of the actual effectiveness or ineffectiveness of classification, for instance, in many areas. They were unaware of the conditions surrounding job and cell changes as these changes actually took place with cigarettes or services in exchange.

The reasons for this unawareness in most instances seemed to lie in the differences in backgrounds between personnel and prisoners, which were so different that many times there was no common ground through which to communicate. Differences in background resulted in differences in sets of values. They were thinking in two or more different frames of reference, with little in the way of similar concepts or ideas transcending. Many personnel lacked that type of empathy to which many psychologists refer as "clinical intuition." The results of this situation are that two groups of people with different values may live side by side for years, interpreting the same behavior in two different ways, each wondering what the hell the other is thinking about. Routines of procedure frequently become so habituated that only with difficulty can they be changed. The situation in some cases may entail ego-involvement, in which case the side with the greatest power in terms of numbers or authority prevails, increasing the frustration on the other side, thereby aggravating the problem by winning the issue. Because of this situation, interviews with most prison personnel are of widely variant value in evaluating a prison program, limited by the extent of their experience and their "clinical intuition."

I do not presume to know the conditions of prisons on a national scale. I have visited only a fraction of the institutions listed in the directory of the American Prison Association. After reading many reports, visiting prisons in several states and the federal system, hearing many speeches, and conversing with many persons regarding prison programs and evaluating each experience in terms of my own experience, I am convinced that few others know conditions of prisons on a national scale, either.

The man usually given credit for knowing national conditions best is Professor Austin H. MacCormick of the University of California and Executive Secretary of the Osborne Association. He has visited more prisons with greater frequency than, probably, any other man in America. Generally quartered in the wardens' residences, he has been most frequently given free access to all parts and personnel in the prisons. He has stated that he knows Michigan prisons probably better than others because he has been invited to "investigate" them more frequently than others. Michigan Corrections is also the system I know best. After reading several of Professor MacCormick's reports on Michigan prisons, I have been impressed by their superficiality, his resorting to description of physical plant and operational procedure, and what I considered to be shallow judgment in recommendations. My thinking was supported by the members of the Michigan parole board who referred to his work in 1952 as "sloppy." I am not saying I could have done as well under similar circumstances. Perhaps the approaches from quarters in the wardens' residences have carried meanings which militated against obtaining the sort of information which would have permitted better evaluations.

The man whom I believe to be the most capable penologist in the country today is Donald Clemmer, Commissioner of Corrections for the District of Columbia. His reports on some of the same areas MacCormick has investigated show greater depth, better discernment of crucial issues, and better judgment. Even Clemmer, however, made at least one recommendation regarding classification that Michigan had already tried and discarded. It is most difficult for any man to know prisons on a national scale, even if he has free access to all of them. It would take too long to build up and keep the confidence of personnel and inmates in order that evaluating data might be gathered.

Face-to-face discussions at conferences yield some information as to conditions in the area being reported. Most of their value is in anecdotal indices which may give clues as to the status of the system. One leaves such conferences with impressions as to the relative progress made in specific areas by specific systems, a general idea of their basic philosophy of penology and corrections. Sometimes it is difficult to get any information at all about a specific area of which one wants to learn. Well do I recall trying to learn about the effectiveness of classification in Illinois during conversations at the meeting of the Central States Correctional Association in 1950. Long and interesting generalities ensued and at the end I wondered about the effectiveness of classification in Illinois. After a couple of exchanges of correspondence with Illinois officials after the meeting was over, some of my questions had been answered.

Another view of the correctional systems of various states can be obtained by interviewing the men who have gone through them. Inmate reporting of fact can be just as invalid as the reporting of fact by other human beings. As a matter of fact, the same personal interests color the reports of inmates and prison personnel and investigators alike, with the directions of their interests varying according to their status in the given situation. When one inmate reports something in an interview, it should not generally be accepted without further checking. When two inmates independently and at different times report the same information, however, it would seem to be more reliable. When three or more inmates report the same information independently, it is reasonable to suppose that the statement is true.

Using this approach, I took the opportunity to learn about other prisons while interviewing thousands of inmates during my ten years (including Army service) of experience in Michigan's prison system. As psychologist at the State Prison of Southern Michigan, I interviewed routinely between 2,000 and 2,800 men each year. When a man who had served elsewhere came along, I asked questions about the system in which he had served. Following up the same approach in other positions, the interviews were less routine and fewer in number. Some of the information so gained is systematically recorded, but most of it remains a matter of memory.

Because of Michigan's geographic location and the persons who migrated to Michigan, the bulk of the information gained from inmates concerns the prisons in Ohio, Illinois, Pennsylvania, Indiana, New York, Connecticut, Kentucky, West Virginia, Wisconsin, Georgia, Alabama, Tennessee, Mississippi, Arkansas, and certain federal institutions. Three or four independent interviews were held concerning Oklahoma, Texas, Colorado, Iowa, Missouri, and Minnesota. At least one interview was held concerning all states except Maine, Vermont, New Hampshire, Oregon, North Dakota, South Dakota, South Carolina, Utah, Montana, Wyoming, and Arizona. Checking on some of the interview information against conditions as they actually existed in prisons subsequently visited has confirmed much of the interview information.

There is no single source of information as to the conditions in prisons nationally. Newspaper reports of investigations, research studies in professional periodicals, officials reports of inquiry, inmates' statements, and the statements of prison personnel must be evaluated and integrated before an adequate statement can be ventured. Certainly, the inmates' statements can not be left out. In my opinion, the inmates' statements are the most important single source of information because they are the persons most directly affected by prison programs of any sort. Attempting to make a statement about conditions in prisons is a daring and presumptuous venture, but I shall try to do it by integrating as best I can all the information I have gleaned from the forementioned sources.

The majority of states do not have any real central control over the prison system. With the exception of appointments of wardens, most prisons are operated by the warden in practical autonomy. The majority of wardens are political appointees without specific training or experience for the job. In some states where the political situation is predominantly a one-party affair, the tenure of the warden may be continuous over a period of fifteen or twenty years. In other states, the tenure of the warden is congruent with the tenure of the elected administrator. As a result, the warden seldom becomes more than a public relations man, leaving the actual operation of the prison to old guards and other subordinate personnel who may have remained from previous administrations. Very few states have set up training and experience requirements for candidacy to the office of warden. Some states which have set up requirements for lesser officials leave the wardens out of the "classified" service for which requirements are set.

In the traditional prison organization, the chain of command goes from the warden to deputy warden to assistant deputy warden to custodial inspector to captain to lieutenant to sergeant to guard. The chain of command is entirely custodial.

The federal penitentiaries, Michigan from 1946 to 1952, and California have given the Treatment phases deputy-warden status in order to bring about a balance between Custody and Treatment. Even in these situations, however, Custody is the prevailing division. All other services are traditionally subordinate.

States with real central control usually exert that control in one of two forms, (1) a Department of Corrections or (2) a Division of Corrections within the Department of Social Welfare. The prison systems generally recognized to be the better systems have real central control. California and New Jersey, considered to have the two outstanding correctional programs in the country, were led by two outstanding penologists, Richard McGee and Sanford Bates, now retired, respectively, both imported for their qualifications to do the job. The approach to corrections in California and New Jersey is in Treatment rather than Custody. California has been pioneering since 1940 in the experiment with Youth and Adult Corrections Authorities in which the court retains the judicial function of determining guilt, but a board of professional people deliberates on the plan of treatment and determines length of stay in an institution. New Jersey has taken the lead in group therapy and has been using the old Lindbergh residence for an unusual experiment in self-controlled group living.

New York has strong central control, strong civil service recruitment and protection of personnel, and good reception and diagnostic centers. Inmates seem also to agree, however, that strong political interference provides an occasional undercurrent of confusion, particularly when a prisoner from the big city with some political influence is involved. Inmates have reported the New York system as "rough," generally because custody is considered to be strong and inmate movement is well regimented. The influence of the treatment aspects so well publicized from New York are said to be localized in a few places. It may be, too, that the classification system in New York is so good that the "unsalvageable" men are grouped in their "rough" prisons and released only to find their way into Michigan's and other prisons, which could well impair the value of our information. More New York prisoners in proportion to their prison population, though, have found their way into Michigan prisons than have prisoners from neighboring New Jersey.

Few states have effective civil service systems or merit programs for the recruitment and selection of personnel for the prison system. In 1952, the states in which a merit system or civil service system selected at least some of the prison personnel were Alabama, California, Colorado, Connecticut, Georgia, Illinois, Kansas, Maine, Maryland, Massachusetts, Michigan, Minnesota, Missouri, New Hampshire, New Jersey, New York, Ohio, Oregon, Rhode Island, Vermont, Wisconsin, District of Columbia. This is true also of the United States Bureau of Prisons. This represents an increase on paper from 16 states in 1948 to 21 states in 1952. Practices vary widely from state to state, even though civil service or the merit system is present. For example, Michigan's civil service is as strong as any, supported by being in existence by amendment to the state constitution together with constitutional provision for financing it. With the exception of top-level positions the Civil Service Commission there has shown ability to protect career employees. Even in Michigan, however, I have observed decisions by the Civil Service Commission which I thought were swayed by the political exigencies. In neighboring Illinois, however, with a merit system three decades older than Michigan's, the protection for the career correctional employee is considered to be much less secure. Some other states have the system on paper.

Salaries in corrections are not attractive. The hope to contribute to the growth of humane treatment or the personal need to express superiority through brutality, condescension, or "do-gooding" are the only obvious incentives to enter correctional work. Guards are the largest number of employees in any correctional system, and their quality in large measure determines the level at which the prison program will function. The lowest guards' salaries I have seen in 1953 were $90 per month and $118 per month under no particular plan. At the same time, California paid guards $325 per month, Illinois $300, Massachusetts $320, and New York $353 under civil service plans. Personnel who would work as guards for $90 and $118 per month during times of prosperity probably would not be the most capable men in competition in the labor market. Certainly, no significant standards of education, intelligence, age, or other standards for recruiting could be maintained at those salaries.

Men are not trained for prison work in the public schools, though a few universities graduate some men from curricula in corrections who then find themselves trained beyond the salaries most prisons can offer. In-service training is a method by which the leading prison systems improve their personnel and, in turn, their programs. The United States Bureau of Prisons, California, New York, and New Jersey have excellent in-service training programs. In-service training programs in the majority of prisons, however, are absent altogether.

The philosophy of corrections varies throughout the country with each state. Attempting to find patterns which emerge from the myriad of laws, policies, and practices is difficult. The terms, "treatment," "classification," and "rehabilitation" are beginning to appear in the correctional laws of the states, but they are slow. Philosophies of punishment, rehabilitation, "out-of-sight, out-of-mind," or public works are intertwined with each other in most prisons, with emphases on each dependent upon the philosophy of top administration. Budget figures show where the money is going and how much relative emphasis is being placed on each program. All states spend more money on custodial personnel than on almost all other personnel combined, though some minimum security institutions within the system may reverse the figures. I was asked one time what we were doing, using up a quarter of a million dollars annually in Michigan for individual treatment. I pointed out that custody was using almost a million and a quarter, to which came the rejoinder, "Well, that's different!" The person who asked the question would have preferred to spend a million and a half on custody and none for treatment. Some of us would have liked to spend a similar figure for both services.

Most prisons spend about $3.00 per man per day on the program. Michigan Corrections spends approximately $11,000,-000 annually with a prison population of 9,000. Other prisons cost the taxpayer less. Mississippi, for instance, has operated at a profit in cotton over the past ten years, having turned back to the state about a million dollars more than the total appropriations granted by the legislature. In general, it is logically observed that the better the treatment program, the higher the per capita budget. California and New Jersey, while still spending more for custody than treatment, have two of the largest "Treatment" budgets in the land, proportionately larger than the Treatment budget of the United States Bureau of Prisons. In emphasizing Treatment, the United States Bureau of Prisons has a continuing in-service training program for all personnel and the psychiatrists, medical men, dentists, and psychologists are furnished by the United States Public Health Service. Education in California prisons is provided by the state educational department on the same population basis as that provided in the public schools. California boasts of one of the best educational programs in American prisons. On the other hand, Nebraska refused to pay for a schoolteacher, and educational services must be paid for from the profits of the inmate canteen, as of 1950.

Custodial practices and discipline differ widely, also. Generally, the effectiveness of discipline and custody is in direct proportion to the size of the budget. Prison rules and regulations have to be scaled down to a level that can be enforced by the available custodial force. States with a full custodial force can maintain rather rigid rules and regulations for everybody. Some states with not so much money for custody tend to maintain rigid rules and regulations for most prisoners, but reserve privileged status for a few who, in turn, assist in maintaining the peace. For instance, Colorado is reported to have such a program in which the administration is considered to be "tough," but some capable inmates have more privileges, on however informal a basis, than others probably less influential. An example of administrative reliance on inmates in Colorado is the fact that two inmates are used at the main entrance for parking cars and for opening and closing the locked gate, of course under the supervision of an officer.

In other states, the legislatures have not provided enough money to hire a full custodial staff. Consequently, inmates are used as guards. I have visited some states where inmates go into armed guard towers in the absence of officers. Armed inmates are frequently used in some states for the supervision of work gangs. Several inmates have told me that in Arkansas, a lifer or long-termer used as a guard is awarded his release if he shoots somebody trying to escape. Several stories have been told about long-termers who told young, naïve inmates that they were too young to associate with these men, that he was the guard and he would turn his back while the youngster made good his escape. After allowing sufficient time for the young inmate to get off state property, the armed guard would turn, shoot the escaping convict, and secure his own release.

At the Mississippi State Penitentiary, where there are very few civilian guards, male and female armed inmates, both colored and white, in vertical striped clothing, keep other inmates in horizontal striped clothing in secure custody. I felt a little unnecessary apprehension while strolling through that situation, not having been accustomed to it. The Mississippi legislature, however, does not provide Superintendent Wiggins with sufficient funds to maintain a civilian guard force. Food costs show the same variation that other phases of the prison programs show on a national basis. The average daily cost per inmate throughout the country appears to be around fifty cents. The highest daily per capita food costs I have seen in a correctional institution was $1.25. The lowest I have seen was 17¢ per day per man. All these figures take into account the food raised on institutional farms.

In most prisons, supplies and materials mysteriously disappear. An official at the State Prison of Southern Michigan has been frequently accused in private conversation of building his fine brick home through theft and graft involving prison materials. Very few prisons have an adequate cost accounting system for the control of the taxpayers' financial investment. After visiting several prisons and looking at some of their financial records, I am convinced that the place to start in improving most prison programs is in the installation of an adequate cost accounting system so that the director of corrections may know for sure where the money is actually going and be really able to control its use.

The Achilles' heel in institutional finance is in the use of the profits from the inmate store or canteen. In the larger prisons, an inventory of $10,000 to $15,000 may result in around $8,000 monthly sales and profits ranging from $1,000 to $2,500. The lowest yearly profit I have seen recorded was slightly under $5,000, but I am sure that there are many totals under that figure. This profit is generally placed in a "welfare fund." From the welfare fund is purchased recreation equipment, music supplies, and other items not provided for by appropriated funds. Many states provide that parolees from the prison may obtain loans to help them get started again, but provide no funds for the purpose. Most of these loans come from the welfare fund, and much of it is written off as bad debt. Because this fund is locally controlled and seldom audited, it can and is frequently used for items that would be difficult to justify, such as a water heater for an official's residence. I saw one monthly report in a medium-sized prison with $504.63 charged to "administration." Nobody seemed to know what it meant, and I did not suggest an investigation to find out—it would not have been courteous. In most cases, the use or abuse of this fund is not illegal, but just careless. In other cases, it is very carefully used for legal and justifiable items with strict periodic auditing, such as in the United States Bureau of Prisons. In some cases, there is room for suspicion of illegal use of the fund. One fund I have seen showed about $50,000 of the welfare fund in securities, with no provision to show what was happening to the dividends. With a salary under $4,000, the warden and his wife were living lavishly with diamonds to match. It would have been protection for that warden to have had his accounts audited so that suspicion as to hidden income might have been allayed. The United States Bureau of Prisons is sufficiently aware of the implications that monthly financial reports of the welfare fund and its use must be sent from each institution in the system to the director's office in Washington.

Some inmate canteens or stores have lunchrooms in which sandwiches, ham and eggs, and similar lunches are sold. In some of these prisons, the amount of food sold is in inverse ratio to the quantity and quality of the food served in the prison's mess hall. Inmates have told me in some prisons that they were forced to use the canteen to "survive," which was, of course, exaggeration, since the men who could not afford to use the canteen were still "surviving." Nevertheless, the inverse ratio seems to obtain.

The most serious problems in maintaining peace and order within the prisons are gambling and sex. Both are controlled, not so much for the activity itself, but because more fights between inmates are caused by these two activities than any other. To control gambling, many prisons make money contraband and issue tokens or scrip for spending at the inmate canteen in amounts determined by the size of the inmates' accounts in the front office. Many other prisons recognize that, with the custodial force they have, they could not reasonably enforce that rule, so they place a limit of usually five dollars, or no paper money, that an inmate can have on his person. Seldom does anybody stop to count the money an inmate has, and gambling goes on hardly slowed down. Many prisons waive the rules against gambling on specific holidays, and on the Fourth of July, an observer can see games and money everywhere in the yard.

Homosexual activity results in fights when the eternal triangle develops between two wolves and a boy. A few fights occur when a boy resists the attentions of a prospective jocker. In prisons with one-man cells, homosexuality can be somewhat controlled or held to a minimum. When the prison has two men or more per cell, such control is almost impossible. Several inmates have told me that in Illinois, where inmate clerks handed out cell assignments—under supervision, of course,—the standard quip for a long time was "Here's your marriage license."

I was visiting a state prison west of the Mississippi one time and observed double bunks in what were intended to be one-man cells. Curtains hung over the cell door from the inside. I asked the official who was with me whether they had a homosexual problem. He said they didn't find any. I believed him.

Inmate informers told me that in the camps maintained by a Southern state visiting days were on Sunday. Each inmate could have visitors on alternate Sundays. Wives and sweethearts could visit privately in the barracks. Blankets hung from the upper bunk gave the lower bunk all the privacy anybody wanted. When I visited that state's correctional system, I made no mention of it. The officials told me about it, however, and pointed out that it solved a lot of problems for them. All the prisons in Latin America do it officially. I have heard of several in the United States that do it unofficially, but only in two states have I had confirmation. In the second state, a room was set aside which was rented for conjugal purposes. Prior to 1952, an inmate operated the concession, but when a state legislator objected to that practice, the inmate was removed from that advantageous position. A custodial sergeant took it over. In most prisons, classification, which has assumed the meaning of "treatment," is not effective. Most prisons have programs they have labeled as "classification," but only a minority of these programs can properly be called classification. State laws limit some programs in classification by providing for classification according to physical ability or inability to work on the roads, such as Florida's statutes. On the other hand, some states have laws which give statutory basis for classification for the purposes of diagnosis and treatment, such as Michigan. In prisons with effective classification programs, social workers or sociologists prepare social histories on incoming inmates, psychologists test for intelligence and aptitudes, and representative staff members meet to determine placement for each man in a program both beneficial to the man and according to the needs of the institution. The classification report is in the form of a recommendation to be translated into action in the office of the custodial deputy warden. In many prisons, the deputy treats the classification committee recommendation as a recommendation and files it in "13." The man is then assigned to whatever job the deputy wants to fill, on the theory that the deputy knows more about the institution than the classification committee, anyway. On occasion, the deputy is a part of the classification committee, in which case his ideas generally prevail. In the better systems, the classification committee's recommendation becomes an order.

Job assignments are generally implemented in the office of the custodial deputy warden. Cell assignments are implemented in the same place. When the economy of the state is such that salaries for civilian clerks are not available, inmate clerks are used. Where inmate clerks are employed, there is always the possibility of "dealing" in jobs and cell assignments. For instance, when I went to the State Prison of Southern Michigan, jobs in the stamp plant were worth four or five cartons of cigarettes, while jobs in the kitchen were worth only one. At the same time, I was a member of the classification committee that recommended jobs. All new men obtained some sort of assignment, but the classification committee was limited by the administration, the work supervisors, or the general exigencies, to three assignments considered to be the most undesirable in the prison—the laundry, kitchen and textile plant. The old-timers in the yard found their ways to the choice assignments by currying favor with work superintendents, by recommendations of fellow inmates, or by cigarettes. It was amazing to me that some of the members of the classification committee did not seem to be aware of what was going on or preferred to ignore it.

Actual psychotherapy or "treatment" in prison is virtually unknown. There is considerable writing on the subject, but it is localized to certain places. Certain of the federal institutions, New Jersey, and a few other places have attempted to employ intensive therapy in a few cases. When I arrived at the State Prison of Southern Michigan in 1942, I talked to a man who convinced me that he had not been spoken to by a civilian, guard or otherwise, since 1922. In the branch prison at Marquette, another man told me in May, 1950, that he has not been spoken to by a civilian, guard or otherwise, since classification was set up there in 1937. When the counseling system was established in Jackson in May, 1949, it was provided that each counselor would interview each man on his caseload, which ranged between 450 and 750 men, a minimum of three times a year. We knew that if we could get a "good morning, Joe" on an individual basis to every man in the prison three times a year, it would in itself be an advance for the treatment program, regardless of any ideas of "intensive therapy." The improvement of morale which could be possible would set the stage for subsequent reduction of caseloads and introduction of some type of intensive therapy.

Several patterns have emerged in the Treatment phase of prison programs. Several states, such as Illinois and New York, have established diagnostic depots, staffed with psychiatrists, physicians, psychologists, and social workers. A complete study is made of each inmate and he is sent to the institution considered most appropriate. Their experience has been that there has been little use of the diagnostic material in the prison. Ohio has attempted the use of psychiatrists who prepare a report on all men transferred from one institution to another within the system. The routineness of these reports has rendered them of less value than originally intended. The value of the Ohio system appears to be that each psychiatrist informally selects several men for intensive therapy. Michigan has introduced a counseling program in which all inmates are assigned to a psychologist or social worker called a counselor. The primary weakness is that so few counselors are available that the caseloads run from 450 to 750 men, thereby rendering the therapy relatively ineffective by sheer volume.

All programs are faced with a custodial force generally unable to understand the treatment approach and unsympathetic with it. This lack of sympathy frequently is expressed to inmates in an aggressive manner, and sometimes is reinforced by similar statements from prison administrators. I heard Superintendent George Morris of the Nebraska State Reformatory say that psychiatry, psychology, sociology, and similar disciplines had not, to his knowledge, helped anybody, and that they were passing academic fads that would pass and be gone from prisons in another twenty-five years.

Federal and state legislation has limited the transportation of convict-made goods across state lines or from being sold on the open market. As a consequence, enforced idleness has become an unwelcome part of most prison programs. I visited a prison once which had no idleness. Instead, they had what they called a "grits mill," which consisted of an officer supervising the unassigned inmates in a certain area as they walked for a half-hour and sat for a half-hour for a seven-hour day. Some institutions have tried to solve the problem of idleness by substituting an expanded educational program, but it is difficult to keep up inmate interest and morale in such a program.

Michigan ran into conflict with the labor union when it tried to inaugurate a brick-laying class in the vocational school. It has been estimated that if all prisons produced materials full blast, they could not contribute one per cent of the nation's production. Yet, the best any prison industries can do is to keep part of the inmates busy part of the time. Arts and crafts programs in many prisons are difficult to control. Custodially, some prisons allow no knives, modeling clay, saws, and such items. Other prisons permit knives, files, saws, electric motors, and almost anything but a bar spreader. The Eastern State Penitentiary in Pennsylvania furnishes power machinery. The equipment is less a problem than the control of production and sale of the items. To reduce confusion, some prisons have imposed a concession system whereby one inmate is responsible for wallets, another for model ships, and similar assignments. When one inmate controls a concession with official sanction, an economical hierarchy is set up so that anyone who wants to make wallets must work for the inmate who holds the concession. Eventually, it becomes big business. I have seen trouble start because inmates were making more money than the guards. Various degrees of administrative control from rigid restriction to *laissez-faire* regarding arts and crafts programs exist in American prisons. There is no obvious pattern.

Recreation programs and athletic teams in prisons are rigidly controlled in only a few prisons. In almost all prisons, the selections to team positions, which involve prestige and in some cases special meals and trips outside the prison, finally remain with inmate coaches. Sometimes, a carton of cigarettes in the right place will help decide a difficult selection. This situation frequently causes other inmates to call men on the athletic assignment "a bunch of politicians." In games with outside teams, most inmates cheer for the visitors, refusing to express any identification or loyalty to their alma mater's varsity. Even in intramural programs, most prisons limit the candidates for participation to those with best athletic or other ability, rather than offering a program for everybody. In only a few prisons does the recreation program serve more than a minority of the prison population.

As stated in the book on penal systems in the world published by the Institute of Comparative Law of the University of Paris, *Les Grands Systèmes Pénitentiaires Actuels,* prisons can not very well be ranked as "good" or "bad" with present knowledge. That volume attempted to rank some American prison systems according to their development and acceptance of progressive ideas in penology. California was pointed out as standing alone, leading all others in the penal program. I would add pre-riot Michigan as a national leader in the development and acceptance of progressive ideas. New Jersey leads a group of "intermediate" prisons that included New York and Massachusetts, and I would add to that group the United States Bureau of Prisons and post-riot Michigan. Florida, South Carolina, and Texas were specifically named as being among the most backward.

The conditions in America's prisons vary widely from state to state and from institution to institution. Philosophies of treatment, custody, punishment, and job-holding vary just as widely. Research, writing, and speaking in the field come from the more advanced prisons. The prisons not so advanced have nothing to contribute or say, unless it is defensive in nature. It grieved me one time to hear prison officials from Iowa devote considerable time to a discussion of whether an inmate should be called, "mister," when far more serious questions were at hand. A few prison systems are outstanding in their progressive methods, like California and New Jersey. The United States Bureau of Prisons, with variations within its own system, ranges from tops at their institution at Seagoville, Texas, to national average elsewhere. A few states are diligently trying to improve their programs, like Ohio, Missouri, and Alabama. The majority of prisons, however, are relatively stable in their tradition, progressing only as rapidly as they are carried by outside influences. An index of the temper of the majority of prison administrations may be found in the fact that Colorado's late Roy Best, who was accused of converting state property to his own use and cruelty in prison administration, who recently beat an indictment on technical grounds, subsequently received a two-year suspension for misconduct, maintains a "blow 'em to hell off the wall" philosophy, boasts of his use of corporal punishment, maintains that a prisoner has no civil rights—Colorado's Roy Best was elected president of the Warden's Association, an affiliate of the American Prison Association!

In the meanwhile, organizations and some prison people throughout the country are working for the improvement of correctional treatment. The American Correctional Association (known as the American Prison Association prior to October, 1954) with its annual Congress of Correction, the National Probation and Parole Association, and the Osborne Association are but a few of the national organizations working for the improvement of prisons and their programs. Such men as Donald Clemmer, Austin MacCormick, Robert Hannum, E. R. Cass, Roberts J. Wright, Dr. Wallack of Wallkill Prison, Reed Cozart of Louisiana, Richard McGee and Dr. Norman Fenton of California, Dr. E. Lovell Bixby of New Jersey, Arthur Glattke of Ohio, are but a few of the many men in the practical correctional field who are capably trying to improve the prisons. Effective also are the local state-wide correctional associations, like the Alabama Correctional Research Association, made up of citizens interested in the improvement of prisons and who are willing to stand up and be counted as favoring improvement of treatment facilities. Like John the Baptist and Thomas Mott Osborne, they must feel at times that they are shouting in the wilderness, but they continue to shout. And their group is growing larger. Things are looking up.

It may be interesting to compare the states which have had some sort of disturbance in their systems since 1900 with those which have reported no disturbances. The following lists show those states which have reported disturbances and those which have not.

States which have reported disturbances in their prison system

Alabama	Nebraska
Arizona	Nevada
Arkansas	New Jersey
California	New Mexico
Colorado	New York
Connecticut	North Carolina
Florida	Ohio
Georgia	Oregon
Idaho	Pennsylvania
Illinois	South Dakota
Kansas	Tennessee
Kentucky	Texas
Louisiana	Utah
Massachusetts	Washington
Michigan	West Virginia
Minnesota	Wisconsin
Missouri	

U.S. Bureau of Prisons

States which have not reported disturbances in their prison system

Delaware	New Hampshire
District of Columbia	North Dakota
Indiana	Oklahoma
Iowa	Rhode Island
Maine	South Carolina
Maryland	Vermont
Mississippi	Virginia
Montana	Wyoming

CHAPTER VI

Conditions in Pre-Riot Michigan

Corrections in Michigan during my tenure there between 1942 and 1952 was considered to be among the best in the nation. This appeared to be the consensus among many prison people. Tangible evidence was that a motion picture producer was steered to Michigan when a film short of modern, progressive prisons was made. Consequently, the film, "New Prisons—New Men" in the series, "This Is America," in the middle 1940s, was based on the State Prison of Southern Michigan at Jackson.

When I arrived at the State Prison of Southern Michigan in June, 1942, the size of the place awed me. Possession of the largest prison in the world was Michigan's hesitant boast. The classification department, of which I had become a part, was headed by Chuck Watson, who had previously been secretary to Dr. David Philips, the psychiatrist who had gone to the Michigan Reformatory at Ionia to head classification after a factional fight between the warden and the parole board split the department. Sydney Moskowitz, who had been psychologist at Jackson, was another parole board supporter along with Dr. Philips, and had gone to the central office in Lansing as the parole eligibility examiner for Michigan's new "lifer law." By the time I arrived, the classification department was generally loyal to the warden and had little to do with the parole board. I thought that was a helluva situation, but I learned all over again that factionalism seems to be just a part of institutions.

Only a few days after my arrival, while the orientation

period was going on and I had no duties, I strolled into the office of Deputy G. I. Francis, formerly school director, on an errand for Chuck Watson. A big man in a guard's uniform looked in my direction and said sternly, "You'd better take a trip to Marquette with us before you start criticizing the way we treat prisoners." I turned around to see who was behind me but he turned me around again with, "Yes, you—I'm talking to you!" Deputy Francis was ready to talk with me then, and by the time I was free to answer the big one, I could see his massive frame lumbering down the hall and decided discretion was the better part of valor.

When I told Chuck what had happened, he identified the big one as "Big Ed" Kaminski, and that he probably had mistaken me for another man in classification who had remarked that the custodial officers who transfer men to the branch prison at Marquette could be a little more humane. Big Ed was considered to be one of the best officers in custody. I never found out really to what Big Ed was referring, except that he chewed garlic and didn't like "crystal gazers." All professional people in the classification department, psychiatrists, psychologists, sociologists, and social workers were "crystal gazers."

The crystal gazers had a rough time at Jackson. Fortunately, I didn't smoke—fortunately, because as I walked through the huge, echoing rotunda with the crystal gazers at the end of the day during that first week, I heard a custodial officer from the hall office desk snap, "Put that goddam cigarette out!" I noticed smoke rising from a cigarette in the officer's hand and was ready to challenge him, but the crystal gazers meekly snuffed out their cigarettes in their hands so they wouldn't dirty the floor, and put the butts in their pockets. I was assured that custody comes first around Jackson.

The inmates who worked in my office taught me a lot about prison administration. These inmates typed psychological reports, scored group tests, and did many other things which, by good professional standards, should have been done by civilian employees. I learned about the factional fight going on between Deputy G. I. Francis and Assistant Deputy D. C. Pettit. I never saw them in conversation nor heard them speak to each other. Every noon, G. I. would lead a contingent of "henchmen" to lunch, and D. C. would have a party for his contingent at night. G. I. supported the parole board and D. C. supported the warden. I wanted to support both. G. I. never spoke a civil word to me, and D. C. never spoke a harsh one, probably because Chuck Watson, my boss, supported the warden with D. C. The inmates supported D. C. because he was humane and courteous to everybody, while G. I. was caustic and personally ambitious.

One of the most valuable lessons I learned was from Chuck A., whom I considered to be one of my chief clerks. Chuck wanted to be transferred to upper 15-block which, at that time, was used for kitchen help. The lights in 15 stayed on till midnight and he told me, tongue in cheek, that he wanted to do some of my statistical work at that time. I thought it all right and telephoned Captain Goodall, whom I had befriended, and Cap said he would put through a cell-change card. Several days passed, I called Cap, and he put through another cell-change card. The activity was repeated several times in the next two weeks. One day, Chuck A. told me that he was in the process of teaching me a lesson in prison administration. "The cons run the joint," he assured me. By default, misplaced confidence, or neglect, the officials, there 40 hours per week, permitted the inmates, there 24 hours every day of the week, to control routines. He told me that the clerks in the hall office, deputy's office, chaplain's office, hospital, and everybody's office were inmates. Inmates controlled cell and job changes more than officials. In order for him to get into 15-block, Chuck said he would have to furnish a carton of cigarettes to the inmate clerk. Otherwise, the cell-change cards would be misplaced, misfiled, get lost, or evaporate. I didn't believe him. He offered to bet me and prove it, provided I didn't reveal in any way what Chuck had told me. Another two weeks went by, during which cards were lost or didn't get typed, and I said, "Uncle." Chuck told me he would be in his new cell in 15-block by tomorrow noon, and asked for a couple hours away from the office that afternoon. He was in his new cell by 11:00 the following morning—a carton of cigarettes poorer. That taught me a lesson in prison administration I never forgot.

I went into the Army just before another of Michigan's political investigations got under way. By the time I was discharged from service, Chuck Watson had been fired. So had Warden Harry Jackson, Deputy G. I. Francis, Assistant Deputy D. C. Pettit, Inspector Walter Wilson, Inmate Accountant Joe Porrier, and Recreation Director Dick Riley. All had enjoyed civil service protection. Chuck had been reinstated after a long lay-off, but he was eliminated just a little while later by a new examination for his job after the civil service commission had refused to abolish the position as long as the same position existed in Michigan's smaller correctional institutions.

Upon my return from the Army, I was given the opportunity to go to Cassidy Lake Technical School, Michigan's new experiment in minimum-security penology. I took that opportunity, too, for the situation in Michigan Corrections was tenuous, and I thought I could pursue my studies for the Ph.D. degree at Michigan State a little easier from the Cassidy Lake vantage point. Corrections didn't appeal as a career except for the thrills that insecurity and turbulence offer.

At Cassidy Lake, I worked diligently and hard in the building of a treatment program such as I thought an institution without custody should have. The absence of walls, weapons, and uniforms and the presence of educational facilities and counselors nestled in the wooded hills of the Waterloo Recreational Area offered possibilities for a correctional treatment program such as I had never dreamed of before.

Corrections was too insecure for a family man, and I didn't consider it seriously for a career at that time. I was making progress in my studies at Michigan State. I declined an offer of the deputy wardenship at Jackson in February, 1947, when Deputy Bacon received his appointment. Also, I declined to be considered for the director of classification job in Jackson in 1948 when Bill Johnson was appointed, though he thought at the time that he was selected over me in open competition. Corrections was just too insecure.

By 1949, the treatment program at Cassidy Lake had matured and had been presented to the correctional world through the *Journal of Criminal Law and Criminology*. The series of investigations had continued, had called Cassidy Lake's Superintendent Miles a "lazy, good-for-nothing," pressured the resignation of Marquette's Warden Bush (Deputy Warden Raymond of Jackson resigned under pressure), had fired Jackson's new Warden Benson, had put Chief Engineer Dan Johnson in jail, had changed the corrections law to eliminate Director of Corrections Dr. Garrett Heyns, had dismissed Assistant Director of Corrections in Charge of Prisons Major "Bill" Burke, had fired other lesser employees, and investigators were in the process of chasing down information to prepare criminal indictments against many officials of the Department of Corrections, including members of the parole board and Superintendent Clemor D. Miles of Cassidy Lake. All had enjoyed civil service protection.

Since Michigan State was to award me a Ph.D. degree in June, 1949, I had started to look for other jobs. I was going to join the faculty of a Midwestern university.

Commissioner Brooks, newly appointed by the new governor, "Soapy" Williams, told me he had heard I was planning on leaving, liked my work at Cassidy Lake, and offered me a better position at Jackson.

At Jackson, I found that I was being paid as assistant deputy warden in custody, but that I would travel the state of Michigan trying to co-ordinate classification. My going into other institutions as the representative of the new political commissioner raised the defenses of the institutional people. They wanted to know what I was investigating, but did not ask me.

They were cagey, and I don't blame them. Co-ordination of classification under such a scheme was next to impossible. I found myself twiddling my thumbs, not wanting to spend time in an institution that was apprehensive, and having no specific duties at Jackson. Then I found what the master plan was. Sydney Moskowitz had become assistant deputy warden in charge of individual treatment at Jackson when Deputy Raymond had resigned. Moskowitz was in line for a seat on the parole board, leaving the assistant deputy's job open. I was to occupy that position. However, Bill Johnson was director of classification and had been at Jackson continuously, except for Army time, since 1939. He was familiar with recent developments, the routine of the job, and had been promised the position by Moskowitz. While my name was at the top of the civil service register for the wardens' series at that level, Bill's was far down the list. The proposition was made to split the list between "Custody" and "Treatment" people, which would have brought Bill to within appointing range. After some haggling, which I did not enter, I was appointed assistant deputy warden in charge of individual treatment in July, 1949.

Major problems facing the treatment program when I took over were (1) the active antagonism of custody, most vividly manifested by refusal of Assistant Deputy Warden George L. Bacon, charged with custody, and my immediate predecessor, Syd Moskowitz, to communicate freely or even remain in the same room together, (2) the passive resistance, or at least the absence of active co-operation, of Warden Julian N. Frisbie, and (3) the open resistance to me and my program by my chief assistant, Bill Johnson, and his clique within the treatment division who had expected him to be appointed assistant deputy warden in charge of individual treatment.

The warden complicated matters for me when he ordered me, "You leave Bill alone!" He amplified that by telling me to let Bill run his own area without interference or supervision, an order he never rescinded. The only concession the warden granted was my request that Bill not be told that this was happening, so that if I could convince Bill in casual conversation to do something, it might be accomplished. For the three years that followed, Bill insulted me, failed to co-operate on new programs I proposed, feigned ignorance when the occasion suited, and tried to split the group that supported me. He never openly opposed a major project the warden favored during working hours, with the exception of in-service training and case conferences for psychologists and counselors. He was most annoying at night, with his numerous telephone calls, in which he repeated monotonously, "I'll ruin you and your program, and you know I can do it, too!"

Repeatedly, I tried to gain Bill's co-operation by telling him that we complemented each other in our viewpoints, by spending an occasional evening with him, and by inviting him to share in major decisions. After bowling one night, he told me he had never had a boss he liked, and that they were getting progressively worse. Dr. Philips didn't know what he was do-ing, according to Bill, but he was acceptable because he was a psychiatrist. Chuck Watson had been "totally untrained" for the job of supervising anybody. Syd Moskowitz was a self-seeker. And now—"you!"

He telephoned me at night, frequently getting me out of bed to tell me with thick tongue that I was a "sonofabitch" or something of the kind. After I returned from Philadelphia, where I had attended the annual meeting of the American Association for the Advancement of Science in December, 1951, Bill set up a schedule of telephone calls. He told me he knew I was tired from driving and that I had a rough New Year's Day at the prison the following morning, and that he was going to impair my efficiency. He said that he was going to telephone through the night at regular intervals, "so you can't sleep," and added that I didn't dare not answer the phone because I was on duty.

His most unusual annoyance occurred on Thursday night, around April 19, 1951. He telephoned from the Meadowlark Inn about 11:30 P.M. to say that several of the boys were having a celebration for winning the bowling match that eve-ning and wanted me to join them. There was no noise in the background. I dressed, told my wife that something was wrong, and went to the Meadowlark. When I entered, Dorothy, a waitress, asked me how much I weighed. I caught her hint. Bill and Glenn Kerlin, Bill's closest friend who was paid as a psychologist, were at the bar, and owner Monte was behind it. Nobody else was there.

Bill and Glenn greeted me profusely and offered me a drink. I suggested buttermilk, but they ordered a double stinger, which Monte prepared over my protests. Empty beer bottles told me what my companions had been drinking. Bill told me that the plan had been to call me, Bill and Glenn would jump me as I entered, and Monte would call the police to have me arrested for disturbing the peace. The plan had been discarded about the time I entered.

When Bill went to the men's room, Glenn told me that the whole plan was Bill's idea and that he didn't want to do anything like that. Upon Bill's return from the room, he wanted to talk about "our troubles." A second stinger was set up for me, though I had sipped only a little of the first—so as to appear nonchalant. Bill shook his finger in my face and told me what to do about civil service ratings and other things. I was convinced that he wanted to incite me to lose my temper and strike at him so Monte could call the police. He told me that if I didn't do things his way, he would get some "guys" to beat me up. "There must be at least three guys in Jackson as tough as you are," he assured me. I didn't leave the Meadowlark until their two o'clock closing time, since I did not want them to be behind me. They walked out first, and I followed. It was six months later that Bill apologized for "that Meadowlark deal."

In January, 1952, I changed tactics with Bill. Instead of being friendly, I remained aloof and called him only when he was needed. In keeping with the warden's order, I "let Bill alone," but I told some of his clique that I was through fooling around with Bill, on the theory that word would get to Bill. It worked. After January, 1952, the nocturnal telephone calls stopped, Bill stopped his delaying tactics and morale-busting activities.

Deputy George L. Bacon, charged with custody, had been pictured to me as a hard-headed man who could not be reasoned with successfully. Sid Smith, chaplain-psychologist from Ionia, had called him a "mule-headed record clerk" when George had held that position at the Michigan Reformatory. Deputy Moskowitz had described him in most uncomplimentary terms. I decided that I would exert every effort to get along with him when I went to his office to meet him.

When I went in, George stood up and accepted my introduction with a broad, genuine smile. He stood six-feet-five, had been an honor student in teacher's college, and I liked him. He was not as he had been pictured to me. The more I knew him, the more I realized that he wanted to be the one to get the ideas to be promoted, but that was easy to handle. He was personally ambitious and sometimes petty in minor issues, but he was generally friendly, reasonable, and able to talk out problems.

Deputy Bacon and I had only three major disagreements, and they were honest differences of opinion. The first one was whether custody should continue to operate the "labor pool" (the mechanics of job assignment) or whether individual treatment should do it. Deputy Bacon's point was that since custody has responsibility to maintain peace and order within the prison, custody should have the authority to assign men to jobs as well as cells and, besides, custody has this responsibility in all other prisons. My point was that if individual treatment should determine the preferred program, which included custodial factors, since custody is represented on the classification committee, individual treatment should follow through to make sure the recommendation for the preferred program is followed. After several discussions, the problem was settled by the warden and Commissioner of Corrections Brooks by placing the labor pool in the individual treatment department.

The second major disagreement concerned the use of modeling clay for hobbycraft (arts and crafts), George opposed the use of the clay because heads could be made of it to place in beds so that when the officer taking count looked in the cell, he would think a man was there when it was only a head made of modeling clay. I pointed out that heads could be made of flour, water, and soot, all already available in the kitchen. The warden and the commissioner again decided the issue, and modeling clay was permitted.

The third disagreement was my request that George permit the counselors access to the disciplinary cells. He became red and told me that if I tried to run his 15-block, he'd run my gym. The riot settled that one.

The warden was at best lukewarm to me and my program in the beginning. Whether he had favored Bill Johnson for my job as a result of Moskowitz' influence, I never knew. The outstanding policy statement he made to me during 1949 was, "To hell with rehabilitation, we gotta run the institution!"

After working together for a year, however, Warden Frisbie began to support me as staunchly as I had supported him. Maybe it was that support that he began to reciprocate. After giving me a rough go for a year, maybe he decided I could take it and liked me for it. I think the reason was that both of us told each other what we thought and our reasons for it even when it would have been politic for me, at least, to keep quiet. We felt secure around each other because we knew each other's positions, that our thinking would be compared on issues, we could argue profusely, but when a decision was made, that decision would be followed. At any rate, we became close friends I think because we considered each other to be intellectually honest. By the middle of 1950, Warden Frisbie was supporting progressive penology stoutly.

The counseling program had been introduced and consolidated. Psychologists, sociologists, and social workers were called "counselors" and were assigned permanent case-loads from the inmate population. It was an attempt to re-align professional personnel so that more permanent contacts could be achieved than had been by the traditional classification system. Each counselor prepared the admission summary on

the men permanently assigned to him, and followed them
through their periods of incarceration. Regular interviews or
therapy sessions were held. The counselor prepared the pre-
parole progress report for the parole board at the expiration
of sentences. This program achieved success within the institution and national recognition.[1]

The State Prison of Southern Michigan had a good custodial force compared to the custodial forces in most prisons.
Custody was strong and enforced rules rather strictly. Individual treatment had emerged as custody's equal in determining prison policy. The inmate store fund was rigidly reg-
ulated and accounted. A cost accounting system had been
introduced. A machine method of processing commitments,
parole lists, releases, and other routines had been developed.
Schools were being integrated with industries through an on-
the-job training program. The intramural recreation program
was becoming more important than the already big varsity
athletic program that included football, basketball, baseball,
and tennis. The library and law library were second to none
of which we knew. We were looking for ways to make new
improvements while consolidating the old.

All the major problems worked out at the institution, the
only remaining problems were in the state political situation.
The legislature was progressively cutting the institutional
budget while the inmate population and costs were rising.
Several moves, such as cutting inmate wage allotments, cutting
inmate scrip issues from weekly to bi-weekly to monthly, cutting food quality, cutting personnel, and eliminating a dentist,
were made in order to accommodate those budget cuts. The
general tightening of the belt, we interpreted, was the Republican legislature trying to embarrass a Democratic governor and his political appointee, the commissioner of corrections. Inmate morale was undermined—as was the staff morale,
wondering who would be cut next. Whenever a cutback of

---

[1] See Fox, Vernon; "The Michigan Counseling Program," *The Prison
World*, January–February, 1950, and Fox, Vernon; "The Effect of Counseling on Adjustment in Prison," *Social Forces*, March, 1954.

some sort was made, inmates seemed to blame the institutional administration for not being able to procure what was needed. "What the hell's comin' off?" was a frequent question asked by inmates.

Even so, by January, 1952, the major problems were worked out, and things looked bright for even more progressive penology in Michigan. The warden and I were optimistic. Deputy Bacon and I were getting along well, entertaining each other in our homes. Bill Johnson was beginning to cooperate. The warden and I agreed on penal philosophy. Everything was quiet. It was in early April, 1952, when the warden remarked in a conversation after working hours in my office, "Things are too quiet—something must be wrong."

CHAPTER VII

The Michigan Riot

On Sunday, April 20, 1952, I was the deputy on duty and had been working at the prison all day. Having gone home about 6:30 P.M., I returned at 9:00. The light was on in the warden's office, which was unusual. Upon my entering the lobby, Warden Frisbie told me that about 7:30 inmate Earl Ward had telephoned Captain Tucker at the hall office from 15-block to inform him that the inmates had taken over the block and were holding four guards hostage. The guards held were Harold Carrier, James Akins, John Holmes, and Thomas Elliott. Guard Hinton had escaped while Carrier was being brought in from the yard. Hinton, at Ward's orders, had called Carrier into the block, and had escaped by running when the door was opened and Carrier was between him and Ward. Deputy Bacon was already at the prison. Armed guards had been sent to the academic school which overlooked the entrance to 15-block from the second floor and to the main corridor gate which protected the entrance from the prison yard to the rotunda and hall office. These strategic points had been covered by armed guards.

Although I had been the deputy on duty, I had not been notified of the riot when it started. Warden Frisbie explained that since this was a custodial matter involving custodial facilities and personnel, they had overlooked the deputy on duty and had called the custodial deputy. This was logical, since the deputies on duty other than Bacon had been instructed to stay out of custodial matters and leave them to custodial people. All custodial assignments were made by the hall office

86

captain under Deputy Bacon's direction, regardless of who was in charge for the week-end.

The first act of the inmate leaders in 15-block, Earl Ward and "Crazy Jack" Hyatt, was to demand the presence of a newspaperman and Deputy Bacon. Ed Smith of Associated Press was available from the *Jackson Citizen Patriot*. Deputy Bacon and Ed Smith had appeared within a few minutes and Ward had his conversation with them while they stood some ten or fifteen yards away from the block. Ward displayed some hand weapons the mutineers had found in 15-block. He termed them "vicious," and had wanted an explanation for their presence. A blackjack and a steel device called a "come-on" or a "wrist-breaker" were displayed prominently, but the single weapon which received most attention was a short length of medium chain, probably fifteen inches long, with both ends attached together to an eight-inch leather strap. I have not yet determined how it could be used, but Ward indicated that it would do a lot of damage if an inmate were to be struck with it.

After displaying the weapons to the newsman and Deputy Bacon, permitting pictures to be taken of them and of the hostages posed with their captors outside of 15-block, Ward went inside the block, locked and barricaded the door. I could not help but wonder why, if force were to be used, it was not used at this point. The rioters or mutineers were not organized. There were guns aimed at the 15-block entrance from the academic school. Custody had had time to prepare, but apparently not the presence of mind. There were manpower and weapons in the corridor immediately behind Ed Smith and Deputy Bacon. Ward was outside the block. One picture shows him at the side of the block, at least five yards away and over a hedge from an open and unbarricaded entrance. This was the time for action! It didn't occur. I shall probably never know why Custody failed to act at this opportune juncture. By the time the 15-block door was closed and the barricade went up after midnight, it was too late for force.

Warden Frisbie said that the three of us should stay apart.
Deputy Bacon was with the men at the corridor gate. The
warden was going to the hall office. I would remain in the lobby at the information desk to handle incoming calls and to assist newsmen. Ed Smith was in the warden's office, answering
telephone calls from reporters and giving out information. I
was bringing the files of the mutineers to Ed and assisting him
in getting the information he wanted. Reporters had been arriving at the prison since 10:00 P.M. About 11:00, a corps of
newsmen were taken inside by the warden. Any who came in
later, I sent through the gates by verbal order.

After midnight, the lobby began to resume its normal
quietness. I went to the Research and Selection section and
made a pot of coffee. The two young ladies who worked there
had graciously left their larder unlocked! Captain Hanson of
the State Police, two detectives, and I sat down to sip coffee
and to discuss the situation. After reviewing the files and discussing what the four of us knew about various men in 15-block
we agreed that there would be carnage if we attempted to
storm the barricaded cell-block now. At least 44 of the 179 inmates in 15-block were already convicted murderers. Earl
Ward and "Crazy Jack" Hyatt had been in the attack on Governor G. Mennen Williams at the Branch Prison at Marquette
on July 10, 1950. Those men would stop at nothing. We estimated roughly that 35 to 40 persons would be killed if we
attempted to storm the block then. The inmates had no food
at this point, however, and we might delay the carnage if we
kept them talking.

I learned later that the inmates had made a tape recording
which included their charges of brutality. It was made with
Ron Milton of Jackson's radio station WKMH in the presence
of many newsmen. As early as 2:00 A.M., Deputy Bacon and
Warden Frisbie attempted to negotiate with Ward by telephone. News reports indicate that they presented Ward with
a nine-point ultimatum, and that Ward countered with six
complaints. I never knew the contents of either.

At 3:00 A.M., a stray reporter strolled in. I took him inside, and we went to Deputy Bacon's office. Warden Frisbie, Deputy Bacon, Assistant to the Commissioner Seymour Gilman, and I sat and talked. We decided that there was nothing to do now but to await developments. I suggested that there would be no school until this situation was over. Warden Frisbie told me not to let any inmates into the school as long as armed guards were there. Factors in the situation were reviewed without decision. The presence of hostages, the inmates' threat to kill them, and our estimate of their ability to carry out that threat was the reason that no action was taken right then. We had three courses to follow: (1) we could storm the block, (2) we could starve them out, or (3) we could negotiate.

These men were not young, first-offenders with short sentences. There was no capital punishment in Michigan. There was no punishment more severe than 15-block, and many of these men had already been there for months without prospect for early release from the block. We decided that it would be folly to storm the block at this point. It had to be starve them out or negotiate. We tended to favor the starvation idea if we could keep them talking enough to save the hostage guards, but none of the ideas actually had precedence. Strategy at this point was in a state of flux. We had to watch and wait, determining our moves as the inmates acted.

The men in 15-block had had homosexual orgies. One homosexual, whose first name is Jerold, co-operated in anal intercourse until he was tired and then was forced and injured. Fourteen men had had anal intercourse with him before he was rescued by the riot ringleaders and sent out of the cell-block to the hospital to have stitches taken in the anal area. Other homosexuals were reported to have opened their cells to business.

As daylight came, Mr. Gilman and Ron Milton from WKMH went out to 15-block. An officer and I strolled behind them. Mr. Gilman talked to Ward and the other inmate ringleaders. I merely wanted to see what the situation appeared to be without getting into it. I had never seen Ward before. He had spent his time in medical and disciplinary status. The Individual Treatment division was kept out of those areas as much as possible. At 7:00, the radio announced on the morning news that 15-block had been taken over by inmates. Shouts cheers, and jeers went up from the cell-blocks where the men had been listening.

Ward was enthusiastically telling Mr. Gilman about the brutality that had been perpetrated in 15-block. During the process, he called Gilman sadistic and inefficient. Mr. Gilman had written six points on a scratch pad, but I never knew what those six points were. It didn't matter because, as Ward told Gilman, "We ain't organized yet." They didn't know what they wanted. Mr. Gilman told Ward that he would investigate those charges of brutality and if they were true, corrective action would be taken.

"Investigate?" shouted Ward. "Don't be ridiculous!"

Investigation by an official means "whitewash" to the inmates. We have to accept the inmates' word as true for a point of origin and go on from there. I called Mr. Gilman away from the window and suggested that maybe we had better accept the statement at its face value and take steps to prevent a recurrence. I suggested that it is better to start with the inmates' word when they hold the hostages. Gilman nodded and turned back to the window. I felt embarrassed for Gilman. It was obvious to me and to the inmates that he did not know how to act when he did not have control by his authority. At that point Ward turned to me and repeated the charges of brutality and showed me the weapons. I had said nothing to Ward yet. When he directed his attention to me, my comment was that I was surprised that the weapons he had shown had been in 15-block. He assured me that this was where he had found them.

Mr. Gilman spoke. He told Ward that if he would release the hostages, he would send Ward to an honor camp. I thought such an offer was inappropriate and a display of poor judgment. Gilman was going to take this man who had threatened murder from Michigan's disciplinary bastion and place him in an honor camp! There were many other things less dangerous to the public that would have been more attractive to Ward. Ward thought it as inappropriate as I did. Infuriated and without hesitation, he turned on Gilman, pointed his finger and told him to "get away from here, and don't come back to this window." Gilman left and he did not come back.

The two others had left and I stayed there alone. With no idea as to what to say and with much less hope than Gilman of ending it, I had not entered negotiations. I just wanted to learn more about Ward. I asked Ward questions about the brutality in 15-block, who had been beaten, how he knew, and attempted to get him to talk as much as possible. It would help me understand and also give Ward emotional catharsis by permitting him to verbalize his aggressions. Ward's underlings were strutting around the room verbally abusing and flaunting the administration. Jerome Parmentier, an obese youngster who had just been transferred from the Michigan Reformatory, was laughing because a big guard was "crying like a baby." He kept repeating, "My mamma's gonna s——t!" Ward asked me about the possibility of getting food. I told him that it would be unusual, but I could not give an answer. I promised to get the warden's ideas about it.

Then I asked him again what the inmates' complaints were. He said that brutality existed in 15-block and elsewhere within the prison, post-operative care in the hospital had been left to inmate nurses, the dental services were poor, and the treatment of inmates in the mental ward was not adequate. I did not press for further elaboration nor question the complaints.

By this time, I favored bringing coffee or something to the mutineers for two reasons. In the first place, I was becoming more and more convinced that Ward and his underlings were fully capable of carrying out their threat to kill, and I wanted his co-operation rather than his animosity. Secondly, I thought that if I could get that door unlocked and the barricades down once in the presence of an official, it would come down easier the second time, and the third, and the fourth. This would tend to reduce the group will to resist by extinguishing or modifying the complete resistance response. I explained my reasoning to Warden Frisbie and Deputy Bacon. Both agreed that it was probably the wiser course, though both had to discuss it. This decision had to wait, however, until after the rest of the prison had been fed.

The problem Monday morning was to determine how much of the routine activity of the prison could be permitted. It was certain that there would be no academic school. Warden Frisbie, Deputy Bacon, and I discussed the possibility of other activities. The question of feeding the inmates on Monday morning was a main topic of discussion. Warden Frisbie suggested using the dining room. Deputy Bacon suggested feeding them in their cells, sending food in trucks pushed by selected prisoners who worked in the kitchen. I tried to stay out of the feeding decision, but suggested that if the prisoners were fed in the mess hall, the lines should be marched down the corridors, rather than over the customary route past 15-block. Either method was satisfactory to Steward Nick Ross. If the feeding were done by the trucks, it was quickly estimated that two meals per day could be fed. Warden Frisbie considered the morale factor. If the men were permitted to go to the dining room, three meals could be served. If the men were fed in the cells, only two meals could be served. Warden Frisbie took responsibility for a calculated risk. The inmates would be fed in the dining room.

The north-side inmates were unlocked, marched down the cell-blocks to the rotunda, down the service corridor, through the kitchen, and into the dining room. They consumed their breakfast, marched back over the same route, and permitted themselves to be locked up again. A miracle had happened! The warden was fifty per cent right already! Then the south side was unlocked. The men marched toward the dining hall. The first five hundred or fewer got into the dining hall, but

an unidentified inmate had put salt in the coffee, someone
threw a tray when he tasted the brine, and the riot was on!
More than a thousand hungry men never got to the dining hall.
As approximately 1,600 (some estimates were 2,600 men—
the exact number was never actually established) men milled
around in the south yard, several of them ran toward the inmate store, where an inventory of more than eight thousand
dollars' worth of cigarettes, candy bars, canned goods, ice
cream and other miscellaneous items were stored. The inmate
store was raided, the windows broken, and the fixtures damaged. More men ran toward the commissary and took canned
goods, baked goods, meats, and other items. They did damage
as they looted. The refrigeration system was broken. In a few
minutes, fires were burning in the yard to roast quarters of
beef and other meats taken from the butcher shop. The band
room was raided. It wasn't yet really a riot—it was a grand
picnic. Nobody was fighting. They had armed themselves
with knives, but nobody was fighting. It was just a big picnic
at this point. Homosexual acts were going on in broad view
for anyone to see, meat was being roasted, games of chance had
started, men were tooting horns, and one man was beating
the bass drum with a brand-new trumpet.

The warden did not know what to do, and said so. He did
not want to send the untrained guards into the melee. In the
Marine Corps he had been accustomed to having hundreds
and thousands of trained troops at his command. Commissioner
Brooks knew less than the warden about such situations. Commissioner Leonard's State Police were not ready yet. Deputy
Bacon was doing nothing. Somebody had to do something.

It was a period of disorganization in the yard. It was not an
organized riot. I thought that this was the time to take advantage of their disorganization and coax as many men off
the yard as possible. There were many men I was sure, who
wanted no part in a riot. Consequently, I asked three people,
individually, to go out on the yard with me to establish face-
to-face relationships with the men on the fringes of that potential "riot" and take them off the yard before they organized

into a real "riot." I asked only a few, not wanting to embarrass those I thought did not have the courage to do it. Those I asked didn't have the courage, either, so I went out alone. Disregarding verbal abuse from some inmates, I talked with them, and started taking them off the yard. In the meantime, Deputy Bacon was signaling me to come in off the yard so they could close the doors for security. I saw a group of officers in the southwest corner of the yard, just standing there, not making any move. I signaled them to come, but they didn't see me—they just stood there apparently confused. I told Deputy Bacon I was going after them, but he indicated that if they didn't have sense enough to come, we couldn't do anything about it. I started for them, but had gone only a third of the way when they started in my direction. When it became apparent that they would reach safety, I started talking with more men. During that period, I took a group of men to 7-block and several groups to my office, the classification room, 6-block, and the visiting room.

Momentum was picking up. It was becoming a riot. I learned later that a colored lifer, James Hudson, had taken over leadership of the rioters in the yard and was directing efforts toward damaging property and capturing officers. The process of taking men off the fringe was too slow for me alone, particularly when there was no apparent support. I went into the service corridor, finally, in response to Deputy Bacon's signals. He explained that the capture of a prison official would be much more serious than the capture of several guards. By that time, inmates were seeking refuge from the yard. I was amazed when Deputy Bacon refused to open the doors to permit inmates to come in from the yard when they were seeking safety. Several inmates appeared at the corridor door and begged for admittance, stating that they wanted no part of the riot. Deputy Bacon refused to let them off the yard. I thought we wanted to clear the yard, and remonstrated with Deputy Bacon. Finally, he permitted a few to come in, but not all. He explained that they could have hidden weapons and formed a fifth column, and started fighting as soon as they got in.

There were enough rifles and weapons in the hands of officers and State Police to take care of that eventuality, I thought. By that time, the inmates who were locked in the north-side cells had begun to yell and throw things from their cells. They broke the plumbing and other fixtures in their cells, and water was running over the galleries in some instances. Men were systematically breaking out all the windows in the cell-blocks on the south side. I watched helplessly while men broke out each pane of glass in the north end of 11-block with a hoe. It was work—but the inmates were having fun. They were expressing much of the pent-up aggression they had been holding for probably many years. How to handle this anarchy was a problem. We didn't have many State Police, but it appeared that those few should throw a wedge through the south gate and the railroad gate. That wasn't our business—that was the business of Commissioner Donald S. Leonard of the State Police, a man with an excellent reputation.

While he was getting organized, I thought that it would be well to speak to the men on the yard through the loud-speakers in order to get them to thinking with us in unison or at least to orient them concerning the situation. I wanted to provide some sort of leadership to compete with the leader-ship of the inmate leaders in the yard. The best idea seemed to be to get someone from 15-block to talk on the speakers. That would be better than to have an administrative person do it.

I went to 15-block again to talk with Ward. When the group gathered around the window, I told them that it would be difficult to deal with them while the rest of the riot was go-ing on—that our attention would be too divided. I asked for a representative from 15-block to appear on the radio with me. Nobody would come then, but a man named Jimmy Bishop would come at 1:00 P.M. It was 10:30 then. I didn't want to wait that long, but there was nothing I could do about it. I promised to come back at 1:00 and grant safe passage to the radio room and back to 15-block.

That two and a half hours was a long time. During that

time, the situation had developed into a full-blown riot. The laundry had been completely destroyed by fire and hacking. That was symbolic aggression, too, for Laundry Superintendent Charlie Ranney had had the reputation of being the most stern disciplinarian of all work supervisors in the prison as far as inmates were concerned. They said that Ranney had three shifts on his assignment at all times, one on the job, one "laid in" and not working, and the third one in the "hole" on disciplinary tickets written by Ranney.

So the laundry was first. The gym was second. There was much talk among the inmates, real or imagined, that cigarettes and bribery in the right inmates' hands enhanced chances for a berth on the athletic teams or favored opportunities for a place to perform certain acts, or other favors. The gym was burned and the equipment with it, with the battle-cry that the gym assignment was a "bunch of prison politicians." The motion picture projectors were next. The inmate who operated them had formerly been head nurse in the mental ward, and had been accused, rightly or wrongly, of taking advantage of inmate mental patients. The library was destroyed, too, for many of the clerks there were accused of saving good books when they came in for their "friends," defined as those inmates who would pay them in cigarettes for the favors. The *Spectator* office, the prison newspaper, was also destroyed because in it was an assignment of "prison politicians," too. The greenhouse was a shambles, because it was the top "prison politician" assignment. Commissioner Brooks had actually ordered some big Detroit gamblers to be placed on that assignment, and whenever he would come into the prison he seldom failed to pay a visit to his "friends" in the greenhouse. The hospital and religious fixtures were untouched.

In addition to all this damage, the 15-block bastion had been made stronger. Food had been put into the block; knives, bats, and miscellaneous weapons had been provided the men there. Many of us watched from the corridor gates when whole bolognas, canned goods, bread, meats of all sorts, and miscellaneous items were pushed through between the bars. Long butcher knives, cleavers, and other instruments were pushed into the block. Even more important, eight guards had been captured by the rioters in the yard and had been pushed into 15-block, so that there were twelve hostages now. The additional guards were Ken Parsons, Emile Hergert, Cecil Lawrence, Joseph Dzal, George Brown, Harvey Robb, James Chaffin and H. W. Curry. Charles Goodyear, aged 68, was sent to safety because he was too old. Mrs. Brown and Mrs. Carrier came to the prison lobby and waited day and night.

Newsmen were all over the prison. They were badgering everyone with questions. On one occasion a newsman asked what I thought the prisoners were protesting against. I indicated that, since 15-block was Custody's bastion, the inmates had called for the custodial deputy and a newsman and demanded explanation for the existence in 15-block of "vicious" weapons, it was obvious to me that it was a spontaneous protest against Custody. The remark was printed.

Commissioner Brooks had been at the prison all morning. He asked me what the prisoners wanted. I told him that they had mentioned brutality, treatment in the mental ward, postoperative care by inmate nurses, and that many of the inmates in the yard and some in 15-block other than Ward had complained about the food. Commissioner Brooks said the main complaint was the parole board. That was the first time I had heard a complaint about the parole board. Their complaints about the segregation of homosexuals did not, as news reports had it, concern having homosexuals in the prison population. Rather, it referred to the housing in the prison of the criminal sexual psychopaths who were under jurisdiction of the State Hospital Commission but were housed in the prison rather than in the Ionia State Hospital. (The criminal sexual psychopaths are committed by probate court for treatment rather than sentenced by a criminal court for punishment.)

At 1:00, I went out the corridor gates toward 15-block. There were many men in the north yard now, whereas previously they had been mainly in the south yard. State Police were on the roofs of the cell-blocks, and institutional officials were gathering on the roof of 5-block. Approaching the window at 15-block, I asked for Bishop. He wasn't there. He had been permitted to leave the block during the riot—I learned then that he had not originally been in 15-block in the first place, but had been let in during the morning.

"You didn't really expect him, did you?" someone asked. I didn't reply. Surely, I had expected him. He gave me his word. My word had always been good with inmates. I had expected reciprocation. I thought that maybe he was returning to 15-block to meet me, so I stepped around in front of the block to see. Armed inmates were gathering there. At this point, I sensed the acrid smell of tear gas. I hadn't smelled anything like it since basic training in the Army. For a brief moment, I identified myself with the inmates at whom it must have been fired. It was too weak to be effective, however, because of the vast area of the prison yard. I thought it must have been fired by some trigger-happy individual and shrugged it off. I continued to walk. On the east side of 15-block, I stopped to look down the side-walk between 15-block and the kitchen into the north yard. I had spoken a brief, "hello," to several inmates, but paid no further heed to them.

Before I knew it, I had been surrounded. Looking to determine whether I should make a break for it, I counted eight or ten deep in the ring that surrounded me. A break for safety was out of the question. I noticed that the men who were next to me had their knives and cleavers dangling toward the ground, while the men on the fringes had their knives raised. If there was a degree of safety, it was right where I was. They were shouting things like, "Abolish the —— parole board," "Get better food," "Fire the warden," "Kill Bacon," and similar rash demands.

I thought the best thing I could do would be to show no fear and to talk about something near and dear to their hearts. I recognized several of the inmates in the group as men I had known a long time. I recognized one man, named Roberts, who had been with me as a boy in the Starr Commonwealth for Boys near Albion, a good training school for homeless, dependent, and problem boys. I directed my conversation to-ward him. As nonchalantly as I could, I reminded them that we could not abolish the parole board because it had been set up by the legislature and could not be abolished without legislative action. What they would have to do if they wanted to abolish the parole board would be to get a senator or rep-resentative to introduce a bill into the legislature whereby the function of the parole board could be reviewed and abolished or modified as the deliberations dictated.

A man paced the fringe of the group, saying, "Grab him! Grab him! Don't let him work that psychology stuff on you!"

After about five minutes—though it seemed to be closer to five hours—I looked at my watch and said, "If you fellows will excuse me, I think I'll go talk with Ward." As I turned to go, they opened a path for me, and I walked to the front of 15-block and around to the window. We had hardly exchanged greetings when a colored man with a knife in his belt came toward me. I stepped back, surveying the distance to the cor-ridor gate and the distance to the crowd of inmates.

He spoke to me, "Dep, I've talked to you over the phone, and now I'd like to get closer to you." I glanced at the knife and stepped back again slowly without making a reply. He stepped slowly forward and I stepped just as slowly backward.

Ward shouted out of the window, "Step back, he's all right—he's a regular guy." The colored man stepped back, the crowd came forward to the hedge at the entrance to 15-block, and I went back to the window of 15-block. I knew I could have been cut off from the corridor gate by anyone who wanted to do so, but in this tense game of nerves, I wanted to convey to the inmates that I wasn't afraid of anything. It would help me later.

Ward said, "For Christ's sake, Dep, you'd better take your own precautions for your own safety. I can't guarantee what this crowd is going to do." That was a welcome admonition as far as I was concerned.

"O.K., Ward, but I'll be back," I said, and thrust my hands into my trousers pockets and strolled slowly toward the corridor gate and safety. Then I went into the corridor, and on into the radio room to make the talk I thought would be advisable to help clear the yard. Officer Wright contacted me to tell me that some of the men in the yard said they would go to their cells if I would be warden. That was not the sort of demand that makes for harmony in administration, so we kept it quiet.

When I arrived in the radio room, James Bishop was there. He had come into the radio room from the south yard. I outlined a little speech for him, emphasizing the idea that the inmates should go back into their cells. "Let us in 15-block finish what we started," was his theme. After he had finished, jeers went up from the men in the yard. He indicated that he wanted to go outside the walls because, now that he had gone on the radio for us, his life wouldn't be worth a nickel in the yard. Commissioner Brooks came in about that time, and I told him the situation. Commissioner Brooks ordered Bishop put on the list of inmates to go outside the walls. I sent Bishop to the visiting room to stay. Commissioner Brooks told me that he had arranged to obtain temporary kitchens from the local National Guard unit, and the men could be fed tonight if they would go into their cells.

By that time, the State Police were organized. A wedge was scheduled to come into the south gate and through the railroad gate at the east end of the prison. I took the microphone and started to talk to the men in an *ad lib* manner. I told them that the kitchen had been destroyed, but that Commissioner Brooks had arranged for a temporary unit from the National Guard. I told them that in order to provide food, we would have to clear the yard so that people would feel safe in the distribution of food. I was trying to get unity of thinking of some sort without arousing the jeers and catcalls that the inmate's speech aroused. As preparation for the State Police, I told the inmates that in order to assist in clearing the yard, the State Police were coming in the south gate slowly and quietly, though armed, and would attempt to clear the yard systematically and in reasonable time. I reviewed the complaints which had been expressed by the inmates and indicated that there might be some basis in fact for some of them, but that the administration did not knowingly permit unhappy conditions to exist. I tried to list the complaints without taking sides. I asked inmates who had other complaints to write them to me in a letter. I asked the inmates please to go to their cells while we were taking steps to correct possible abuses and wrongs! There were no jeers. The State Police moved in.

During the riot, two inmates took H. W. Curry out to the end of the walk in front of 15-block. I learned later that inmate Darwin Millage had been killed by State Police and Curry was being sent out so he could be killed in the yard in retaliation. Machine guns clanked on the window ledge in the academic school above. The inmates dropped Curry's arms and returned to 15-block. Curry ran through the corridor gate to safety. He said that he was sure the convicts in 15-block would bargain in good faith, but "those guards don't stand a chance if there's any reneging."

A telephone call to me at the hall office from Earl Ward had jarred me. Ward said that the State Police were manhandling a man right in front of 15-block. If he was killed, they were going to kill an officer hostage. Ward was yelling frenziedly. This was the first time I had heard him yell that way. It worried me. I told him that I hoped that he would realize that the killing of a hostage would mean a murder charge. He seemed not to hear me, and continued to insist that the State Police cease manhandling the man. I told Ward that I could not order the State Police around, but that I hoped that he would realize that a murder charge would result from the death of a hostage. I indicated that I would investigate right away, and hung up. I went to the corridor gate, but all was serene, in a relative sense, that is, by that time.

A couple of hours later, everyone was in a cell—some cell. There were five men in some cells, but everybody was locked up. The State Police had performed magnificently. They had pushed the men into the cell-blocks. Under the supervision of Commissioner Leonard after they were in the cell-blocks, the men were distributed to the galleries and to the cells. Institutional guards locked the cells. It was marvelous to watch. During that riot, I developed admiration and respect for the Michigan State Police. Four State Troopers, seven guards, and eleven inmates had been injured, and one inmate had been killed.

After everyone was in his cell, I called the counselors—the group of psychologists, social workers, and sociologists who form a large part of the treatment program. The counselors went to the mail office to pick up incoming mail for the inmates and brought it to the rotunda. Then I went on the radio again. I told them that counselors would bring their mail to the cell-blocks. Because many men were not in their blocks, it might be difficult to locate everyone, but the counselors would find them all in time. They would distribute the newspapers in the cell-blocks, too. I thought this would help in rebuilding morale. A uniformed officer was more unwelcome in the cell-blocks than anyone else, so the counselors were selected to do the job. After the mail was delivered, I asked the counselors to go with me into the north-side cell-blocks where inmates were raising havoc and try to establish these face-to-face relationships with as many men as possible. They went into the north-side blocks and did a good job. Some men were not quieted by the counselors, but some were. The total result was improvement in 5-block, 4-block, 3-block, and part of 2-block. Those were all the blocks they were able to work in that day. Returning to the rotunda, I asked them to go into the blocks as they felt able to do so as long as the men in 15-block held out.

Now that the yard was clear, I went back to the window at 15-block. I had been there but a few minutes when the corridor gates opened. Out strode Deputy Bacon, flanked by three State Troopers on either side, with guns at ready. The entourage walked into the north yard, and disappeared around the kitchen, and apparently around the yard and into the corridor gate again from the south. The scene was anti-climactic, and elicited laughter from 15-block and yells from the north side cells. My reaction was one of amazement. Here was this big man, six-feet-five in height, weighing about two-fifteen, who did not venture into the yard when there was danger, and signaled me off. Now that the yard had been cleared, here he was for all to see strolling in the yard with a heavy police escort!

Back at 15-block, Ward told me that an inmate had died in the riot. He wanted to know how he died. If he was killed by an official, Ward would kill a hostage. He had to do it— there was no choice. His only problem now, he assured me, was in determining how the inmate had died. He had called the warden. If Warden Frisbie told him that Darwin Millage died of violence from other than an inmate, he would have to kill a hostage. The warden had said Millage had died of cancer! Absurd! Ward was trying to put me to a supreme test. He was daring me to tell the truth. He had no faith in anybody else, he told me. He said he had had some faith in Deputy Bacon and Commissioner Brooks before the riot, but not now. I told him that before we could really tell what Millage died of, we would have to wait for an autopsy—that while highly improbable, it was still possible that Millage may actually have died of cancer. He agreed that an autopsy was needed, but smiled at the idea of cancer. At his insistence, I promised to bring him the results of the autopsy.

About an hour later, after I had obtained the autopsy results, I went to 15-block. Ward was waiting anxiously and with obvious suspicion. He spoke, "What did Millage die of?"

"Gunshot. Ruptured aorta," I replied.

Ward called to "Crazy Jack" Hyatt. Jack was in charge of the hostages on the fifth floor of 15-block. There were eleven hostages now. During the afternoon, the crowd had called for officers to be killed. Ward had protected as many as he could because he wanted his part of the mutiny to be orderly. Officer Curry had been taken to the crowd, but an alert wedge of State Troopers and the clank of a machine gun had saved him. The eleven hostages were locked in individual cells on the top floor of 15-block. Ward and the other inmates informed me

that they were all right, but that locked in with each officer
was an armed inmate who was to kill at the signal from "Crazy
Jack" Hyatt, who spent his time sharpening his knife on the
cell bars.

I told Ward that the institutional officers were unarmed.
Millage was not killed by an institutional guard. Nobody had
been killed by an institutional guard. "If you're going to give
justice, you'd better get a State Trooper, not a prison guard,"
I said. "Do you have a State Trooper in there?"

"That's logical," Ward whispered in some amazement.
When "Crazy Jack" Hyatt arrived, Ward told Jack that Millage was killed by a State Trooper and that they would have
to get a State Trooper. "These guys didn't do it," Ward said.
They agreed not to harm a hostage at that point. I had saved
and even improved my relationship with Ward, in that I would
not lie to him even to save a guard and, simultaneously, the
guard's life had been saved. Time was on our side. The longer
we could keep them talking, the safer were the lives of the
hostages, particularly if that safety could be reinforced by frustration of anticipated killings, induced by the introduction
of new ideas or goals.

Ward asked for food. I suspected that they already had
enough food for two weeks. I had discussed the question with
Warden Frisbie and Deputy Bacon, and they had agreed that
it might be well under the circumstances to give them food
to keep them talking, if for no other reason. I called to the
boys in the kitchen, and asked them to bring food and coffee.
A push-truck of sandwiches and coffee was prepared. I went
to the kitchen and pushed the cart to the front of 15-block.
Ward wanted the sandwiches pushed through the bars so he
wouldn't have to open the door. After a brief conversation,
however, he agreed to open the door. I pushed the truck in
front of the block. The barricade came down, the door opened,
and two inmates came out, got on either side of me, and the
three of us pushed the truck into the block. I stood inside the
block for a moment, turned my back and walked out.

I went to the window to talk with Ward. I asked him how

he expected to feed 179 men and have it come out even. He indicated that all the men would be crowded into the corridor outside the disciplinary cells on the first floor. The truck would be placed beside the narrow door leading into that corridor. As the men emerged through the door, they would be given their portion, and they would go upstairs to eat it. I watched some of it. It worked with precision. That gave us one of the answers we needed. Ward was obviously the leader, in that he carried on conversations and any statement made by the other inmates had to have Ward's approval. The other inmates would glance at Ward while they were talking to obtain approval. Now, Ward had demonstrated that he could handle a mundane and practical problem like mass feeding in an anarchical situation. Ward was the leader. Ward was in charge. We could deal with Ward and know that the negotiations would have the support of the group. Natural or otherwise, Ward had emerged as the leader.

It was dark by the time I returned to my office. My office wasn't my office any more. I could hardly get into it. Newsmen had been using it for their headquarters. Five temporary phones had been installed. There were a corps of newsmen at the prison, wire service men, special correspondents for newspapers, staff writers, photographers, magazine men, radio commentators and television men. All had questions, wanted interviews on tape, or something. We were courteous to them. We took the attitude that they could see anything they wanted, we would answer their questions, and that they would not interfere with our handling of the riot. There were some officials who thought they should not have been permitted in the prison during the riot. No other prison riot had had so many newsmen on the scene. This was what Ward and the rioters wanted, however. They wanted "plublicity," as they called it. The more newsmen, the more "plublicity."

Warden Frisbie and Deputy Bacon tried to make arrangements for surrender by telephone to 15-block. They promised that an investigation would be made into the grievances and that there would be no reprisals if the guards were released unharmed. Ward rejected these terms, but made no counterproposals.

Late Monday or early Tuesday, Commissioner Donald S. Leonard of the State Police indicated that immediate plans to storm the block had been dropped. "Maybe this can be settled by conference," he said.

It was midnight when I telephoned my wife, Laura, and suggested that we go downtown and get something to eat. I hadn't had a meal since Sunday night. We went to the Mayfair Grill and ordered a meal. As we sat at a table near the counter, three newsmen came in and sat at the counter. They didn't notice us. The only one I recognized then was Jack Pickering of the *Detroit Times*. They were talking about the riot and the administration. One thing they said startled me. "Fox and Frisbie don't see eye to eye," made me wonder what they were talking about. I decided to see the warden at the first opportunity to see what he knew. If we could put our bits of information together, we might be able to see the origin of any misunderstandings. Warden Frisbie and I had been in agreement much more frequently than not, and any disagreements were talked over and the warden's final decisions were always accepted.

Nothing of importance happened during the night, and Tuesday morning, we began talking with the rioters about specific terms. All the time we talked, I had been trying to delineate in my own thoughts what the inmates wanted. I had come to the conclusion that they didn't know what they wanted and were trying to crystallize their own thinking so that they could get as much as possible out of this situation. I asked the group in the window of 15-block concerning the items about which they had talked with Mr. Gilman, who had jotted down some information about brutality on a pad early Monday morning. They shrugged off Mr. Gilman's notes as "Gilman's notes, not ours."

It seemed obvious to me that they had not organized their own minds, and that if I could help them do it by questioning, suggestions, and conversation, then the terms could be made acceptable to everybody and impotent as far as "damage" to the state of Michigan was concerned. Actually, the issues had to be built up on which agreement could be reached. These issues had to be built on real or imagined complaints of the prisoners as a point of origin. I continued to talk with Ward and the others in generalities about brutality, conditions in the disciplinary block, and other factors which seemed to be relatively less important to them at this point. When I thought the time was right, I mentioned that Donald Clemmer, Commissioner of Corrections for the District of Columbia, had prepared the Report on Corrections for Michigan's "Little Hoover Commission," and that he had attacked the structure of 15-block. I suggested that the disciplinary cells could be made more sanitary by removing the steel doors from most of the cells and putting grilled doors in, and by making the windows larger. Ward and the other inmates listened intently. After further talking over a period of several hours, Ward finally said, "Look, Dep, you know prison administration. We know the inmates' gripes. Between the two of us, we ought to be able to work up a good set of demands."

He was letting me guide his thinking to some extent. I agreed, and said that we would work up the demands here at 15-block. I would make notes of the points of agreement, and I would draw up the demands for the inmates. In an attempt to reduce resistance, I suggested that when the inmates gave up, they should march directly to the dining room for a hot meal—maybe steak. I knew that the entire prison was to be served a utility grade of steak that evening, something frequently on the menu. The portion allotted to 15-block could be held until they gave up. They agreed to that, and asked for ice cream, too. That was all right, for ice cream was served frequently. I had already asked the warden about it and he had approved the meal as bait.

During early Tuesday morning, I told the warden what I had overheard at the Mayfair Grill and suggested that we compare notes before radio talks were made. He agreed. He said he would review my talks so we would be together on them. I told him I wanted to talk now, and I was going to put it on tape. Joe Dellinger had the tape recorder ready. I told the inmates that we were going to have a man from 15-block explain the terms and the procedure we would follow in giving him safe conduct from and to 15-block. Everything was all right, so it went on the central radio system to all cell-blocks immediately.

The inmates in 15-block had sent out two typewritten reports about conditions in the prison. In part, the reports said, "Nowhere have prison probes been so numerous—nor more politics and corruption been uncovered than in this model system. . . . For a nonjudicial body, the Michigan parole board has the most judicial power of any body so conceived. From their decision there is no appeal. . . . Here is a surprise: 'Michigan's happy convicts' don't appreciate the so-called honor camps. They know that the more housing the Corrections Commission commands, the more prisoners can be held and for a longer time."

We began discussing terms, point by point. It was a long and laborious process, beset by discussion among the inmates, with frequent need for clarification, and untold patience. It was a trying and tense situation in which emotional control was of utmost importance. Finally, the points of agreement emerged.

1. 15-block should be remodeled to provide for adequate lighting and treatment facilities. This was my suggestion as previously mentioned for the purpose of achieving an alignment with the inmates so that they would permit me to help them with the terms, thereby enhancing their reasonableness and their acceptability to the state of Michigan. This was not a new suggestion. Donald Clemmer called 15-block "archaic" and had made remodeling of the block a recommendation to the Legislative Committee on State Government Reorganization the year before. Dr. Russell Finch, medical director for the Department of Corrections had previously recommended the remodeling for "sanitary reasons." Several months before, I had outlined a plan to remodel the block, using fenestra steel detention windows, grilled doors, inset lighting covered by

tempered plate glass, and redecorating to make the detention block serve rehabilitative purposes. I had been told to hide the plan, or somebody might get the idea to do it. Obediently, I had hidden it. I don't think Ward considered this term particularly important, but it was important to me in that my suggesting a term in that area helped to align inmate thinking with my thinking.

2. Counselors should have free access to the disciplinary cells in 15-block. This term originated with the inmate demand that all officers who had ever been suspected of engaging in or condoning brutality in 15-block be dismissed. I had insisted that such a procedure would be unfair. There was not enough evidence on any one case to bring it to a court and, further, we should not act on suspicion. The most advisable term, I explained, would be one that would provide the chaplains or counselors, or anyone else in whom the inmates had trust, with the privilege of entering the disciplinary section of 15-block. In this way, someone in whom the inmates have trust would be able to view the fresh bruises and to hear fresh stories of brutality and take the evidence to sympathetic ears in the administration, preferably to the warden because I suspected that the assistant deputy warden in charge of custody had "covered" some cases of custodial officer misconduct in this area.

The inmates in 15-block wanted nothing to do with the chaplains because they said that Chaplains Ray Barber and Al Saunders had been quoted in a Chicago newspaper as saying that Earl Ward and "Crazy Jack" Hyatt were "mentally dead" as far as religion was concerned. This left the term to be covered by the counselors, though there was no particular enthusiasm among the inmates about the counselors, either. Few of them had ever had experience with either the chaplains or the counselors because of their 15-block status. At least, the permitting of counselors to enter the disciplinary section of 15-block was a far more acceptable term to the state than to dismiss all guards who had been suspected of engaging in or condoning brutality in 15-block!

3. Revise segregation policies and give Individual Treatment a place on the segregation board. This term arose in response to the inmate dissatisfaction about being placed in "segregation" in 15-block and being left there for months without information or orientation and without an adequate program. Actually, this had been an area of contention for some time. In early 1950, the segregation board had been made up of two representatives from Custody, the psychologist, and two representatives from Individual Treatment. One day in early 1950, Deputy Bacon had summarily excluded the representatives from Individual Treatment from the board without discussion, reason, or warning. My appeals to the warden were futile. One of the major departments in the prison engaged in the treatment of inmates had been excluded from deliberation in this meeting.

I told Ward that I didn't know whether his complaint was justified or not. Similar to the brutality complaint, however, I thought that the counselors or Individual Treatment should be represented on the segregation board to provide another viewpoint during deliberations concerning the need to segregate a man. It was agreed that the segregation board could be made up of the assistant deputy warden in charge of custody or his representative, the assistant deputy warden in charge of individual treatment or his representative, and the clinical psychologist.

4. Eliminate inhumane restraint equipment and dangerous hand weapons. This term was based on the finding by the mutinous inmates in 15-block of the chain-on-the-strap, "wrist-breakers," and lengths of rubber hose. There was little I could do about that one. The weapons were there and I hadn't known they were there. I suspect that Deputy Bacon didn't know all of them were there, either. Ward recognized the need for some weapons or implements of restraint, such as a blackjack and handcuffs. His terminology was to eliminate the "inhuman" restraint equipment.

5. Pick only guards for 12-block who would not be inhuman in their treatment. 12-block is reserved for semi-mental

cases, epileptics, blind and physically handicapped, and senile cases. Because of the nature of the population in this cellblock, care had been exercised in the assignment of officers to this block. It is a difficult assignment for an officer, however, and there had been several "incidents" there. These incidents had ranged from accusations by inmates of homosexual behavior or "shakedowns" for cigarettes on the part of officers to outright physical brutality. All incidents had been investigated and handled. One which occurred shortly before the riot involved Officer Blaine Lovette, who had allegedly struck an inmate. Feeling had been intense for some time, and expressed itself in this term. Since Deputy Bacon and his assistants already exercised much care in the selection of officers for 12-block, the inclusion of this term merely served to appease the aroused inmates. It would not change actual practice.

6. Adequate and competent personnel for handling mental cases and a more adequate screening. The original demand was to dismiss all the inmate nurses who had worked in the mental ward during periods of alleged brutality. The brutality was a constant allegation, so that it would mean that all inmate nurses would have to be dismissed. Ward cited specific instances of brutality and mishandling of inmates, but was ready to concede that not all nurses were involved. As a consequence, he withdrew the demand for dismissing all who had worked in the mental unit before, and accepted the promise that all nurses in the mental ward now would be re-screened for temperament and capability of brutality and that all new nurses would be similarly screened. I told him that one of my friends, Greg Miller, now chief psychologist for the Traverse City State Hospital was due to be here on Wednesday, and that we hoped Greg would be our new clinical psychologist. Greg Miller would not tolerate brutality.

7. A letter on prison stationery asking the parole board to revise its procedures to give equal treatment to all parolees. This was the most difficult of all the terms to bring from the ridiculous to the acceptable. The term was originally to abolish the parole board and either let everyone do flat sen-

tences without parole or have everyone automatically released
on parole at expiration of a specified part of the sentence and
to be returned in case the parole was violated. I told the inmates in 15-block that such a term could not possibly be agreed
to by the administration in good faith because the prison administration had nothing to do with the creation or abolition of
the parole board nor with the establishment of parole policies.
It took considerable time to discuss that point, though everyone realized its validity. The frustration aroused in the inmates by being rendered helpless concerning a point that had
become major in their thinking needed considerable venting
and catharsis before the inmates could accept the fact that the
parole board was there regardless of what the prison administration agreed to do. Neither Ward nor the other inmates
were ever satisfied on this point.

8.   Post-operative care should be given under the direction of the medical director. This term originated in Ward's
personal experience, and I was able to alter it only slightly.
When Ward was transferred to Jackson from Marquette
several months before, he had been transferred for medical
attention to his foot. When the foot had been operated on,
post-operative care had been left to inmate nurses. Ward had
been highly dissatisfied with the sort of care he had been
given by the inmate nurses, and sought this term to correct
the situation for others. Subsequently, I asked the inmate nurses
about Ward's foot, and they told me that he had received the
same care as other patients. One of them told me about
coming into Ward's room one time and discovering a knife. He
had attempted to get the knife from Ward. Ward had told
him that he shouldn't worry, though, since the knife was not
for him. Rather, he was going to kill the officer who had told
him to stop complaining—that he was no better than anybody
else. After he killed the officer, the nurse could have the knife.
In a little while, however, the nurse succeeded in getting the
knife.

When I explained that the medical program in Southern
Michigan was one of the best prison medical programs in the

country, that the physicians left some post-operative band-
aging to inmate technicians they had trained in order to have
time for more pressing medication and surgery, it made no
difference. The term was altered only slightly from having
post-operative care performed by the medical director to having post-operative care performed under the direction of the
medical director. I thought that at least there was enough room
for definitions of "under the direction" to make the term
acceptable to the medical director.

9. Equal opportunities for dental treatment for all prisoners, with special regard to elimination of buying preference
or obtaining it through friendship. This was, in my estimation,
a just term. I made no effort to change it. There had been
several instances in which the evidence was fairly sound that
dentures had been made on week-ends or during the week
for men who had been far down the waiting list, and that the
work had been purchased for cigarettes or other consideration.
I explained that such did not occur when our former dentist,
Dr. A. G. Davis, was on the job, but that we had not even
been able to employ a civilian dentist for several months.
That fact was recognized, but Ward indicated that it didn't
take a dentist to control a waiting list so that everyone took
his fair turn. He was right.

10. Creation of a permanent council, elected by inmates,
to confer periodically with prison officials. This term began
with the demand that Ward and Hyatt appoint a committee
to review all the rules and regulations pertaining to inmates.
The council would be empowered to veto any rule with which
it did not agree. They mentioned the names of some of the
inmates they wanted on the council, including "Crazy Jack"
Hyatt and "Red" Walshfer, a long-termer who had just been
transferred from Marquette. I told them that they should not
try to appoint such a committee, but that it would be more
fair and democratic if they permitted the inmate body to elect
their own representatives. I was thinking that such an election
process would give an opportunity for research to learn more
about social stratification and prestige in the prison popula-

tion. Further, I contended that it would not be administratively sound to provide the inmate body with the power of veto.

I reviewed briefly that New York had been experimenting with self-government since the time of Thomas Mott Osborne, in 1914, and that they had found the "inmate advisory council" much more workable. Even there, however, inmate self-government had been abandoned. Michigan had actually been the first, as far as we can tell, to experiment with self-government, back in 1854, but not much progress was made. The federal prisons and some state prisons have the inmate council idea in force at the present time. Consequently, this was not a damaging term. As a matter of fact, I considered it a fairly good one, since it would give the inmates and administration another channel through which freedom of communication could be made so that each could better be understood by the other. I suggested that the inmate council be an advisory council, elected by the prison population, to meet with me once a month in the classification room to go over matters of interest to the inmates and to the administration. If nothing else, it would be a form of group therapy. "Crazy Jack" Hyatt objected to the compromise from a council with power of veto to an "advisory" council, but finally yielded to Ward's persuasion.

11. No reprisals against any ringleader or participant in the revolt. I had explained to Ward at the beginning that the prison administration was in a position to waive institutional rules and punishment by agreement but, like the abolition of the parole board, the prison administration did not have the power to waive state law. Consequently, the term "reprisals," in this term would have to refer to punishment within the institution. If someone were killed, for instance, the prison administration could not prevent the attorney general, the sheriff of Jackson county, or any other citizen from issuing a warrant and demanding trial for murder. The prison administration could agree to disregard the riot as a cause for further punishment. Since the men involved were already in the punishment block with no immediate prospect of getting

out, and since we could not waive state law, I thought that this term was empty and of no consequence. However, it seemed to be reassuring to the inmates in 15-block, and I favored almost anything that would make surrender easier for them. I suggested that one of their number come with me at 2:00 P.M. to put their terms over the central radio system so that all inmates would know our progress, and since the day before we had asked them to return to their cells while 15-block negotiated with the administration, I wanted them to announce their own terms to the world through the press and radio. The reason was that the terms were not as mundane and specific as most of the inmates wanted. If they announced the terms as their terms, however, they would be forced by their pride to make those terms the basis of their negotiations. Russell Jarboe agreed to come to the radio room that afternoon. Ward said that to reciprocate evidence of good faith, he would release a guard as soon as Jarboe was returned to 15-block under safe conduct. I asked whom he would release so we could notify his wife, but Ward immediately became defensive, indicating that they would decide that at the proper time. I could see that I had made him uncomfortable, which I did not want to do at this point, so I changed the subject.

I told Ward that I would be back with the agreement in time for him to review it and make whatever corrections to which we mutually agreed, and Jarboe could come with me and put the terms on the central radio system at 2:00 P.M. for the inmates in the entire prison to hear.

By default of the rest of the administration, I had become the leader as far as dealing with the 15-block situation was concerned. Commissioner Leonard's State Police had cleared the yard on Monday and were just standing by. Commissioner Brooks and Warden Frisbie were seemingly lost. Badgered by newsmen on one occasion, Frisbie was quoted as saying, "Go see Fox—he's running this show." I hasten to add, however, that I was *not* running that show! All major decisions were approved by majority in conference with Commissioners

Leonard and Brooks and Warden Frisbie. I was acting under their approval and encouragement. Even though the terms had been verbally agreed upon, it was obvious to me that the group of rioters in 15-block were yet too strong, were enjoying themselves too much, and were not sufficiently tired and irritable to surrender the hostages and their position.

It was about this time that inmate William Manus was released from 15-block because he was ill. Ward had written the diagnosis, "neurotic, subject to hypersensitivity and neuro-tremors, with one- to three-minute spells of dizziness and black-outs."

The rest of the prison was noisy. Yelling and banging could be heard all the time. There was no attempt to feed more than one meal a day until the kitchen could be repaired. That wasn't all that was smashed. Cots and furniture were destroyed, plumbing was pulled out, mattresses and clothing in the cells were burned. The library, laundry, theater, gym, tailor shop and other facilities were destroyed. In 11-block bars were sawed. Early estimates of damage ranged between two and two and a half million dollars.

After getting the notes ready on the terms of agreement, I went to the lobby to ask Franklin DeNato, Jr., my secretary, to come to an office where I could dictate the prisoners' terms. I had located Frankie when Commissioner Brooks called me. Governor G. Mennen Williams wanted a conference with him at noon regarding the prison riot. Brooks said he wanted to take me along because I knew more about the inside of the prison and the inmate mind than anyone else at the prison. I was to be ready to leave the prison by 11:00. It was almost 10:30 then. I had already told some newsmen that Jarboe would go on the central system at 2:00. I told as many as were available that it would now probably be later than 2:00, but did not tell them why. Frankie and I went into Frankie's office and I dictated the prisoners' terms as accurately as my notes and memory could reconstruct them. I told him I would be back as early this afternoon as possible, and asked him to have copies double-spaced waiting for me so I could go to 15-block with them. After going to 15-block to explain to Ward that I had to go to Lansing and that I might not be back by 2:00, but would be there as soon as I could, I went to the lobby to meet the commissioner.

During the ride to Lansing, Commissioner Brooks reviewed several past events at the prison. In many of the major controversies between Deputy Bacon and me, he had decided in favor of Deputy Bacon. He said, "Custody had operated the prison, Custody had had its way, and now, look what has happened! As soon as this riot is over, you are going to have your chance to run the prison with your Individual Treatment." At another point, he continued in this vein, "When considering promotion potential (for civil service examinations), we thought Deputy Bacon was a more forceful man because he operates like a bull in a china shop. We thought you were too reserved and co-operative to be forceful, but the events of the past few days has shown us that we were wrong all around. Bacon hasn't done anything—he's been dead weight. You've proved yourself capable of handling any situation."

I thanked him for the immediate compliments, but pointed out that prior to the riot the Individual Treatment program at Jackson and throughout the state had progressed recently farther than it ever had before, and that we were still going. I reminded him that I could be forceful if necessary, as I had been at Cassidy Lake, but that progress could be and had been made faster at Jackson by gaining co-operation. He agreed, but said that he hadn't stopped to realize it until the riot started. There were several things he wished he could do over again.

We went to the governor's house, rather than to the capitol, so that we could avoid newsmen. Commissioner Brooks and I arrived first and waited. When the governor and his entourage came, Commissioner Brooks introduced me, explaining that he had brought me along because I knew the inside of the prison and the inmate mind better than anyone else. We sat down to lunch. Besides Governor Williams, Commissioner Brooks, and I, there were Paul Weber, the governor's public relations man, and Larry Farrell, secretary to the governor. Listening to the conversation, I got the impression that the governor was worried because this was an election year—he wanted to know how he could explain away the prison riot in terms that would satisfy the voting public that the riot was not the result of his political administration. That seemed to be the extent of his concern!

I suggested that he call in the Osborne Association to make an impartial survey. Commissioner Brooks was not in agreement, apparently because he thought penal experts would criticize Williams for appointing a politician who knew nothing about prisons or corrections as Commissioner of Corrections. Governor Williams asked how he could get in touch with the Osborne Association. I indicated that Commissioner Brooks had the address in his office in Lansing, that I had the address at Jackson, or that he could telephone Austin MacCormick, Professor of Criminology at the University of California at Berkeley, since MacCormick is also Executive Director of the Osborne Association. The governor decided to telephone Austin MacCormick and ask the Osborne Association to make an investigation.

After leaving the governor's house, Commissioner Brooks and I went to the offices of the Department of Corrections, where the commissioner had some work to do before returning to Jackson. When I went in, my friends greeted me and asked me questions about the riot. A. Ross Pascoe, a member of the parole board whom I consider to be one of the most capable release men in the country, invited me to sit down. He said that there was considerable comment within the parole board about news reports of my talk to the inmates over the public address system to the rioters Monday when we were trying to get them off the yard. The objection was that the newspapers had reported that I had "admitted the validity" of their grievances against the parole board and other phases of correctional administration. I explained to Ross that such was not the case at all. While I had no script nor recording of it, I assured him that I had merely listed the grievances as I had interpreted them, that I had heard them before, that some of them may be justified, and that I think they may be representative of the grievances of all the inmates. Further, the ad lib talk was designed to "coax" rioting men into their cells, and I was careful not to make any final statements except to assure the rioters that we were sympathetically aware of the nature of their grievances.

Ross said that he had actually thought that to be the case. My reaction was that people not at the scene of a riot cannot understand the tenseness and explosiveness of the situation and that almost anything within reason has to be done to save lives; and at the same time, we who are in the riot have reciprocal difficulty in understanding the intellectual calm with which people outside the area of violence can criticize our efforts.

Back at the prison, I found that two inmates had been beaten up mercilessly and thrown out of 15-block. Ellsworth Roberts and Jerome Parmentier had been struck with the weapons found in 15-block, especially the chain-on-the-strap. These two had apparently tried to get notes out of 15-block to the prison administration, and had been caught by the other inmates. Regarding the beatings, Ward told Warden Frisbie by phone, "We have a very strong organization here. The discipline is terrific. We've locked up the rough boys and we're getting rid of those that don't believe in our policy."

Frankie gave me the terms of the agreement, typed double-spaced, and I took them to 15-block. A few of the inmates wanted to argue about some of the terms. They were not happy about the failure of abolishment of the parole board. They complained about the food, laundry service, hobbycraft, and miscellaneous items. I told them that they had already agreed to these terms, and that all these other things were minor items that could be "janitored up" later.

They wanted to add more terms. I reminded them that if the agreement was lengthened, it might lose its effectiveness; that these terms were major principles that covered many areas, and that they might go down in the annals of history like the resolutions of the American Prison Congress of 1870 that hung framed on the walls of my office! Most important was that they had already verbally agreed to these terms and that I had taken time to have them prepared—we didn't want to junk them now.

"Besides, the world is waiting for one of you to come out of 15-block to go on the radio with these terms." They agreed to send someone out, but they didn't think that Jarboe could pronounce some of the words in the agreement. Ray Young volunteered to go with me on the radio. I agreed, but asked that Jarboe come, too, because it had been announced that he would be there. I asked them to get the officer they would release ready so there would be no waiting when I returned. The barricades came down, the door opened readily. With repeated performance, it had become easier for them to take the barricade down and open the door. Young and Jarboe emerged from 15-block, and we walked slowly toward the corridor gate. Newsmen and photographers lined the corridor.

Upon request of the inmates, I had asked the State Police to put their rifles behind them so they would not be in evidence when the inmates came through on their truce mission. Most, but not all, observed the request.

We walked to the parole board hearing room, where the radio panels and their outlets were housed. We sat at the end of the table before a microphone. The room was filled with newsmen, radio men, and photographers. Just before we went on the radio system, Young checked the terms. He noted that the one regarding reprisals had been omitted. I penciled it in, and we went on the air. Young read the terms haltingly, and with some mispronounced words, while Jarboe chewed gum vigorously. After the program was over, I asked again that inmates who had additional grievances should write letters to me. We started back toward 15-block. As we emerged from the corridor gate to go to 15-block, a spontaneous cheer arose from the north-side cell blocks. As we were halfway to 15-block, some photographers asked us to walk through the corridor again for some pictures. As we turned around to go back, the cheers from the north side turned to hoots, and Young signaled that all was all right. After the pictures, we returned to 15-block.

As I accompanied Young and Jarboe to the door, I asked for the hostage they would release. Ward and inmate Ken Moore came out with Officer Thomas Elliott. Ward held Elliott by the belt while pictures were taken. After a short period of picture taking, Elliott was permitted to go. Captain Harold Tucker had come out to meet him. Elliott was taken to Deputy Bacon's office where he was interviewed by Commissioner Brooks, Warden Frisbie, Deputy Bacon, Mr. Gilman, and Commissioner of State Police Donald S. Leonard. By the time I arrived, the interview was over, and I knew nothing about his reports, except that Commissioner Brooks and Warden Frisbie had decided not to tell the newsmen what he had said.

I found out later that Elliott had reported excellent treatment at the hands of the inmates in 15-block, and that the administration did not want that made known to the public. Newsmen were waiting outside the front door. Captain Tucker took Elliott out the back door, gave him a cap, and they walked through the rotunda by the crowd of newsmen, and out of the prison without being recognized. Elliott was not at that time interviewed.

In order to get the yard cleared of debris, counselors went into every block except 15-block to select men they trusted to work. With the selected crew, the kitchen was opened and the yard was cleaned. The counselors also kept mail and newspapers going out and in for the men as a matter of maintaining as high morale as possible.

Political reaction had already begun. Attorney General Frank G. Millard had said that he would prosecute all crimes he could find as soon as order was restored. Harry W. Jackson, head of the attorney general's criminal division, was appointed to find crimes among inmates and to determine if there was misfeasance or malfeasance in administration. Speaker Victor A. Knox announced that house and senate appropriations committees would investigate. Democratic Governor Williams charged that the riot indicated the unwisdom of the legislature's action in cutting appropriations. Republican legislators replied that the administration and its appointment of an ineffective corrections commissioner were responsible. Representative Robert Montgomery announced that he would ask the Michigan legislature to consider a death penalty, at least, for any prison inmate who killed a hostage guard. Attorney General Millard said, "Somebody must be punished."

I was called to the personnel office. Upon arriving, I met Harry W. Jackson, an assistant attorney general who headed the criminal division. Warden Frisbie, Commissioner Leonard, and others were there. Mr. Jackson began with a report from Attorney General Frank G. Millard that the prison could not agree to a "no reprisals" term, as the newspapers had reported, and that it was the function of the attorney general's office to enforce the laws of the state. I had begun to explain that that was no secret, that the inmates understood that, and that our reprisals referred to institutional punishment only. At that point, however, Captain Tucker called me to go to 11-block and try to convince the inmates to permit themselves to be locked up.

I went to 11-block with Captain Tucker, wondering on the way what I could do. When I waded through the water on the floor, the inmates cheered. I took off my shoes and stockings because of the condition of the floor, and the inmates warned me to watch out for broken glass. They shouted that they wanted me as the next warden. I shouted back that we wanted to bring food to them, but that some people were afraid to take food up to the higher galleries when all cells were not locked. Rightly or wrongly, they were afraid of being attacked and thrown off the gallery. (This was actually true in some cases.) I asked them to permit a length of chain to be placed around the bars so that the door could be locked with a padlock. They agreed to permit this, and the locksmiths went to work. They cheered me as I left the block.

This sort of relationship, I was sure, would not only settle the riot, but would also calm the prison in the months of reconstruction that would follow. It was a simple formula. Treat men as men, whether they be inmates or not, and always make your word good. If a man can trust the administration, then the relationship will be good.

A brief emergency arose Tuesday when banging and pounding was heard in the tunnel leading from 15-block to the basement of the administration building. The inmates in 15-block had removed the metal cover and had broken into the tunnel. They were trying to work their way to the basement of the administration building next to the arsenal. State Troopers were stationed where they could guard the tunnel and protect the arsenal. Because of the presence of heavy steel grating at strategic points, it was actually not a serious threat.

During late afternoon, Ward called me and said that they had beaten up a man, and suggested that I come after him. I called for a rolling stretcher. They were going to throw him out of the cell-block. When I arrived, the barricade came down, the door opened, and two inmates dragged a body out, and returned to the block. I recognized Pawlak, who opened his eyes and muttered, "Thank God, Dep, you're here." After a pause, he asked, "Shall I try to get up?" I told him to lie there until the stretcher came. We didn't wait long. The stretcher came, we lifted Pawlak on it, and he was taken to the hospital.

Ward told me to go home, that nothing would happen until I returned. He thought I needed the sleep. I went into my office and talked with newsmen. About 8:00 P.M., Ward telephoned to see if I was there. He said that as long as I was here, they were going to beat up another man, but if I had not been here, they would have had to wait until morning when I would have arrived in order to keep their promise. He was glad I was here for the sake of the man, who would have had to spend the night knowing he would be beaten up in the morning. I asked Ward to be sure not to kill him because that would mean a murder charge. Ward said that they would throw him out in a little while, but that they would give me time to get a stretcher before they went to work. I called nurses and stretcher, got Captain Tucker, and we went to the corridor gate. Ward waved us back, indicating that they hadn't done their job yet. We watched in silence without seeing anything. We could only assume that in the shadows behind those big doors and bars there was a beating taking place. Then through the window we saw Ward go to the desk, get a ball and peen hammer, and go back into the shadows. We learned later that he had used the hammer to break the victim's arms and legs, and to pound on his head. Soon the barricade came down, the doors swung open, and the unconscious James Glenn was thrown out. Captain Tucker, the nurses with the stretcher, and I went out and got him. He was taken to the hospital, all limbs broken and skull fractured.

Through the night nothing happened. All was relatively calm—a tense calm. In the morning, at Ward's request, I brought another truck of coffee and rolls to 15-block. Ward promised to release another guard at 2:00 P.M. in response to the fine way the administration had treated the mutineers. This time, I didn't ask who would be released.

Early Wednesday morning, the inmates gave me a five-page treatise on parole prepared by Richard Bellew, a very capable inmate in 15-block. Dissatisfied with the term concerning the parole board, the inmates had decided to expand their thinking in this area.

By Wednesday morning, Commissioner Brooks had decided to set up his office at the prison. He took over the parole board hearing room, and assigned tasks specifically to supersede any previous orders. I was to be responsible for 15-block. "That's your only responsibility," Commissioner Brooks said, "and you report to me periodically." This order superseded all previous orders, he told me. He followed it with the comment that 15-block was a pretty big responsibility.

Warden Frisbie was disgusted with Deputy Bacon and his inability to hold up under pressure. I hadn't seen Deputy Bacon since Monday, but had thought nothing of it. Frisbie said that Bacon had had nervous exhaustion and had had to be taken home twice. He said that Commissioner Brooks had vehemently expressed the desire to have another chance at marking the promotional potential in the recent civil service examinations in the wardens' series as far as Bacon and I were concerned.

At 2:00 P.M., Officer Harold Carrier was released from 15-block as a token of good faith. There were pictures of the releasing, and 15-block was getting their "plublicity." Carrier said, "I thank God I am safe today. I hope my friends in 15-block have as much luck. I don't know whether they will. Those boys inside mean business."

State Senator Charles Blondy arrived at the prison Wednesday. Senator Blondy was the only legislator or high state official outside the State Police or Corrections Department whom I saw visit the prison during the time of the violence. Greg Miller, chief psychologist at Traverse City State Hospital on educational leave of absence to study at Michigan State University, had arrived Wednesday morning, and had accompanied me during the day. I had arranged for him to meet Dr. Russell Finch, the medical director. Donald Clemmer, Commissioner of Corrections for the District of Columbia, also had arrived.

During Wednesday afternoon, we met almost continuously in the parole board hearing room. Commissioner Brooks, Commissioner Leonard, Warden Frisbie, and I had actually constituted the "board of strategy" for handling the riot. While the technique was based on my recommendations, it had received approval from this group. All our relationships had been very friendly. Wednesday afternoon, however, Commissioner Leonard said that it was time for a show of force, and he wanted to make it. I didn't agree, nor did Commissioner Brooks and Warden Frisbie. The inmates and administration had agreed on general terms, but we had not prepared a document for signatures yet. Two officer hostages had been released in the past two days. It was entirely out of context to have a show of force now.

The idea struck me at that time that Commissioner Leonard had an ulterior motive for wanting to provide a show of force at that time. He was to retire from the State Police on May 1

and enter the Republican primaries for the office of governor
of the state of Michigan. If he could retire in a blaze of glory
just before a political campaign, it would enhance his chances
to win. If he could express the aggression of the people of the
state of Michigan against those convicts who dared to rebel,
he could be elected governor. Could he possibly be thinking
in that direction?

Later that evening, preparations were made by the State
Police to blast the block when the signal was given. TNT had
been moved into the prison for the purpose. News reports,
such as those in the *Chicago Daily News*, estimated the quantity in hundreds of pounds. The explosives were in large
wooden crates, which were carried by two State Troopers. An
abundant supply of guns, tear gas, and ammunition was moved
in. Greg Miller had overheard State Troopers saying, "Nine
guards for 170 inmates—that's not a bad ratio at all. If we
could get that in Korea——"

During Wednesday afternoon, several things were suggested. One was that I conceal a small pistol in my clothes, lure
Ward and Hyatt to the window for conversation, and then
shoot them both! What sportsmanship! What tact! Commissioner Leonard wanted a conference with the inmates at
15-block to tell them that they'd better come out or else—I
decided that the yard was fairly free, and that if Leonard
wanted to do that, he could walk out there and do it himself,
but I would not be a party to it. Warden Frisbie, Donald
Clemmer, Commissioner Leonard, and I agreed to go out to
15-block at 6:00, Wednesday evening.

Fatigue and strain were beginning to show among us. While
previously there had been a unanimity of purpose among us
and differences of opinion were talked out to everybody's acceptance, that cohesiveness was now gone. Men who had previously operated in conference as a group now began to emerge
as individuals. The interpersonal relationships that gave cohesiveness to the group were disappearing. I began to wonder
which group, the increasingly aggressive and irritable official
leadership or the threatening inmate leadership, was going to

be most difficult to prevent from precipitating a blood-bath. I found myself defending the inmates in some instances to avoid such an event. That placed me in the position of being accused by some of letting the inmates win me over instead of my winning them. Men were not thinking clearly.

It was on Wednesday that Governor Williams asked Austin MacCormick and the Osborne Association to investigate the prison situation in Michigan to determine the cause of the riot. He added that the appropriations had forced a reduction of 60 guards at Jackson since 1949 while the prison population was increasing. The legislature had turned down a request for $600,000 to build housing facilities at Ionia for aged and infirm inmates so that overcrowding at Jackson could be reduced.

About 4:00 in the afternoon, I asked Senator Blondy and Greg Miller to come to 15-block with me. Greg Miller talked to the inmates about his plans for the mental ward, and Ward seemed to be happy about it. The inmates were really excited when I introduced Senator Blondy. The inmates gave the senator their complaints about the parole board. Senator Blondy promised to take up their complaints on the floor of the senate, May 14.

At 6:00, Commissioner Leonard, Donald Clemmer, Warden Frisbie, and I met at the parole board hearing room. We started to 15-block. Donald Clemmer and Commissioner Leonard waited at the corridor gate, while Warden Frisbie and I went to 15-block. "Crazy Jack" Hyatt was waiting. Knife in hand, he waved it and verbally abused Warden Frisbie in a shrieking voice and in terms too vulgar to repeat in print. Warden Frisbie handled it well, without getting excited, and without losing his poise. After the first tirades from "Crazy Jack" and Ward had been spent, they talked more reasonably. Hyatt retired and Ward talked with the warden. Ward was angry because of the warden's replies to reporters concerning the 11 points that were agreed upon. He reviewed each one, point by point.

Replying to the demand that 15-block be remodeled, Warden Frisbie had been quoted as saying, "Granted. The first gallery has already been repaired, only a lack of steel and money have held up the rest." Ward insisted that nothing at all had been done. The warden said he had been misquoted.

Concerning granting counselors access to 15-block, Frisbie had been quoted as saying, "Okay, no argument. They've been allowed in there regularly; this means only that the frequency of their visits will increase. The only thing I'm going to insist on is that they not be made 'errand boys'—called in every time a man wonders why he hasn't got an answer yet to a letter he mailed three days before."

Ward told the warden he knew this was a lie! I knew that by custodial order the counselors had not been allowed access to the disciplinary cells, and that my appeals to the warden had been in vain. I didn't understand the quote in the paper, either. The group therapist had been permitted access to the upper four floors of 15-block, but had experienced annoyances even when he went there.

Newspapers had also reported that Deputy Bacon had taken issue with one of my statements over the loudspeakers to the inmates on Monday while I was trying to help get the yard cleared. He had said that "we have a counselor for the top four floors, and the men on the base tier appear every two weeks before an administrative board where their cases are reviewed and they receive counseling." The "administrative board" to which he referred was the disciplinary court. The counselor for the top four floors to which he referred was the group therapist, and not the man's regular counselor. The issue behind this term was whether or not an inmate might be visited by his personal counselor when he went into 15-block. The counselors had never been permitted to visit their men when they went to 15-block.

Regarding the segregation board and Individual Treatment representation on it, the warden had replied, "They already have a representative on the disciplinary board; there's no reason why they can't have one on the segregation board." I wished he had taken that view two years before.

As to hand weapons and inhumane restraint equipment,

the warden had been quoted as saying, "No officer is allowed to have any weapons inside the walls; no officer is ever permitted to lay a hand on an inmate except in self defense. I am completely befuddled by this charge. I've been through the cell blocks, 15 in particular, making thorough GI inspections, looking everywhere. I have never found anything of this nature. However, I will investigate further." Ward showed the warden the chain-on-the-strap, the "wrist-breaker," and rubber hoses, and asked what he thought these were.

At this point, Warden Frisbie interrupted Ward, "Look, fella, have you ever been misquoted?" Ward shouted that he had been misquoted all right, but not that frequently and consistently.

Ward wadded the paper up and threw it, turned to Frisbie and shouted, "Okay, so you were misquoted! Where do we go from here?"

Warden Frisbie talked to him calmly about the preparation of the terms on which we had already agreed, reviewed the hiring of Greg Miller as psychologist, and repeated his complete personal opposition to mass punishment and reprisals.

The situation was much too tense now for Commissioner Leonard's show of force. We could not prevent him from coming to 15-block if he wanted, but I didn't want to invite trouble by asking him to come to 15-block when he wanted to threaten men like Earl Ward and "Crazy Jack" Hyatt. I told Ward that Donald Clemmer from Washington, D.C., was present, and that he'd like to talk with Ward. I signaled to Donald Clemmer, who came from the corridor gate. Ward told Commissioner Clemmer about the complaints. He started to tell him about the "Little Hoover Commission" report that 15-block was archaic. I reminded Ward that Donald Clemmer wrote it. Ward apologized to Commissioner Clemmer, and showed him the weapons. After a brief conversation, we returned to the corridor gate.

I didn't signal for Commissioner Leonard to come. I thought that if he really wanted to come, he could do it. Nobody was holding him back. Further, he held more rank than either the warden or I. I didn't want to accept responsibility for trouble I was sure he would start. Later, however, he complained that "through some oversight or otherwise, I was not invited to participate." With all the State Police around, all his rank, and all his verbiage, an "invitation" would have been anti-climactic.

It was some while later when I was in the lobby that the warden told me that maybe I'd better go to 15-block because "Crazy Jack" Hyatt had taken over. Ward and the warden had been talking over the telephone, when scuffling was heard, the phone banged around a little while, then quiet, and after a pause, a voice came into the receiver, "This is Jack, I'm in charge now. We want action." Hyatt had called for Captain Tucker to get the personal effects of two officers they threatened to kill. Something didn't sound right to me. I had thought Ward was so completely in charge that I couldn't accept the idea that Jack could take over.

I told the warden I didn't think it wise for me to go over to 15-block yet, because I was working on the agreement. In the meantime, newsmen were writing frenziedly, telephoning, telegraphing, and waiting for a line. Captain Tucker was worried. He said that Jack had given him the personal effects of the officers, and then slammed the windows shut.

After about an hour, I went to 15-block. Ward was sitting in the corner. He had not been deposed. Hyatt was at the window, but he was following Ward's strategy. They had staged the scuffle! I talked with them at some length about when they would come out. They were vague, but they wanted publicity in the newspapers above everything. No date could be approached. I asked them who should sign the agreements. They said that my word was good enough for them, but that I might be overridden by my superiors. Consequently, they wanted the signatures of my superiors on the agreement. They listed Warden Frisbie, Commissioner Brooks, and Governor Williams. I told them I didn't know whether the governor's signature was available. They insisted on it.

The governor's signature was a little difficult to get because of the distance to Lansing. Rather than send the agreement up, it was agreed by telephone between Commissioner Brooks and the governor's office that a letter would be prepared accepting the terms, the governor would sign it, and a State Trooper would bring it to Jackson to be included with the rest of the agreement. It was after 1:00 A.M. Thursday morning when the letter arrived. It was written as follows:

Earnest C. Brooks, Commissioner
Department of Corrections
Jackson, Michigan

Dear Commissioner Brooks;

This will acknowledge the telephonic report to me tonight stating the 11-point terms, prepared by Dr. Vernon Fox, upon which the inmates in Cell Block 15 agree to evacuate the block and surrender the hostages unharmed.

It is my understanding that the 11 points are unchanged from those which were shown to me this afternoon, except that the final point has been amended to read as follows: "No reprisals of any sort shall be initiated or perpetrated by personnel of the Michigan Department of Corrections."

If this, in the judgment of yourself, Julian W. Frisbie, Commissioner Leonard and Assistant Deputy Warden Fox is in the public interest and necessary to restore order and save the lives of the hostages, I approve your acceptance of these terms to effect the release of the hostages and the cessation of resistance.

Sincerely,
(Signed)
G. Mennen Williams
Governor

Similar letters were sent to Commissioner Leonard, Warden Frisbie, and to me.

Two typists, Mrs. Kate Koning and Miss Joan Jacob, had

typed the material. To meet the first term, I asked Joe Dellinger to draw up a plan for remodeling 15-block, knocking
out brick at the side of the wall and installing Fenestra steel
detention windows, putting grilled doors in to permit circula-
tion of air, insetting lights behind tempered plate glass, with
the controls at the end of the gallery, and painting the interior
a light color. To meet the second term, I prepared a Warden's
Special Order providing that counselors would have free access to 15-block. I drew up another similar order for the warden
to specify that the segregation board would be made up of the
assistant deputy warden in charge of custody or his representative, the assistant deputy warden in charge of individual treatment or his representative, and the clinical psychologist. The
fourth term was met by an order by the warden for full rations
for everyone, whether in detention or not, and the elimination
of all but the standard restraint equipment.

The warden prepared a short letter to the parole board
indicating that the inmates had some complaints against their
policies, and enclosed the five-page treatise on parole prepared
by inmate Bellew. A memo prepared by the warden to Dr.
Finch directed that the list of inmates needing dental care be
maintained and work done on priority of request, and ordered
that "in no case and at no time will one inmate's name be
moved ahead of another inmate's."

I drew up a short plan for the inmate advisory council, to
be elected by coupon ballots printed in the prison newspaper,
to meet with prison officials monthly and discuss inmate grievances and problems. I did not provide at this point for more
careful selection of guards for 12-block, post-operative care,
and more adequately trained men in the mental ward because
we had already been doing as much as we could in these areas.
If, after the inmates saw the agreements as prepared and
wanted these other points fully covered, I would have done
it.

I then prepared an agreement to go on the brochure. The
agreement was as follows:

We, the undersigned, agree to all items in this brochure. After the agreement has been signed, the institutional officials will present it to the available newspapers and the inmates will start cleaning up 15-block. After the newspapers carry the story, a newspaper will be presented to the inmates of 15-block. Immediately after receiving the newspaper, in daylight, four inmates will be stationed at the door to shakedown for weapons. The inmates will then file into the dining room to be served an abundant meal of steak, ice cream, and appropriate trimmings.

During the meal, counselors will enter 15-block, followed by unarmed institutional guards to restore the cellblocks to acceptable use.

After the meal, the inmates will file back into 15-block, enter their originally assigned cells; institutional officers will lock the doors and the new rules will be in immediate effect.

Earl Ward, #72646

Earnest C. Brooks,
Commissioner of Corrections

Julian N. Frisbie
Warden

Vernon Fox,
Assistant Deputy Warden

Commissioner Brooks and Warden Julian N. Frisbie signed the agreement with my pen because they had forgotten their pens. My pen had green ink in it—perhaps left over from Michigan State. This incident assisted me later.

When I took the agreement over to 15-block with the governor's letter, I met considerable resistance. They had decided that the agreement wasn't what they wanted at all. Ward was beginning to have difficulty with the group. He hadn't got enough. I tried to support him by indicating that they had won a great deal—that these were major principles that would go down in the annals of history. They objected because nothing at all had been said about food! Brutality in 15-block wasn't even mentioned! They wanted to abolish the parole board, and for us to write a letter advising that the inmates do not agree with state policies! Jack Hyatt began to doubt that it was actually the governor's signature. They began to doubt that the officials would make good on their promises. I insisted that Governor Williams, Commissioner Brooks, and Warden Frisbie, who had signed the agreement, were trustworthy men whose word was their bond. After about twenty minutes of argument, I finally asked Ward if he would do me a favor. "What is it?" he asked.

I moved closer to the window and prepared my pen for signature. "This is a historic document," I began. "It will go down in the annals of history. The commissioner signed with my pen, the warden signed with my pen, and I signed with my pen. Will you sign with my pen?" I handed him the pen in signing position. He signed the document. Then he would not give the agreement to me. There was further argument. I told them again that these terms were far-reaching principles that would go down in history like the resolutions of the American Prison Congress of 1870. Somewhat reluctantly, they agreed to let those terms stand, weak as they were from their vantage point. I took the agreement and my pen, thanked them, and left.

I was some what perturbed later when *Life* indicated that Ward had seen that all signatures were in green ink and that he demanded green ink, too, and got it. I had told a reporter that such was not the case, that I had green ink in my pen—left over from Michigan State—that Commissioner Brooks and Warden Frisbie had forgotten their pens and used mine—and that I had asked Ward to use my pen because this was a historic document. The reporter had looked at me and said, "Yes, but this makes a better story." So they printed a better story!

I had purposely inserted in the surrender agreement the words, "Immediately after receiving the newspaper," preceding the specific arrangements for surrender. Even though I doubted that surrender would be immediate, I considered it worth the chance. I knew that dislodging the inmates from their position in 15-block would be difficult. Issues had been built up and agreement reached. The terms had been announced to the world by the inmates. Their "propaganda reason" for holding out was gone. Even though the agreement had been signed, however, none of the terms were what the inmates really wanted. I had driven a hard bargain as far as they were concerned, but I had dealt honestly. I wanted to honor to the letter every term we had built up in the signed agreement. The inmates, however, were reluctant to come out on those terms. Governor Williams and Commissioners Leonard and Brooks did not realize this.

I returned the agreement to Deputy Bacon's office, where Commissioner Brooks, Commissioner Leonard, and Warden Frisbie waited. I gave the warden all the papers. He opened the door, and gave them to the newsmen. Newsmen scattered in all directions to find telephones. Some were angry because there were not enough copies to go all around. We had made as many carbons as we could.

At about 4:30 A.M., I decided to get some sleep and rest that had been interrupted since the previous Sunday. I started into the parking lot after my automobile, but I couldn't find it. I was so tired I was seeing flamingos. A systematic search of the lot was fruitless. I debated asking for a car from the garage to take me home, but that would be embarrassing—a deputy who couldn't even find his car! I decided to telephone my wife and ask her to come after me, and I started to the prison entrance to use the phone. Just to the left of the entrance, I located my car! I got home at 5:30 A.M., and went to bed.

After a bath, a shave, and breakfast, I returned to the prison at 7:00 A.M. The *Detroit Free Press* had flown a special edition to the prison at the request of Governor Williams, which included the story of the agreement and its acceptance by Governor Williams, Commissioner Brooks, Warden Frisbie, and me for the administration and by Earl Ward,

#72646, for the inmates. Actually, the *Free Press* had arrived just before I had gone home that morning, but I had been so tired that I took no action. I remember thinking that if the warden wanted the papers in, he could send them in. I remember, too, that he had said that they could wait until morning. Now, with a little rest, the papers had more significance to me. The headlines said, "Governor's Promise Settles Prison Riot." How I wished that were true. The riot was far from settled yet. We had only laid the basis for the final major problem of actually dislodging the inmates from their position. But the papers ran headlines, "It's Over!" With Captain Tucker, I picked up a bundle of papers and started toward 15-block. *Free Press* photographers followed. After several pictures were taken of our passing the papers to Ward and of his reading them, the photographers left.

I asked Ward when he would surrender. Ward said that the boys had talked about it and had set Friday noon as the time. I pointed out that the agreement said, "Immediately after receiving the newspaper," they would surrender. Ward said that the "immediately" meant that the steps toward surrender would be started. I accepted his interpretation, for there was no alternative that could be forced. The men were determined to remain in the block until Friday noon. In the first place, the agreement provided for cleaning up the block, Ward pointed out, and that it would take them until evening to do that. It would be dark by that time, and the agreement said that the surrender would take place in daylight. I said that the dining room would be crowded with other inmates on Friday noon, and that there was no use adding to the congestion, and that Friday morning would be better than Friday noon. Ward agreed, and the time for surrender was set at 10:00 A.M., Friday morning, April 25. "A birthday present for you, Dep," Ward said, since it did happen to be my thirty-sixth birthday.

Returning to the prison rotunda, I told the warden, Commissioner Brooks, and Commissioner Leonard that they had agreed to come out Friday morning at 10:00. Commissioner

Leonard wanted to storm the block or blast it. I argued against it. When asked why they wouldn't give up, I said I thought they wanted to bask in their publicity a while longer. I thought it was cheap effort for the lives of the 169 inmates and 9 guards who remained in 15-block. Twenty-four hours didn't make that much difference. Commissioner Leonard became almost abusive.

Some newsmen wanted to talk with Ward about the surrender. I went to the 15-block window with Jack Pickering of the *Detroit Times* to talk with Ward. Jack asked Ward why he wouldn't give up until Friday morning. There were several reasons besides the ones given me. In the first place, the men wanted to see *all* the papers, evening as well as morning. There was nothing to prevent us or the governor from having a special paper run off to bring to 15-block, while the regular editions ran other stories. If all the papers carried the same story, and the radio newscasts agreed, then the inmates would be sure that their story was being publicized. A second reason came out as Ward half-smiled—while incongruent, I thought of the Mona Lisa—some of the inmates wanted another night with the homosexuals who were locked up in 15-block with them. I could think of no argument that would put down the aroused lust in uninhibited men. Ward promised to give Jack Pickering a "scoop" on their surrender, and we left.

Not long afterward, a telephone call from Ward came. Officer Akins had had a nervous breakdown, and they would release him if I would come after him. I called Captain Tucker, and for a rolling stretcher, and went to 15-block. Akins was crying, sobbing, and shaking. Jarboe was trying to comfort him. When the stretcher arrived, two inmates carried Officer Akins out, and Captain Tucker and I put him on the stretcher. One of the inmates returned to 15-block. The other inmate, Ken Moore, raised his hands and headed toward the corridor gate.

"Bring that man back," Ward shouted. I started after Moore to ask him what was happening. Moore told me that there was going to be no surrender at all, that the surrender would be a double-cross. I had to ignore that because we were progressing sufficiently well that, while it remained a possibility, we could not assume that it was a double-cross until the deadline they had set for surrender had passed. I returned to Ward and told him that nobody had captured Moore, that he had just raised his hands and walked. Jimmy Breeze, an inmate ringleader in 15-block agreed, and told Ward that he had seen it himself. Ward decreed right then that the door to 15-block would not be opened again until the surrender Friday morning at 10:00.

At that point, I was called to the commissioner's office in the parole board hearing room. It was 9:00 on Thursday morning. Inmate Moore was there. Also there, were Commissioner Leonard, Donald Clemmer, and Warden Frisbie. Commissioner Brooks sat at the end of the table and told me to sit down. I sat. Commissioner Brooks said that Moore had told him that the inmates were not going to surrender at all, and that the agreement to surrender was part of a planned double-cross. Consequently, he was going to turn 15-block over to Commissioner Leonard and the State Police. I insisted that we couldn't accept the word of one inmate on something that serious. Moore had double-crossed Ward after being one of the ringleaders since the beginning of the riot. Now that surrender had been arranged, how could we be assured that he was not double-crossing us, too? I insisted that we wait until the deadline for surrender at 10:00 Friday morning, and if they didn't come out, then we would have given them every chance, and we could turn it over to the State Police and Commissioner Leonard.

Commissioner Leonard interrupted, "I'm not going to sit on this powder-keg for another twenty-four hours!" He said, "I don't think we should coddle these people any longer. My suggestion is to give them a one hour's ultimatum or the deal is off." Two hundred armed State Troopers and "hundreds of pounds" of TNT were waiting.

I remonstrated, but to no avail. Commissioner Brooks said, "I'm going to give you one hour to get those men out of 15-

block." I could not possibly have got those men out of 15-block in one hour. At the same time, I didn't want to see the block blasted or stormed! It would have been carnage—sheer carnage! I protested vigorously.

An accumulated total of four hours' sleep since Sunday morning had left me thinking less effectively than usual. What I should have done was to call newsmen and call Commissioner Leonard's bluff—if it were a bluff. If he had taken responsibility for blasting and killing, he could have had it. I wanted no responsibility for taking the lives of citizens of the state of Michigan. I didn't think of that action, however, until the riot was over, and I was rested. At this point, I felt pressured. I was being pressured by Commissioner Brooks, who was beginning to permit Commissioner Leonard to influence his thinking. Newspaper friends in Lansing told me later that Governor Williams was putting pressure on Brooks to get the men out of 15-block, now that Williams had accepted the terms. Whether his concern was political in nature or not, resulting from the newspaper headlines that the governor's promise had settled the riot, I can only conjecture. Under apparent pressure from Governor Williams, Commissioner Brooks was contemplating permitting Commissioner Leonard to use force if the inmates did not evacuate 15-block "immediately." I resisted a show of force.

Finally, Commissioner Brooks said, "Vern, you're tired and nervous. Why don't you go home and get some sleep? We'll meet again at 1:00. We won't do anything until then." I was frenzied. Because he was my boss, however, I went home. One doesn't sleep in a situation like that. Why couldn't they wait another twenty-four hours? Why did they have to blast just at the verge of bloodless evacuation by negotiation on the basis of terms which were not only harmless, but were actually progressive? These terms constituted a victory for inmate and administration alike—a victory for progressive penology. Maybe that was the trouble! These terms constituted a victory for progressive penology and a defeat for the old school of custodial discipline! At this point, the telephone rang.

Ward had reached my residence through the institutional switchboard. I was startled for a moment, then remembered that all telephone calls coming out of 15-block were being recorded, and that the connection must have been approved by the warden or someone in charge. Ward said that there was someone ill at 15-block, and he asked for medicine. He said it was not necessary to send a nurse or physician. I told him that my birthday was the following day, some of my friends in Albion wanted to give me a party, and I'd like to have tomorrow free. I asked Ward to give up this afternoon. Ward asked what had gone wrong. I told him nothing had gone wrong. I couldn't tell him to come out or Commissioner Leonard would blast him out. I knew what kind of answer Ward and "Crazy Jack" Hyatt would have for such a threat!

"This isn't like you, Dep. Something's gone wrong!" Ward kept repeating. I tried to assure him that tomorrow was my birthday, and I wanted to give my friends in Albion an answer. Fearing that I was making little or no progress, I thought that if I could get Ward on the proposing end of the idea, he would sell it to himself, and if he sold it to himself, he could sell it to "Crazy Jack." I asked him to talk it over with Jack and call me back. He agreed hesitantly and hung up.

About twenty minutes later, the telephone rang. Ward had talked it over with Jack, and they had agreed to surrender today, but that I'd have to do something to "take us off the hook with the boys." After promising the boys they would have until Friday morning, they'd think they'd been "sold down the river" if surrender occurred without explanation. At this point he told me that this was to be my idea, not prompted by him. I agreed. I'd have to prepare the boys with a speech. I told him I'd do it, and that I'd be right out to talk with him about it.

I went to the prison, told Commissioner Brooks that they had agreed to come out today, and not to let Commissioner Leonard blast. I went to 15-block. Ward told me what he wanted. I took some of his ideas down on the back of an envelope. I was to tell the boys that their leaders had done a good job. He told me further not to tell anybody that he had dictated that this speech be made. I agreed. In addition, I was to have the speech typed, have it approved by Ward, and leave a carbon copy with him so he could follow it word for word as it came over the loudspeakers. I felt as though I were a puppet. Then I thought of the carnage that would result from blasting. I couldn't see why we couldn't wait until Friday morning—we'd already waited this long. I felt that I was between the devil and the deep blue sea—between the specter of Commissioner Leonard and his TNT on the one hand and the lives of the hostages on the other. I had to obey both Ward and Commissioner Brooks in order to keep Commissioner Leonard from blasting. They would come out at 4:00 P.M. if my speech went on the air at 3:30.

I knew that the speech had to be given. Ward's demand for it, however, was the lesser of two reasons. The more important reason, as I subsequently explained in *Collier's*, was that the inmates were not ready to come out of their 15-block position. Yet, they had to be dislodged to prevent Commissioner Leonard's "show of force" which, in my opinion and that of many others, would have produced carnage. They had to be dislodged by ideas rather than force, if they had to be dislodged on Thursday. Had the governor and other officials been willing to wait until Friday, it would not have been necessary. Under the circumstances, however, it was necessary to avert bloodshed. Even without Ward's demand for it, the speech would still have been necessary!

Resigned to the necessity for the speech, I told Commissioner Brooks that I would be in the Research and Selection office for a while, and that I had to prepare a speech to get the inmates out of 15-block a day early. He said, "Okay," and I left. The speech was a term of early surrender and Ward had given me some ideas to incorporate. In preparing the speech, I had to remember that the inmates were not ready to come out of 15-block, there was still considerable resistance among the inmates against coming out, so I had to make the speech a bit of psychological warfare to coax the

men out of the block. Because I was fatigued, it took a long
time to compose the speech as I wanted it. I composed it for
the boys in 15-block, not for the world! I composed it to coax
mutineers from their bastion, not as Labor Day platitudes!
It was past 3:00 before I finished it. The warden was in a
press conference with all the newsmen. I didn't see Commissioner Brooks. I thought of checking with Warden Frisbie for
suggestions on the theory that a double check would be best.
I thought that Commissioner Brooks' assignment of responsibility order on Wednesday morning superseded the warden's
previous request during our conversation on Tuesday morning
to check speeches with him so that people would not think
we didn't see eye to eye on prison policy. I *had* to check with
Ward and the deadline was approaching. Because of the limited
time, I went to 15-block, asking Joe Dellinger on the way to
get the recording equipment ready in the labor pool room.
I showed the carbon copy to Ward. He approved it without
change, kept the carbon copy, and said he would follow it
word for word. I put it on tape with Joe Dellinger's help in the
labor pool room because I was too tired to try to fight the
noise in the hall office. Joe put the speech on the loudspeaker
at about 3:35. The speech was as follows:

Counselors have passed newspapers to the blocks.
There were not enough for everyone, but Mr. Dellinger
read the news over the radio system. You know by the
newspapers that the boys in 15-block have won. They have
won every single demand they made. Most of the demands
will be put into effect immediately.

Remodeling 15-block will need budget operations,
but the procedures will be started. The grievance concerning the parole board is under jurisdiction of the legislature and is now in the hands of Senator Blondy of
Detroit who says he is going to present it to the legislature
on May 14th.

Earl Ward, Jack Hyatt, Jarboe and all the others in
charge are men of their word. In accordance with their

agreement, the boys from 15-block are going to file out into the dining hall at four o'clock. No State Police will be in evidence. With Ward's permission, institutional custodial personnel will take positions on the roof in order to ensure adequate room for every one of the large staff of newsmen, and to afford them all a good vantage point. Earl Ward is a natural leader. He and the other boys are to be congratulated on the good faith with which they have bargained. Their word has been good. My word has been good.

This may presage a new era of good, sound interrelationships between inmate and administration in American prisons. They have done a service. Congratulations to you, men of 15-block!

It worked beautifully. They could not have refused to come out after that, for it would have been an enormous anti-climax.

The time between the speech and the surrender seemed to be an eternity. Warden Frisbie had come to the front of 15-block, smoking cigarette after cigarette and stamping them out with his foot. Deputy Bacon was very much in evidence now for the first time during the riot. I waved three State Troopers off the north yard in compliance with our assertion that no State Police would be in evidence. People lined the roofs of the cell-blocks, newsmen and prison personnel.

Exactly at four o'clock, the doors of 15-block swung open. It couldn't have been timed better by Western Union. Six inmates emerged, two on each side of the door, one of whom was Ward, and the other four took positions so the emerging inmates would pass through to be searched. The inmates were backed out with their hands up, and were well searched by the selected inmates. Some were the recipients of patting with homosexual connotation. All were searched well. As they backed up about ten feet, Captain Tucker sent them toward the dining hall. After all the inmates except the ringleaders had been searched and sent to the dining hall, the ringleaders went back in and closed the door. After a few minutes, the doors opened again, and the ringleaders brought out weapons they had picked up in the block. Some were in bags. All weapons were thrown in a pile on the lawn. Then the ringleaders went inside again. The hostages were brought to the office of 15-block. Then I was to go in to accept the surrender. It was very dramatic. It was also pregnant with possibilities.

If there was a time for a double-cross, this was it! The hard core of ringleaders was there without any obvious dissenters. The food that could have lasted two weeks for a large group could last indefinitely longer for a small group. There was no assurance that all the weapons were out of 15-block. Eight guard hostages remained, and the addition of the assistant deputy warden in charge of individual treatment would have augmented their bargaining power, except, perhaps, as far as Commissioner Leonard was concerned. It was a calculated risk. I swallowed hard and walked in as nonchalantly as I could. Warden Frisbie started to step in after me, but Deputy Bacon grabbed his arm. In a little formal ceremony, Ward turned over the keys of 15-block to me. It wasn't a double-cross. Ward was playing straight. The ringleaders walked out. The hostages walked out. Then, in a final bit of drama, with Earl Ward at my left and with "Crazy Jack" Hyatt at my right, we emerged from 15-block to end the most dangerous prison riot in American history without the loss of a single guard.

CHAPTER VIII

The First Month After

The most unforgettable scene for many persons who saw
it occurred when the last eight hostage guards emerged from
the main gates into the lobby of the prison. Loved ones who
had been waiting greeted the men with hugs, kisses, and
tears. Big men and mature women cried unashamedly and
lumps clogged the throats of those who watched. Photographers recorded the scene. Commissioner Brooks told the eight
guards to go home to their families and that they did not
have to return to work until they felt like it. The tension was
over for the guards and their families. It was time for joyous
tears.

The *Detroit Times* reported, "Between tearful hugs and
kisses they told their stories. The stories coincided exactly in
one particular: Their treatment had been splendid. Whatever their many past sins, Ward and Hyatt had proved themselves leaders. They had kept at bay other convicts who would
have torn the guards limb from limb."

Back at 15-block, I wanted to go home and to bed. If I ran
out now, though, the inmates would tend to doubt my interest in them. I thought it best at least to look into the dining
room. As I strolled in, they were eating the promised meal.
They were steaks in name only. It was utility grade of beef
prepared in mass. I had been in many cheap restaurants in
my day, but I'd never seen anything like that served in any
restaurant. Visions of a shoe repair shop flashed across my
mind. These steaks had been saved over from Tuesday night
when the rest of the prison had had steaks. This was not un-

common at Jackson. Steaks or pork chops regularly appeared on the menu at least once a week. The potatoes looked good. I don't remember the vegetables. The packaged ice cream looked good, too. They had their "steak and ice cream," as they had been promised. Several armed custodial officers supervised the eating.

The rumbling of many footsteps attracted our attention. As we looked outside, custodial officers with rifles at ready were trotting in formation, imitating the State Police, toward the door and into 15-block. The inmates laughed. I thought it inappropriate, too. I had gone in there unarmed when inmates were there. The counselors would have done the same thing, as agreed. 15-block was empty now, and custody would not let the counselors go in. Custody was taking over. They charged the empty cell-block with ready rifles!

Inmates looked up from their eating and smiled. They extended their hands to express their appreciation for my efforts in resolving the tense conflict in which they were as much confused as anyone. I took their extended hands in greeting and heard them verbalize their appreciation. Ward was looking at me, apparently wondering if I would speak to him now that it was over. I walked back and spoke to him. He extended his hand and I took it, placing my other hand on his shoulder. No matter what others may think, Ward was a man of his word to me throughout the riot, and I shook his hand. One man in the center of the group began acting peculiarly. Some of the other inmates told me he was an epileptic and was apparently about to have a seizure—he was experiencing his aura. I went to the center of the group and helped him out where he could sit by himself and have room for his seizure if he were to have it. At that, I waved, "good-by," to the group and left.

The situation appeared to be very favorable at that time. All inmates I saw went out of their way to greet me. Prison personnel did the same, with the exception of Deputy Bacon. The means to quiet the prison situation further lay peacefully in my hands. Years of pushing for progressive penology began to return their rewards. Individual Treatment had paid off in a crisis of violence when Custody was helpless.

Now, as stated by one of my psychologist friends from a child guidance clinic, I had the prison situation in the palms of my hands, and could work for a full therapy program with in-service training for personnel. More immediately, however, I knew from the treatment I received when I walked into a cell-block and from the prison personnel, that it would be an easy matter to bring the prison to normal. I had some reservations even then, however, for I knew that when one person suddenly gains so much popularity, the jealousy and envy of his ambitious peers will militate against him. The interaction between Brutus and Julius Caesar in Shakespeare's play merely symbolizes similar interaction that takes place frequently in everyday life. There was nothing to do but await events.

I walked to my office, but it was filled with newsmen, so I went on. I was called to the hall office—I don't remember what for. Things were getting hazy now, the tension was over, and I was beginning to relax. I don't remember all the activity. I was behind the hall office counter when Ed Smith of the Associated Press, working out of the *Jackson Citizen-Patriot*, asked me if I had a copy of the talk that had been given the inmates. I said "sure," and handed him the copy from which I had put it on tape. Without a word, he half-walked, half-ran toward the front gate. I didn't see him for a long time after that.

While it was still daylight, it was long past time for me to go to bed. I went out the front gate. In the lobby, Commissioner Brooks stopped me and told me that the governor wanted to meet with the men who had worked to end the riot. We were to go across the street to the State Police post. I went with Commissioner Brooks. When we went in, there was Governor G. Mennen Williams with his press secretary, Paul Weber, and his executive secretary, Larry Farrell. There were

Warden Frisbie, Captain Harold Tucker, and a corps of newsmen.

Commissioner Brooks took me by the arm and we went out front. He said the governor had been asked by some newsmen about my radio message to the inmates. Of course, the governor knew nothing about it. He wasn't at the riot. We went back inside. The governor was making a statement, slowly, deliberately, cautiously, with one eye always on Larry Farrell. He said that the state would carry out to the letter the agreement we had made. He subsequently made the statement to the papers as, "The terms of the agreement, of course, will be honestly adhered to." He commended the work of the brave men who had helped end the riot. He mentioned Commissioner of State Police Donald S. Leonard, Captain Harold Tucker, Warden Frisbie, and the brave custodial guards. That was my first inkling that the period of strain and stress was not over for me. I paid little heed, however, because I wanted to go to bed more than anything else. Little else mattered. Toward the end of his statement, the governor recognized my work in delineating the issues and crystallizing the agreement.

The newsmen wanted a picture from the conference. Ray Girardin of radio station CKLW and one of the Detroit newspapers, Governor Williams, and Captain Harold Tucker lined up for the picture. The newsmen called for me. I noted a fairly well-concealed look of uneasiness on the governor's face. I wondered who had set the policy. Whose advice was the governor following? I lined up on the end, next to the governor, recognizing by this time that they would want, for some reason, to cut my picture off. I wondered later what would have happened if I had been stubborn and taken a position in the center, as I could well have done. The picture was taken, everyone shook hands, and I went back to the prison with Commissioner Brooks. I drove home, my wife fixed me something to eat, and I went to bed about seven o'clock.

The following day was April 25, my thirty-sixth birthday. I called the warden. He told me to take it easy, rest, not listen to the radio, no newspapers, just relax. I didn't have to come to work—I'd done enough for several men. I deserved a rest. I thanked him and told him I would drive to Detroit with my wife, not read any papers, no radio, just relax. We drove to Detroit, called on relatives, had lunch, and drove back. We were planning on having a big evening together, my wife and I. I had heard about the big steaks and French fried onions they serve at the West Point Inn.

It was about a quarter to six in the evening when we arrived home. I turned the radio on. "Fire Fox!" That was the first statement I heard on the six o'clock news. Aspiring and yet small-time politicians were attempting to gain publicity by getting into the prison scene which was the center of public attention at that time. Auditor General John B. Martin Jr., already noted among my acquaintances for talking before thinking through the issues, was issuing press statements, though he had never been closer than thirty-six miles from the violence. Republican gubernatorial candidate John B. Martin, Jr., called loudly for "Dr. Fox' summary dismissal and for the resignation of his superiors." A county prosecutor from Grand Rapids named MacMahan, with whose rigidly conservative and uninformed opinions I had not agreed on a narcotics panel at Albion College a few months before, had issued his vociferous solution. While it was an opportunity for publicity, I wondered whether there would have been a difference in degree of intensity had not the narcotics panel so well emphasized our differences. Other comment was reported. I wasn't hungry any more. The steak and French fried onions at the West Point Inn could stay there.

Attorney General Frank G. Millard, Republican candidate for re-election, said that he acknowledged that he might invite more trouble in the riot-wrecked prison, but he was going to prosecute to the fullest extent of the law. Deputy Attorney General Harry W. Jackson said that any inquiry would have to wait until the prison got nearer to normal. Prosecutor George Campbell of Jackson county was frankly reluctant to take any step that would break faith with the rebels, saying, "I am aware of the tense situation within the walls. I am wondering whether there should be any action from a reprisal angle." Millard indicated that his investigation would cover any crimes committed at the prison either by convicts or personnel.

When this turn of events occurred, two of the employees in the Individual Treatment Department took tape-recording equipment to the homes of those released hostages they could locate in one day. On Saturday, Miss Joann Volakakis and Joe B. Dellinger interviewed four hostages. Each hostage enthusiastically supported the manner in which I handled the riot. When the warden found out about these recordings, he ordered them to his office to be locked up, and did not release them. According to my information, they were never made available to anyone, not even the governor's fact-finding committee. This action on the warden's part was a clue that I was to be left out on the limb alone, while Commissioner Brooks, Warden Frisbie, and the governor were going to return to conservative safety. While it was they, rather than I, who made the final decisions during the riot, it was I, rather than they, who was destined to accept full responsibility. Since all of their final decisions had been in accordance with my recommendation, it was right that I should have my share of the responsibility. Since they had set final policy, however, I thought they should share with me in that responsibility. The confiscation of these tape recordings indicated that such was not to be the case.

As the tempo of criticism increased, Deputy Raymond Buchkoe called me from Marquette and asked for a copy of the letter he had written about Ward when he was transferred to Jackson. The letter diagnosed Ward as a homicidal and dangerous person. He could not find his copy, and he wanted the letter to use in Marquette. I suspected he wanted to show others the sort of man with whom I was dealing. I telephoned the prison to have the request complied with. When it was discovered that the request came through me, the warden had the file locked up and refused to permit anyone to see it! Prior to that time, it had been practically public property!

About the same time, the warden told Joe Dellinger to cease supporting me. He told him that if I were to be criticized, that there was no need for Joe to be identified with me. Further, the warden told Joe that his defense of me was futile! He did not elaborate. Personnel were instructed not to contact me at home or anywhere else. That did not stop them. Many continued to come to the house. Others stopped coming to the house, but contacted me by telephone.

Politics was foremost before and after the riot—not during it. Commissioner Brooks announced that one of the first problems facing the prison, now that the riot was over, was where to cut guards. The legislature had cut the budget from $11,982,000 to $11,021,000, which meant a cut of 45 to 50 guards and a proportionate cut in other employees. It was pointed out that when the riot started in 15-block, the complement for the block was four, when the block usually had five officers. Governor G. Mennen Williams blamed the Republican legislature for the trouble. The legislature blamed the Democratic governor's administrative practices. The qualifications of Commissioner Brooks for his job were questioned, since his experience had been in insurance and in distributing soda pop in fourteen western Michigan counties. Republicans vizualized the prison riot as a major issue in the coming political campaigns and elections.

United States Senator Homer Ferguson, Michigan Republican, issued a statement from Washington accusing Governor Williams of "appeasing" convicts. The governor is the chief law-enforcement officer in Michigan, and as such has demonstrated conformity with the "pattern of irresponsible government so familiar here in Washington." He denounced steak dinners and granting immunity to rioters. Rep-

resentative Hoxie filed for introduction a bill providing for
life imprisonment for any inmate who destroyed property val-
ued at over $100,000. Bills appropriating $1,000,000 to repair
damage at the prison and $30,000 for the attorney general's
investigation were filed.

Representative Charles E. Potter, Republican candidate
for the United States Senate, said that a new federal law
would make it possible to transfer unruly felons like Earl
Ward and Crazy Jack Hyatt to Alcatraz. He said that Governor Williams should enter into negotiations with the United
States attorney general to arrange transfer of some Michigan
prisoners to federal prisons. Governor Williams replied that
he knew of no law permitting such action. He agreed to enter
into negotiations if such a law existed. He warned that the
state's rights must be respected.

The "steak and ice cream dinner" also was attacked, now
that the riot was over. Max Barnes, a restaurant owner in
Grand Rapids, advertised "riotous steaks." I saw his error in
another sign in which he advertised, "Convict Quality." I
wouldn't have a steak in his restaurant if I were sure it were
"Convict Quality," or at least the quality the inmates had
following the riot. Of course, a steak is generally thought of
as big, tender, and well cooked, so I suppose his advertising
did sell steaks for him. However, I can assure Mr. Barnes
and his eating public that the "Convict Quality" steaks I saw
were neither big, tender, nor well cooked!

Several bills, resolutions, and motions relating to the riot
were prepared or offered and tabled when the legislature
convened on May 1. Representative Montgomery of Lansing
prepared a bill to provide the death penalty for any prisoner
who killed a hostage guard. Senator Charles Blondy offered
a resolution that the senate pay me its respects for the coura-
geous service I had rendered during the riot.

Carl Saunders of the *Jackson Citizen-Patriot* had a scath-
ing editorial in Friday's paper, entitled, "It's No Nursery."
Parts of it went as follows, "All of this yielding to criminals
was as nothing to the utterly asinine statement put out

Thursday afternoon by Deputy Warden Vernon Fox! If the authorities want to know what has been wrong, if anything, at the prison to bring on this catastrophe, we suggest they call Dr. Fox. He can tell them. He's what's wrong!" Then he went on to accept the theory, apparently by lip-service, that felons may be mentally sick, and agreed that psychiatry and its associate sciences may offer help for some. "But a prison is no nursery!" he continued, "No prison administration can control 6,500 major criminals of all categories if saddled with the extremist philosophy which Dr. Fox expounds." After indicating that I may have led people to think that the riot leaders were heroes just back from Korea, he concluded with, "Excuse me while I vomit."

I was amazed. I decided that Saunders had no idea as to when nor why the speech was given, which was later confirmed by a reporter with the remark that it didn't make any difference now, for once Saunders took a position, he considered himself stuck with it. The editorial brought criticism from many persons. Reverend Hoover Rupert of the First Methodist Church in Jackson attacked the editorial on grounds of fair play, the continuing trend from custody to rehabilitation, and the general spirit of the editorial. Among other things, Reverend Rupert said, "It does seem lacking to me in evaluative judgment to condemn a man for one sentence uttered in a highly volatile situation after hours and hours of negotiation, when his primary concern was the saving of the lives of nine men. That his choice of words was questionable does not remove the praise due Mr. Fox for his continued effort to bring the negotiations to a successful close—success in that instance lying in the end of the riot and the release of nine men, alive."

Another editorial in answer to Reverend Rupert repeated that the statement was asinine and inexcusable. He concluded with, " 'vomit' is a perfectly good English word which appears a half dozen or more times in the King James Version of the Bible. And there is no other respectably accepted word to describe the retching in the stomach which such coddling and inflating of rebellious criminals brings on." The same paper carried information that Captain Tucker, who had been with me through much of the time during the last two days of the riot, had been praised by prison and state officials because he sacrificed self for the safety of the captive guards. It was beginning to shape up already. I was to be sacrificed. Captain Tucker was to be the hero. He was a hero, but I thought it wrong for me to be sacrificed! On the same page, an article indicated that I had called Ward a "natural leader." The next statement was, "Fox's own files contain this information: Ward is a potential homicidal maniac who was once declared criminally insane." The policy of Editor Saunders' news slanting had been set!

The phone rang. Warden Frisbie said that Earl Ward had wanted to get in touch with me all day. He wanted me to go to 15-block to talk with him. I wasn't fond of the idea, but the warden said that I'd better go. I went to the prison and to 15-block. Officer Neil Oakley, whom I had considered a friend since my days at Cassidy Lake, when he kept my car running by servicing it at his other employer's gas station in Stockbridge, was on duty. Oakley, by the way, had been a central figure in stories of brutality. I told Neil that the warden wanted me to talk with Ward. Officer Oakley said that he was the only one on duty and that he would prefer waiting until another officer came, but that he would open the doors if I said so. I told him that if he were apprehensive, he shouldn't do it, that I wasn't anxious to go upstairs anyway, and certainly would not insist on it. I went back to the hall office, told Inspector Cahill that Officer Oakley was afraid, and that I wasn't anxious to go in anyway. I was ready to go home and stay there till summer. Inspector Cahill called the warden to give him that information, but the warden said that I'd better go into the block.

Returning to the block, Oakley and I went upstairs. Officer Oakley opened the gate at the end of the corridor. He didn't want to go inside with me, so he stayed out while I went in. When I stopped at Ward's cell, the latter said that the boys had heard over the radio about the rough time I was getting and that he wanted a press conference. I told him that it would be difficult to get one in 15-block now. He asked me to tell the warden what had happened as far as the speech was concerned. I told him that I had promised secrecy within bounds of good taste and that I wouldn't do it. He asked me to call the officer. I called Officer Oakley.

I watched Officer Oakley come down the corridor. He stood in front of Ward's cell as Ward told him why I had given the speech. He told Oakley to tell the warden so that the newsmen would get it. I didn't hear all the conversation. I was too busy watching Neil Oakley. He was shaking and perspiring in an exaggerated manner. I was amazed. I had seen many scared men, but I had never observed fear such as that.

Oakley was saying periodically to Ward, "Yes-yes, sir-yes, sir," and shaking like a leaf in a high wind. He was beyond control. Their conversation ended while I was still watching Oakley shake. As Oakley left, I walked with him. Ward said that "Crazy Jack" Hyatt wanted to see me. Oakley and I went to another floor, and I talked with Hyatt. Jack said that the boys knew that I was being criticized now, and that if anything serious happened as far as I was concerned, that I was to be sure that the "boys" were behind me and that they'd really have a riot next time. I left 15-block and went to the warden's office.

I asked the warden what all the criticism was about. He said that some editors had picked up my speech and were criticizing it. I asked him how it could have been different under the circumstances. He said that if he had seen the speech, he might have changed a couple of words, but that was all. He assured me that "mistakes" are bound to be made in times of crisis like that; and in a political hotbed, we have to expect criticism if we do anything, constructive or otherwise. Then he referred to an even graver "mistake."

"Why did *I* let the men out of their cells for breakfast Monday morning?" he asked. That procedure had let 1600 to 2600 (nobody had counted them—these were estimates) men out and had resulted in the major riot which caused millions of dollars worth of damage. As far as mistakes were concerned, he said, "You made one and I made one." We had had to make decisions fast and we couldn't take time to deliberate and discuss them. The warden's "mistake" had resulted in a major riot and millions of dollars worth of damage done. My "mistake" had resulted in saving lives of at least eight guards, and probably more by preventing Commissioner Leonard from blasting 15-block. He told me not to worry, though, that he and Commissioner Brooks would handle everything.

After I returned home, Warden Frisbie called to ask if I had seen any straight razors in 15-block. I told him that I had not, but that I wouldn't be surprised at anything. Safety razor blades would be easy to conceal in any number of places. I didn't know why he called at the time, but I later discovered that Neil Oakley, the Trembling Terror of 15-block, had reported that Ward had threatened him with a straight razor. While I don't think he actually saw a straight razor, he could have "perceived" anything. Oakley's perception could hardly be depended upon for accuracy in his emotional state!

I read in front-page headlines printed in red ink, GOV. REBUKES WARDEN FOX. Naturally, it interested me. I read his statement.

Assistant Deputy Warden Fox performed magnificent work for the state in bringing about the surrender of the convicts in Block 15 and saving the lives of the guards. Except for this fact, his choice of language in addressing the inmates would be utterly inexcusable.

I am keenly aware that Dr. Fox had just come through a period of the most crushing strain and that he was concerned only with the successful evacuation of the cellblock and the rescue of the guards.

At the same time, his statements to the inmates must not be allowed to stand as the position of the Corrections Department or of the state.

Therefore, in accord with our discussion over the telephone, I hereby direct that a reprimand be issued to Dr. Fox for this statement and that appropriate steps be taken to make sure that such a mistake does not occur again.

The phone rang all night. Visitors and newsmen came. Ken McCormick, a *Detroit Free Press* reporter with an unfriendly reputation in the Corrections Department, called to ask when I was going to resign. Paul McClung of the Dell Publications asked for material for an article, and I gave it to him. They wanted to use my by-line, which appeared to be all right at the time, but later I declined. I didn't know anything about the magazine business. Bill Fay from *Collier's* suggested an article, which subsequently appeared in its issue of July 12, 1952. *American* Magazine wanted an article, but it had to be exclusive and I was already committed to *Collier's*. Joyce Selznik and Big Jim called from Detroit—they were going to arrange a special showing for me of "My Six Convicts," which never materialized.

Among the callers were newsmen. They seemed to be lining up for and against my position. Ken McCormick of the *Free Press* and Allen Schoenfield of the *Detroit News* appeared to be against my position. Supporting me were Al Kaufman and Jack Pickering of the *Detroit Times,* Ray Girardin of CKLW, Bob Hoving and Sue Aderhold of the *Jackson Citizen-Patriot,* and Bill Burke of the *Lansing State Journal.* The editors of the papers, however, seemed to be almost unanimously against my position, referring to any treatment program as "coddling" and particularly so the manner in which I had handled the riot.

Sidney M. Smith, the ex-chaplain serving as psychologist at the Michigan Reformatory, got into the act, too. He prepared a complaint to Governor Williams, which was signed by him and six other friends from Ionia. He wrote, in part:

We strenuously object to having psychopathic prisoners who mutiny, congratulated on their leadership.

We deplore the tendency to permit prison inmates to dictate to the state its corrections policies. The serious breakdown of morale is endangering the lives of all who work with the inmates.

That type of statement by men who had never seen a riot seemed inexcusable because of hasty judgment without the facts. I ignored it.

Rae Corless of the *Battle Creek Enquirer and News* telephoned Dr. Floyd Starr, president of Starr Commonwealth for Boys. He reported that Uncle Floyd had said,

> I know Vern does not condone violence in any sense of the word and he could not have been commending the inmates for their seizure of prison guards and destruction of property. But he was at our school here four years and knows our methods of trying to rehabilitate boys who get a wrong start. I am sure he has tried to put the same Christian principles to work at the prison. It was unfortunate that he made a wrong choice of words in his extemporaneous radio talk to the inmates, but it should be remembered also that anyone else who had been subjected to the tension which he underwent all the week might have made a similar mistake.
>
> Some people abhor the idea of the "beefsteak and ice cream" on which he traded. But I think it was a cheap price to pay for the lives of men. Certainly if one of those guards had been my son or brother, I would not have condemned Vern Fox for promising the meal in return for his safe delivery to me.

Dr. Lowell J. Carr of the University of Michigan pointed out that the chief difficulty with prison administration in Michigan was that the public had failed to decide on the objectives. He said, "Citizens have not decided whether they want to protect the public, reform or rehabilitate prisoners, or merely punish criminals. Until they do, successful prison management will be difficult." Professor Carr described the current administration at the State Prison of Southern Michigan as "the most enlightened we have ever had there." He expressed fear that "the state will kick back at the prison administration for the incident by transferring them and putting in someone who is tough."

Some of the papers began "helping" me. Al Kaufman of the *Detroit Times* said they were attempting to fix it up for me and that if I had any information, I could tell him. I told him I would answer anything I was asked, but I didn't know anything in addition to what I had already told him. The paper carried front-page headlines in red ink, "Fox Sorry He Congratulated Rioters." No such thing! I wasn't sorry for what I had done. However, the papers had made it look as though I had congratulated them in a sportsmanlike manner during emotion, and that now I was sorry. Actually, I had done what I had had to do to save lives under the circumstances. If I were sorry for anything, it was for the existence of the circumstances.

The *Battle Creek Enquirer and News* carried an editorial entitled, "Greater Mistakes Were Made Than Mr. Fox's," which pointed out the carelessness of the inexperienced guard who opened the way for the riot. It was contended that the subject was being treated with more emotionalism than it deserved. The editorial accurately quoted me as saying, "I congratulated them for capitulating a day earlier, for keeping their agreement, for sparing the lives of the hostage guards. But I certainly did not and could not congratulate them for their violence and usurpation of authority in the prison." The editorial said that it is ". . . too bad the public had to be listening in when Mr. Fox 'congratulated' the convict leaders, but let's remember that this happened before the surrender agreement had been carried out. Maybe Mr. Fox thought he had to appeal to the convicts' ego to make sure that they delivered on their promise. Quite possibly he knows more about how to talk to convicts than some of the critics . . ."

Apparently, the newspapers and critics had not stopped

to realize that there were two different situations, though closely related at one time. The riot in the yard had caused an estimated $2,500,000 worth of damage. The State Police had handled that riot. The riot, insurrection, or mutiny in 15-block had caused probably $10,000 worth of damage and had held the hostages. I was handling the riot in 15-block. It was to the group in 15-block that the speech was directed in order to get them out of the block. The critics had apparently transferred the action to the yard, and left the public with the impression that I had congratulated all the rioters after "victory" as a good loser! The technique seemed to serve their purposes.

Some papers had come out emphasizing my position by going beyond what I had said in the speech. The *Detroit Times* attributed to me the phrase, "Good old Ward," which I had never said, even under stress. *Life* surprised me as much as any of the periodicals. I had heard that a *Life* reporter had been in Wednesday afternoon, had taken some notes, and had borrowed pictures from the photographers who had taken them. I never saw the *Life* reporter. Yet, *Life* came out with the story, "Convicts Bully a Sovereign State," in its issue of May 5, 1952. How could that be defended? I had written the terms, put on another hat and accepted them, and there wasn't a mention of brutality, food, or unwarranted mistreatment! There wasn't a term in the entire list that I didn't want myself. Yet, here was a major periodical slanting its story to fit the title, "Convicts Bully a Sovereign State." Maybe that is as much as the reporter got on Wednesday afternoon.

Austin MacCormick, Executive Director of the Osborne Association, flew to Lansing on one of his trips between his home in Berkeley, California, and New Jersey, where he was investigating the prison riots and consulting in a manner similar to that in which Michigan had invited him. MacCormick knew Michigan prisons, since he had been called to Michigan more frequently than to any other state. In an interview, he said that it was generally better not to send inmates to the mess hall during times of tension, which is generally accepted as axiomatic among prison administrators. MacCormick said that the problem is to strike a balance between firmness in prison administration and leniency. That, too, is axiomatic among prison administrators. He was measuring his words cautiously and well. He realized that he had to be perfectly neutral and favor neither extreme in a controversial situation.

He was asked if he thought the riot was handled properly. He replied, "I know the determining factor was your hostages. In a Colorado riot in 1929 I remember that the prisoners did send out some heads on platters." He said that the Michigan riot was much more serious than the riots in New Jersey. "At the Trenton riot this year, they were pretty sure the prisoners wouldn't kill. They were a much more stable group than you have here. They were bitter but they weren't likely to cut any heads off." He said that there was no fixed rule for dealing with a prison riot. "Each one is different and you just sort of fly by the seats of your pants."

"At times we wish our pants were asbestos," Governor Williams interjected.

A television show on the situation was presented by the *Detroit Times* station WWJ-TV on Sunday. Jack Pickering and Al Kaufman interviewed Mr. S. J. Gilman, assistant to the commissioner of corrections, and Attorney General Frank Millard. During the program, my position was defended. Mr. Gilman emotionally said that anybody who saw those officers come out to their families would not object to my handling of the riot. We'd rather have that than eleven funerals, he said.

It was on Saturday that Officer Neil Oakley, vice-president of the guards' union, Local 1333 of the state, county and municipal workers, A. F. of L., called a meeting of the afternoon shift before they went to work. They called Commissioner Brooks downstairs from the lobby. They told him that I had aligned myself on the side of the inmates and that I had made it dangerous for anyone else to work there. They complained that the prisoners feel that they have a friend in Fox and that he would save them from punishment no matter what they do. They wanted me dismissed (this was later denied by the union and by Oakley). Commissioner Brooks told them that he would assign me to duties outside the walls, and that I should not come inside the prison, at least for a while. They further refused to go to work without police protection. Of the 60 guards, many refused to go to work. News reports were that only 40 remained to work, the shift being augmented by men on the previous shift. One State Trooper was assigned to each guard. As the guards made their rounds, they were covered by State Police rifles. Guards also demanded the transfer of Ward and Hyatt to Marquette Prison, but Brooks and Frisbie did not accede immediately. The guards demanded that newsmen be admitted to the guards' conferences with Commissioner Brooks and Warden Frisbie.

Frisbie, presumably acting on consensus that newsmen had confused the issues during the riot in their driving search for news and their partial reporting without complete interpretation, declined to admit newsmen on grounds that it was strictly an institutional matter. The guards demanded segregation of sexual deviates, indicating that forced and voluntary homosexual activity was still going on. The guards expressed fear of going into the prison. One guard was not scared, and ex-hostage Officer John Holmes won sub-headlines for it. The guards complained about the counselors, with whom some of them had had conflict. Commissioner Brooks assured them that he would "keep the counselors out of your hair." That was a tip-off to future policy—aggression and custody over rehabilitation and treatment. The guards demanded equal pay with the counselors, who were trained psychologists and social workers.

Within a week after the riot ended, three ex-hostages had resigned, two had returned to work immediately, and two returned Saturday. Elliott, Dzal, and Curry resigned. Holmes and Carrier had returned to work, and Brown and Parsons returned Saturday, May 3.

In order to get the prison back to "normal" again, gradually and as soon as possible, the administration selected two cell-blocks to be marched to the newly opened dining hall. When the order was received to march 4-block and 5-block to the dining hall, Oakley was indignant. "Whoever gave that order?" he demanded. "The thing is to keep these cons under locks. When they get together and loose they're dangerous."

Religious services were provided over the central radio hook-up. Newspapers were kept out of the blocks on Sunday because the inmates were throwing debris from their cells. Newspapers would have added to the debris, the warden said.

Guards and State Troopers searched the prison for weapons. Their findings included "bushels" of weapons. In 1-block alone, there were several bags of weapons and pieces of metal. The search was thorough, going through all cells, men's clothing and bodies. Dozens of hacksaw blades were found. In 15-block, about Saturday, the men apparently decided that they weren't being treated fairly. They started hitting the steel doors with their shoulders until they bulged. In order to prevent a mass break or another riot, State Troopers with walkie-talkies were placed inside the wall with the riflemen, and riot-breaking equipment was prepared for use.

The newspapers reported that I would be assigned to duties outside the walls. The "special duty" was not specified. Brooks told me just to go home and take it easy, that he would cover the public relations angle. He asked me to write up a report on the riot, since neither the governor nor anyone else had any report on what had happened other than what had appeared in the newspapers.

Patrick A. McCabe, the union's international representative, subsequently showed the union that I had saved the lives of some of their members, and that the union should not try to make things rough for me. Neil Oakley, the Trembling Terror of 15-block, was the only leader of the union who opposed me. I was convinced that Oakley had a personal interest, in that he had been named frequently in stories of brutality. One of the terms involved permitting the counselors free access to the punishment cells in 15-block to get fresh stories of brutality and to see the fresh bruises. Did this threaten Oakley's manner of handling inmates? Was this why he was so vociferous? President Matthew L. Maki was sympathetic and friendly to me throughout. The union had abandoned its position against me by the following Tuesday. It was just one of those things that occurs in times of crisis, they told me. McCabe was apologetic and expressed regrets that such a thing had happened.

A speech on Monday noon at the Optimists Club in Lansing had been scheduled for a couple of months. I called the warden on Monday morning to see what I should do about it. I wanted to appear or send a substitute, whichever was thought best. I didn't suggest a substitute, but wanted them to be reminded of the appearance in view of the tense public relations situation. The warden said that Commissioner Brooks was here and that I should check with him. I went into the lobby, but it was filled with newsmen and other people. We sat in the commissioner's car to talk. He told me to go to the Optimists Club, but to give the talk I had planned to give. "Don't talk about the riot," he said. He gave me permission to answer questions about the riot, however, provided I did it in a guarded manner. The commissioner told me to be quiet, take it easy, and that they would handle everything for me.

When I arrived at the club, I said that I did not want to talk about the riot now because we were too close to it. We should wait at least two weeks before we can talk objectively. I found, however, that about half the club members thought from the publicity that my speech had been voluntarily given *after* the riot was over. The newspaper reports had given that impression to much of the public. I told them that the speech was given before the riot was over *as a term of early surrender*. That was all I said about the speech, but I thought it was enough. When I finished talking and sat down, the Optimists gave me a standing ovation. The newspapers reported accurately my statement that the speech during the riot had been given as a term of early surrender. I thought that would help clear some of the confusion the public was experiencing.

Bill Burke reported in the *Lansing State Journal* on Monday in a rather comprehensive analysis of the riot situation. He indicated that Governor Williams had said the rebels had agreed to give up on Thursday when he signed an agreement with them on Wednesday night. Later, "the arrogant convicts told Dr. Fox they would wait until Friday." Then he reviewed the events leading to the speech which, as he reported, had caused me to go from "hero to villain" in two minutes.

Subsequently talking to Bill, I learned that Governor Williams was particularly indignant because the inmates had not readily agreed to come out immediately after he had signed the agreement. Paul Weber, his press agent, had apparently set up a news release program which would have given the governor credit for ending the riot. They probably became frustrated when the plan seemed to be backfiring.

Warden Frisbie's job was still a provisional appointment. Civil Service had sent the letter of certification to Commissioner Brooks on April 18. The riot started on April 20. Commissioner Brooks wasn't available for comment when the newspapers called. He was not certified to the job. He remained "acting warden," as he had been since 1948.

When the criticism mounted, I talked to Commissioner Brooks. He was cautious. I told him that apparently the talk and its purpose had been misunderstood. He replied, "Yes, my boy, but everybody has misunderstood." I decided that it would be futile to talk with the commissioner. As a politician, he was just going to measure the forces at work in terms of Democratic votes, rather than justice and right.

Upon orders of the commissioner, I remained quiet. Not only upon his orders, but because I considered it the best for me. I was in a dilemma. I could have defended myself from the start as far as the public press and radio were concerned. If I did, however, I would have ruined my relationships with the inmates. If, by any chance, I were to remain at the prison, my relationships with the inmates had to be good. Commissioner Brooks and Warden Frisbie had assured me that they would defend me, so I let them do it. Brooks and Frisbie handling the public relations would not impair my relationships with the inmate body. That relationship was needed in order to maintain a treatment program. Some of my friends told me that they watched the paper every day for a comment or defense from me, but none appeared, which surprised and disappointed them. One man summed up further comment with, "Your silence has been most eloquent."

On Monday, April 28, Warden Frisbie made the following speech over the prison radio system:

> Men, I don't make a practice of talking to you over the radio hookup and only do so when in my opinion there is something to say. Today I have several things to talk about in which you probably will be interested. First, let's talk a little about what has happened and then about what we plan to do.
>
> The agreement we made the other day is binding and will continue to be so. We expect to carry it out as rapidly as order is restored. But let's have no misunderstanding about it—the agreement was to cover the time up until the men came out of 15-block. No mention was ever made, no promise given, nor implied that any acts after that would be overlooked. During our shakedown, we have taken no names of people found with contraband and will not do so during the shakedown. However, after the shakedown is completed and any weapons or contraband are found, the usual penalties will be invoked. This is another chance for you, should any of you have any weapons, tools, or other contraband in your possession to still get rid of them. Just toss them out on the gallery or on base and no questions will be asked.
>
> The shakedown is not yet completed but when it is the usual order of events will go into effect. Threatening bodily harm to employees or using insulting or threatening language will not be condoned nor tolerated either.

We are trying to feed hot meals as rapidly as possible. Five-block has been eating regularly for three days and we have started 4-block today. The plumbing and heating have been repaired in 2-block and 5-block and are moving into 1-block now. The other blocks will be completed as soon as we are able. We have been slow about your scrip books; the entire $25,000 stock in the Inmate Store was destroyed. We are reordering and will start issuing as soon as possible. If you are afraid you will lose your scrip forget about it. Your scrip is still good and we will see that you can make use of it.

However, we are not responsible if your scrip was lost or destroyed during the recent trouble. Our procedure will be to pass around store orders to the blocks. The orderly quiet ones first. You fill out the order, attach the scrip to it and the goods will be delivered to you. For the present we can only distribute cigarettes, candy, toilet articles, etc. A list of the items and prices will be furnished to you with the order form. For those who do not have scrip, when the store orders are delivered using the same form, put on it your store request, and if you have the credit in Inmate Accounting, then it will be delivered to you as if you had the scrip.

Remember you will get your privileges back as rapidly as we can orderly restore them. But that is dependent upon your action. The more orderly and quiet the institution remains, the quicker we can restore our normal process.

It appeared at this time that the agreement might be honored. The governor had said it would. The *Detroit Free Press* had printed full headlines, "Governor's Promise Settles Prison Riot." Warden Frisbie had repeated that the agreement would be honored.

While there was much attacking and criticizing, I had also much support. The support from the professional and academic centers and from those who were at the scene of the riot, with the exception of Commissioner Leonard who was frustrated in his desire to blast, seemed to be unanimous as far as I could tell. My attackers were newspaper editors and aspiring candidates for political office trying to make political capital out of the situation. I noticed at the beginning that the news reporters were generally favorable. As Saul Sheifman, public relations expert in Detroit, wrote, "I was happy to notice that the reporters who actually covered the prison all seemed to see your side of the story, in contrast to the editorialists who warmed their chairs and did their masters' bidding to impale you." Division of opinion was intense. Arguments on street corners, in taverns, in barbershops, and elsewhere were rampant. They weren't just for or against; they were *damned for* or *damned against!*

Groups were aligning. A police department in a small town in southwestern Michigan stated that the riot was handled in a "cowardly" manner. That surprised me. Going into the yard unarmed among the rioters during the violence was cowardly! I suppose brave men would have gone in with guns blazing and blown up the cell-block as the commissioner of State Police wanted to do.

The Michigan Area Unitarian Council, meeting at the Congregational-Unitarian Church of Flint, Michigan, took the stand in a general memorandum in support of the general objectives enumerated by the rioters. They made specific mention of "1.) the unthinkably medieval building, Block-15, and its use, 2.) the lack of an inmate council as a means of providing constructive experience in democratic group action, 3.) the absence of any thoroughgoing awareness, either within the prison or in the public mind, regarding the difference between rehabilitation and punishment, and 4.) the deficiency in treatment of mental cases.

"With the rapid progress of events, it was our feeling, too, that Dr. Vernon Fox deserved greater consideration and higher commendation than shelving. If there must be a scapegoat, let it be the people of the state of Michigan at large, for letting our public institutions go inadequately supported, without questioning the higher costs and severer consequences of neglect."

Reverend Edward H. Redman, minister of the First Unitarian Church of Ann Arbor, reported his observation of the counselor system during his visits to the prison as follows:

> I was much impressed with the counselor's duties, and pleasantly surprised by his first-name acquaintanceship with the men, met in passing on the grounds, who were his special responsibility, because his "case load" was in excess of five hundred, and this seemed high under the circumstances. I realized that the usual tension was good-humoredly present, since the divergent methods of the care of "souls" and the cure of "psyches" is not easily resolved. But, I also realized that the "rehabilitating" motives of the chaplains and counselors alike were being frustrated by the "punitive" motive of guards. It was felt that the "guards" tend to view "counselors" as competitors for prestige and pay. It looked to me as though some progressive reforms had been instituted somewhere along the way, but the official personnel of the prison were still unclear or divided as to the goals to be accomplished with the individual prisoner, i.e., whether punishment or rehabilitation.

His observations, I thought, were quite accurate.

Even Chile got into the act. Dr. Julio Olavarria, director general of prisons in Chile, was at the University of Michigan, and had visited the prison a few weeks before. In an interview on Monday, April 28, he decried the American practice of feeding men in large mess halls which give them opportunity to plot escapes and mutinies. He advocated individual feeding in cells at all times. He further stated that an outsider should have conducted the negotiations. I couldn't help but think while there were plenty of "outsiders" available, they didn't volunteer until *after* the danger was over!

I received about two hundred letters during that first

week. Of the mail I received, only two letters were unfavorable to my position. After the first week, more letters straggled in, some favorable and some unfavorable, but the letter-writing phase of such a crisis apparently exhausts itself at the end of a week. Many persons from whom I did not receive letters said that they had written to me. This made me wonder whether some of my mail had been confiscated at the prison.

Letters came from various parts of the country and from other countries. A letter from Paris indicated that a good job had been done on the riot and that the terms were identical with the principles advanced by the International Penal and Penitentiary Congress. One from Kansas City, Missouri, was as follows:

> Congratulations on the principle you displayed and your courage in standing up for human beings. We need more men like you in *all* American penal institutions. All Kansas City seems to endorse your actions.

Similar letters were received from all parts of the country.

Editorial comment was vicious. A Detroit editor attacked the very idea of having a "reform-school graduate" as a deputy warden. Apparently, he was referring to my experience as a boy in the Starr Commonwealth for Boys, a very good school for underprivileged boys near Albion, Michigan, and on whose board of trustees I now hold membership. The editor apparently wasn't very well acquainted with the school.

Armchair editors like Carl Saunders of the *Jackson Citizen-Patriot* wrote emotional editorials. Saunders' choice one, previously mentioned, ended with "Excuse me while I vomit." Warden Frisbie was concerned with that editorial and told Saunders that I was a reasonable guy. He made tentative arrangements for me to meet Saunders, but the meeting never occurred. Knowing both of us, Frisbie said that he knew that we could get along well if we had a chance to talk with each other. It never happened. Perhaps the other editors could be viewed similarly, but I never had a chance to find out. All I know is that here were a bunch of armchair opinionists telling me and the world how prisons should be run and how the riot should have been handled after everything had quieted down!

News stories were colored and changed to meet the desires of the editors. A reporter for the *Jackson Citizen-Patriot*, for instance, wrote up a case study of Earl Ward, which showed his assaultive history and emphasized the unpredictability of his behavior. The editor refused to let it run. I thought I knew why. Reporter Sue Aderhold of the same paper interviewed me by telephone soon after the riot. During that interview, I said, "I should get a job in some nice, quiet university where they don't have riots." Before press time, Sue Aderhold called me to tell me that my statement had been changed at the editor's desk to read, "I should get a nice, easy teaching job in a university." It had gone over the Associated Press wires that way. The reporter wanted me to know that she had reported it accurately, but that it had been changed at the editor's desk. I could visualize the reaction of university administrators to the changed statement! I regarded it as an effort to undermine my position in one of the areas of its greatest support. Based upon comments about the editor by members of his staff, my suspicion is that the comment was altered deliberately and with malice aforethought over the reporter's objections.

Some editorial comment was favorable. The paper of the University of Michigan, the *Michigan Daily*, was most outspoken in its praise. Parts of an editorial by Bill Wiegand were as follows:

> Seeing a man do his job well is always a source of peculiar satisfaction. Occasionally, this ability is of crucial importance. At Southern Michigan State Prison for four days this week, the lives of thirteen men hung on the special skills of a few penologists. The men whose lives were at stake were the prison guards who were held hostage in the detention block by a group of mutinous

convicts. The procurement of the release of these men was the most impressive story to come out of the Jackson Prison riot.

Why was the situation kept under control? Simply because Warden Frisbie and Deputy Warden Fox never jeopardized their trump card among the mutineers—rebel Earl Ward. This was expert psychology. The publicity-hungry Ward maintained control only because officials restrained overt police action against the block which could have easily stampeded the nervous convicts into crowning a new and more maniacal leader. While Ward was in command, Fifteen Block remained rational and willing to bargain. In any other hands, it would probably have turned into a butcher shop.

If the practical psychology of the officials was great, their patience was almost superhuman. More three day prison managers appeared on the scene or spoke from Lansing swivel chairs than existed on the four floors of Fifteen Block.

A Pulitzer-Prize-winning newspaperman from Detroit was mortally offended when a guard touched him once in order to keep him out of the line of fire. He swore "to take this place apart brick by brick, and you know I can do it, too" should any further indignity be committed. For the entire week, his paper misreported, sensationalized, and deliberately warped the news from the prison. They have asked editorially that Dr. Fox be fired.

Certainly the rewards for these men do not come from the state legislators who call for immediate investigations of the administration, or from newspapers who think that the state has bowed to a criminal king, when "the king," shorn of everything but a meaningless piece of paper is returning to a plank bed in a bare cell tonight and every night.

Still there must have been moments that made all the criticism seem unimportant to the warden and his tireless assistant. Like when the first of the eight hostage guards met and embraced his wife and child at the main gate. The flash-bulbs popped, the reporters shouted—and it did not matter much whether Earl Ward was eating steak or caviar.

The Pulitzer-Prize-winning newspaperman was Ken Mc-Cormick of the *Detroit Free Press*.

The *Battle Creek Enquirer-News* carried an editorial under the title, "Greater Mistakes Were Made than Mr. Fox's." The *Manchester Guardian* had me associated with Dostoyevski and John Howard as penal reformers. The *Christian Science Monitor* was not unfavorable. The *St. Petersburg* (Florida) *Times* editorial of April 28 supported my position most enthusiastically, pointing out that the demands were basically points that a progressive government should have provided years ago.

Letters to the editor became excellent reading. They were pretty evenly divided in their for or against positions. Some referred to me and my supporters as "well-meaning but ignorant reformers and sob-sisters." Others were well summarized by one which said, "Deputy Warden Bacon used the 'hit 'em over the head' method; that, my friends, is the only way to handle prisoners."

Part of a long one was quite poignant when it said,

> I ask you to remember, Mr. Editor, that Commissioner Brooks, his assistants and even the warden himself willingly took a back seat because they realized, as did everyone else, that Dr. Fox was the one and only man who could bring those guards out alive and in one piece. What would you have done if it had been your son, or brother or father? Would you have sent the State Police in there, guns blazing, and had those men killed and thrown out piece by piece, or would you have done just as Mr. Fox did? You, yourself, have stated that those men were criminally insane. They were capable of doing anything, even as they said, "cutting off the head of

a guard." You cannot reason with men like these in the
manner you would normally use. You must treat them
as they are, insane, and often you are called upon to do
things that may seem wrong at the time. Dr. Fox knew
all of this and yet he, and only he, had the courage to
meet those men face to face and bring this dreadful
thing to an end without shedding the blood of those
guards. For this I congratulate you Dr. Fox.

Others were not so favorable. One in particular warned
that "the public, through the carelessness of Dr. Fox, might
become a prey to those murdering, careless, raping scape-
goats." Continuing,

Remember, Dr. Fox was hired for that class of people
belonging in Kalamazoo or Ypsilanti institutions for the
insane. We should not hire a psychologist for the prison.
What effect do you suppose Dr. Fox's congratulations
had on the other inmates who did the burning and destroying of buildings? Dr. Fox, when he was shaking
hands with Ward, the rebel, could have given him the
message personally and not broadcast it.

Back to my defense came other letters to the editor. There
were several in the vein of the following one from the *Detroit
Free Press.*

Everybody, it seems, is against Deputy Warden Fox
and is yelling for his dismissal. We would like to come to
his defense. During the riot and conferences between
the convicts and prison officials, Fox stood out as the only
person able to keep the prisoners under control and the
guards alive. Everybody was solidly behind him and
agreed to the prisoners' demands for better treatment.
Now that the guards are free, the state says: "The convicts be damned!" The very reasons the prisoners rioted
are again part of the prison scene. Governor Williams
and State Police Commissioner Leonard, after okaying
the demands, are ready to forget their bargain.

Several letters to the editor suggested that it might be well for the governor to consult with me in prison affairs in view of demonstrated ability.

One of the letters expressed my sentiments regarding Commissioner Brooks and Warden Frisbie at the time when it said, "But now that the riot is over, or so we are told, and they are content to sit back and watch Dr. Fox being literally torn into quarters and thirds, and thrown to the wolves to save their own skins."

Barbara Ellerby, in the *Albion Evening Recorder*, wrote,

> That same editor who was so quick to condemn Fox, asked the question "Why was Fox talking and making deals instead of the warden?" Why, indeed! That would be a good question to do a little research on, wouldn't it? Vernon was in close contact with the convicts every minute, negotiating between them and the prison officials, and I think he deserves a lot of credit for a job well done. We should all be proud of him.

A letter in the *Detroit News* was as follows:

> Due to the brilliant strategy, the great moral and physical courage, and the tireless effort for six days and nights, of Dr. Vernon Fox, ten men are now alive. Dr. Fox was the only man in Michigan capable of saving ten women from widowhood, and many children from becoming orphans. The way he applied his psychology at that crucial moment—the turning point—was to flatter and cajole. It worked. The guards were freed. But because he used the words, "congratulations" and "great leaders"—and, because it is an election year—this most honest and conscientious public servant has been made a political football. Had he performed an equal act of heroism while wearing Uncle Sam's uniform in battle, he would have received a presidential citation. Instead, the ambitious political opportunists have twisted his words—and are howling for his blood. He understands the workings of the criminal mind as few men do. He

believes that with proper facilities and adequately
trained personnel, great good may be salvaged from this
tremendous, tragic human scrapheap. If he had not
been physically and mentally exhausted, he perhaps
would have chosen his words differently. But why care?
They worked! He is a crusader, and a martyr to a great
cause—Humanity—and the preservation of life—and the
rehabilitation of unfortunate humans.

One of my former students at Wayne University wrote in
glowing terms about my work and my handling of the riot.
The student remarked that if the state of Michigan lost Fox,
it would be losing its most competent and progressive penologist.

Again, in the *Jackson Citizen Patriot*, there was defense
for me and a direction of the aggression elsewhere. Parts of
one letter were as follows,

> It would seem to me that they need more people out
> there who can use their heads as well as did Dr. Vernon
> Fox. He certainly did a fine job and should have praise
> and thanks sent his way rather than relieving him of his
> duties. Dr. Fox certainly has shown his ability in han-
> dling a touchy situation.
> Warden Frisbie is the man to be relieved of duty.
> Anyone who shows the poor judgment that he did is not
> the man to be head of such an institution. What did he
> expect when he let the men go to a dining hall and then
> announce there was trouble in cell block 15? It was a very
> stupid move on his part, I think.

Taking the opposing viewpoint, another type of letter to
the editor condemned me and praised Warden Frisbie. Typical of these is the one that follows in part,

> I have been through the prison many times, as my
> father is a retired prison guard. . . . In my opinion, it
> can't be called a penal institution, it is a glorified hotel!
> They have always given the inmates too many privileges

and too much freedom. I think if Warden Frisbie were left alone to run that prison he could do a good job. He is an old army man and knows the meaning of discipline, as army men all know.

* * * * *

As for Deputy Warden Fox, what I and a good many others think about him just isn't printable. I can't see him given credit for anything except endangering the hostages lives further when he was so "quick to point out to the inmates, that the agreement, signed by the governor meant only that there would be no reprisals on the part of the prison or corrections commissions." After the inmates were satisfied with the whole thing, he pointed out to them that the state would still punish them. It could have caused the inmates to hold the hostages until they had a paper signed that there would be no reprisals from the state. If Deputy Warden Fox claims to know so much about the inmates, what was his motive in trying to stir them up again by pointing out flaws in their agreement? Pardon me while I vomit with the editor!

One man said, "As long as neither Hopalong Cassidy nor Roy Rogers was on hand, Dr. Vernon Fox had to do the best he could. Really this is not his specialty. He would have let any of his critics do the job if they had stepped forward with some sound advice and demonstration of ability."

The letter to the editor among those which gratified me most was one written by Armond V. Prater of Stockbridge. He wrote:

> When I wrote my previous letter to this column I guess I was a victim of the mass hysteria fostered by incomplete and prejudiced news reports.
>
> Since learning the truth of the matter I regret my hasty criticism. When I implied that Dr. Fox was crazy, I should have added, "crazy like a fox." If here is a man who can so influence people, I guess a lot of us have been prize chumps in demanding his ouster.

Opinions had me as a hero and as a heel. I was accused of causing the riot, stopping the riot, and of doing nothing at all! I was credited with having started riots among the Communist prisoners of war on Koje, just off the coast of Korea. I was charged with responsibility for all riots after the Michigan riot and some before. Friends told me that custodial personnel in Michigan and some other prisons had said that if anyone is killed in future riots, the corpses could be laid at my feet. The obvious answer to the latter statement is that had I done nothing to save the lives of the hostages in Michigan, then their corpses could also have been laid at my feet.

The letters to the editor were voluminous, vociferous, and represented myriad viewpoints. They were frequently highly emotional, but just as frequently they were considered and well thought out. My impression at the time was that my support among the people who wrote to the editor was much stronger than was my criticism.

Inmate opinion was unanimous as far as I could tell. Typical excerpts from the numerous letters written by inmates are:

(1) Words have failed me in order to define my sincere congratulations to you for your courage and consideration. I have been keeping abreast with the latest news and I beg of you to maintain your position. You can rest assured all inmates are for you 100%.

(2) Had it not been for your patience along with your consideration, I flinch from the thought of what fate had in store for all. I have heard several news announcers, quoting Governor Williams' request for your resignation. I beg of you to maintain your position. For you may rest assured the entire population of Jackson is in your corner.

(3) But I for one feel that you have done one great job in this case, I'm sure that there isn't anyone who could have done better for either side of this mess.

All the fellows should be grateful that there was someone like you, who could keep this thing down as much as you have done.

(4) I wish to extend my thanks and gratitude to you for the intelligent and comprehensive way that you alone have solved this situation that has existed here in this prison the last few days. Many of the inmate body, also, the loved ones of the prison guards, have no one but you, to thank for their lives. There may be some who don't realize what could have happened if it hadn't been for you.

There were many others of similar vein. Letters going out to relatives from the inmates had much the same tone. An example was:

You remember my mention of Dr. Vernon Fox? I heard his words to the boys in fifteen block over the prison radio system and remarked to myself, at that time, that I thought he would be called to account for them. He certainly is. You must remember, Hon, there is a lot more to this subject than the public is apt to hear about. It will become a political football, . . . never forget the type of mentality he was dealing with. Don't forget that the guards were still being held as hostages. Don't forget that Fox spoke as a psychologist and that he had to make a quick, decisive, and climactic sales talk that would result in the rescue of eight human lives. He had to do all this in the face of conflicting official opinions between State Police Chief Leonard and others. All this happening in one of, if not the largest, walled prisons in the world. Fox succeeded, thank God, and God will reward him for his efforts and humanity and intentions. But it looks like Fox is to be crucified for his work. I wonder what the released guards think about it? Millard is acting like a spoiled child, maybe because he feels that he has to get some publicity too.

My impression of public opinion throughout this period was that the news reports went out without interpretation during a period when the public was indignant with the "rioting convicts." Editors took their positions. After the news stories began straightening themselves out, and additional facts were printed, public opinion began to shift in my favor. By the time one week had passed, all the information that ever came out had been printed somewhere, sometime, in some paper. It has never been integrated, however, into one story. Consequently, only those who read much and digested it were able to interpret what had happened. Those who did not read so much just went on original impressions. Editors, however, had taken their stands, and did not want to reverse them. Like umpires, they stayed with their decisions! The public in general, I am convinced, was shifting to my side. Letters to the editor supported that observation. One which appeared in the *Jackson Citizen-Patriot* was as follows,

> In your editorial, "Security Comes First," you stated that the public reaction to Dr. Fox's statement was the same as yours. Have you interviewed "the public"?
>
> Most of the "public" I have talked with feel that Dr. Fox is getting a slap in the face to repay him for the tireless and wonderful work with which he saved lives in the riot. Only fuddy-duddies and people not intelligent enough to understand could take the stand you say the "public" does.

When the support for my position began to be expressed, Saunders of the *Citizen-Patriot* returned to the editorial page. In an editorial on Tuesday, April 29, he recognized that I had support. He said that he had no desire to

> persecute Dr. Fox nor to get into an argument over psychology with men who had studied in that field. We realize he was exhausted and under a great strain when he spoke to the prisoners. But in the minds of the people of the state of Michigan, security and discipline must come

first at the prison. Last week we saw what happens when that security is lost.

If there is any misunderstanding it stems directly from the statement itself, which was given to us in typewritten form by Dr. Fox.

He and the psychologists who are supporting him should have been able to anticipate the reaction of the public as well as that of the warped minds in cell block 15 when he congratulated the leaders of the rebels and said their violence might lead to a new era in prison administration.

He concluded by repeating that psychologists should approach their jobs with the "immediate security of the institution and the safety of society in mind." On the same page was an editorial asking again for capital punishment in Michigan.

Dr. Lowell J. Carr of the University of Michigan consistently analyzed and predicted events throughout the entire period of the riot and its aftermath with uncanny accuracy. Regarding my speech to the inmates, he said,

> Vernon Fox is being ripped to pieces by public opinion and cannot lift a finger to defend himself. Fox's controversial prison broadcast was a psychological tool used Thursday at 3:30 to pry Ward and Hyatt out of the block 15 at 4 o'clock. To the man-on-the-street the message was irrational. Of course it was intended for Ward and Hyatt—the blustering, boastful, swaggering psychopathic leaders.
>
> It must be understood that a psychopath is basically empty, behaves in a disorganized and impulsive manner, and is among the most difficult of all cases to treat. Vernon Fox did not know if Ward and Hyatt would stick to the 4 o'clock surrender agreement—a psychopathic personality is impossible to predict. The 3:30 broadcast, publicly pronouncing them men of honor was a brilliant and dramatic scheme calculated to end the block

15 siege quickly and without bloodshed. Fox literally
goaded the brazen convict leaders out of the doors of
block 15 to meet their public.

In my opinion, Fox was justified in using every
means at his disposal to end the seige—from the steak
dinner bait right down to the public challenge to Ward
and Hyatt that they were men of their word. There is no
doubt in my mind that a massacre would have occurred
had the block been taken by force.

I had had no contact with Dr. Carr, and yet he was able to see
what had happened from a distance. He was right, and I
could not have defended myself without risk of losing my
working relationship with the inmates. I did not defend myself, either, until I had decided to resign. Dr. Carr wrote a
letter to the governor as follows:

April 26, 1952.

Hon. Mennen Williams, Governor
Executive Office, Capitol,
Lansing, Michigan.

Dear Governor Williams:—As a member of your Study
Commission on the Deviated Criminal Sex Offender—
and as a sociologist with some acquaintance with the
field of criminology—may I appeal to you

1. To continue to handle the aftermath of the Jackson
   prison riot as fairly and objectively as you handled
   the riot itself?
2. And to utilize this golden opportunity to open up the
   whole question of the basic purposes of imprisonment in Michigan and the antiquated nature of its
   prisons?

On the first point: Frisbie and Fox during the last
three years have given us the most enlightened administration Jackson ever had. The Monday morning quar-
terbacks and the political opportunists are in full cry
after Fox for his so-called congratulatory speech to the

rioters. As you know, Fox when he gave that speech was engaged in a kind of psychological warfare (a) to hold the riot leaders to their surrender agreement, (b) to hurry up the surrender itself, and (c) to forestall Don Leonard's proposal for the State Police to shoot their way into Block 15. Fox wasn't congratulating rioters on their victory; he was trying to build up their ego to stick to their agreement. You repudiated the speech quite rightly as a statement of administration policy or views, which it was never intended to be. But Fox himself is in a dilemma: if he explains why he said what he did, he will lose his moral hold on the convicts—a hold more important than ever at the moment. If he doesn't explain it, he stands convicted of being a public enemy of prison discipline. I trust you will not throw him to the wolves over this unfortunate public misunderstanding.

On the second point, as I suggested in a memo, to Neil Staebler yesterday for transmission to you, the riot opens a golden opportunity *if the political difficulties can be overcome*, for making a decisive advance in public understanding of and public support for a modern penal philosophy and modern methods of implementing that philosophy. I sincerely hope you will find some way to make the most of this opportunity.

Respectfully,

L. J. Carr,
Professor of Sociology

I was cheered when Governor G. Mennen Williams announced that he had asked for investigations by the Osborne Association through Dr. Austin MacCormick and also for a local investigation by a fact-finding committee made up of reputable men not connected with state government.

Austin MacCormick is a well respected national penologist. I must admit, however, that my impression of him is that he plays politics in a shrewd manner. After reading several of his reports, I concluded that he outlines his report using data he thinks proper, and then after evaluating the political situation, reports out only what he thinks will be accepted. I have never read one of his reports that I considered to be particularly "expert." However, he was an impartial outsider with a national reputation among prison people as being sound.

Minor flare-ups continued at the prison. What would ordinarily be called riots were going on continuously. I was sure, and it was confirmed by friends from the prison, though officially denied by the warden and commissioner, that the continuing difficulty was at least partially related to their unkind treatment of me. I was sure that the prison at the end of the riot would have settled down had the "get-tough" policy not been instigated. I was sure that I could have quieted the prison down, but the policy had changed. I predicted in speeches that flare-ups would continue as long as they maintained the "get-tough" policy.

Explanations given for the riot were varied. Everybody could explain but me. Editors and political candidates had many reasons for the riot, and I was one of them! I didn't know what caused it. In answer to questions from legislators, the warden had named overcrowding and the mixing of criminal and mental types in the inmate body. He said that he would like to have a "flying squadron" of guards ready for any eventuality. He suggested that 15-block be used for other purposes and that a new detention building one story high be built to house only the "tough guys." Frisbie said that there had been no hint of trouble prior to the riot. I had not known of any inkling of impending riot, either, other than a "general tightening of the belt" because of budget restrictions. The legislators interjected the parole board as another factor in causation of the riot. Guards expressed opinion that the counselors caused it by writing "bad reports."

Governor G. Mennen Williams had started a third quiz, in addition to that of Austin MacCormick and that of Attorney General Frank G. Millard. Williams appointed as chairman of a governor's fact-finding committee, Lester P.

Dodd, Detroit, President of the Michigan Bar Association; and as members, Talbot Smith, Ann Arbor attorney; and Richard Rogers, Chief of Police at Midland, Michigan, and former president of the Michigan Association of Chiefs of Police. The fact-finding committee, the governor said, would work merely on determining the facts as to what happened when the riot broke out and how it developed. I welcomed that committee! While I recognized the existence of much public criticism, I knew that an impartial and competent investigation would bring out the facts in their true light. In view of that, I could ride a lot of criticism while biding my time, awaiting action by impartial bodies.

In the meantime, I was given opportunity at many service clubs to discuss the situation. At each club, I merely narrated in an unsensational manner my view of what had happened during the riot. That had the clearance of the warden and commissioner. I attacked nobody. Commissioner Brooks mildly criticized me after a week and a half had gone by for not attacking anybody. He implied that one can be too gentlemanly in a public brawl. My assumption was that he was referring to Donald S. Leonard who was taking every opportunity to publicly denounce and criticize me, as did also some of the other aspiring politicians.

Governor Williams dictated a "get-tough" policy for the prison. On Monday, April 28, Commissioner Brooks broadcast over the prison's central radio system the announcement of this new policy. He threatened to bring in the National Guard as well as the State Police. Williams was doing this in obvious response to newspaper editors and Republican candidates. He was symbolizing the aggression he thought the public wanted expressed, and was directing it toward the inmates.

The leaders of the riot were taken to other places of confinement on Wednesday, April 30. Earl Ward was taken to the jail in Howell. "Crazy Jack" Hyatt was taken to St. Johns. James Hudson, who was the self-admitted leader of the yard riot, was taken to the jail at Ithaca, Michigan. The disciplinary block was returned to a bread-and-water diet for the first time since that practice was abolished in 1948. Water hoses were brought into the cell-blocks to subdue the men. Under the new "get-tough" policy, custody reigned supreme. Commissioner Brooks had forgotten his thinking that custody had got us into this, and now Individual Treatment would get a chance. Counselors were relegated to the low social status in the prison that they had had ten years before. Furthermore, the agreement following the riot was being ignored, despite the governor's promise and the warden's assurance.

The prison was slowly beginning to restore order. On Saturday, April 26, the inmates who had been locked helter-skelter in whatever cell into which they could be driven the previous Monday were unscrambled. The relocation of cell assignments was a big job, necessitating constant checking, with officers taking groups of men from block to block according to the cell assignments. Many men who had not wanted any part of the riot had been herded into the visiting room, and shunted outside the walls without screening, as an emergency measure. These had now to be accounted for. Fifty more men were sent outside on Saturday. By Saturday evening, at least, the hall office people believed that they knew in what cell every inmate was locked.

On Sunday, May 4, I appeared by invitation on a television program for the *Detroit Free Press* station WXYZ-TV. On this program, I defended my criticized speech on the basis that it was needed to "goad" the rioters out of 15-block. It was a bit of psychological warfare.

Commissioner Brooks, responding to questions asked by reporters, said that he could not dismiss me because I was under civil service. Arthur G. Rasch, civil service director, announced that Commissioner Brooks "is talking through his hat when he says he can't fire Vernon Fox." Rasch said that all he has to do is to dismiss the worker he wants to dismiss and to notify civil service of the action.

The legislature was in a "get-tough" mood, too. Senator Elmer W. Porter, noted for conservative emoting, was chair-

man of the senate appropriations committee. He said, "If the
governor won't get tough with them, I guess we'll have to."
Porter said that if he had his way, the prison would get nothing but the $400,000 the "little legislature" had provided
for emergencies when the legislature is out of session. State
Building Director Langiur said that the estimates would not
be ready when the legislature opens. Senator Porter said that
it didn't make any difference "because we won't give them
what they want anyhow." Getting into rare form, Porter continued,

> I believe we should give them enough money for
> new laundry equipment and let them install it them-
> selves. If they don't like that they can get a bucket and
> a plunger and wash their own clothes.
> And there'll be no "complete law library" replaced.
> All those men do is use the law library to flood our courts
> with legal papers and appeals. The man in the street
> doesn't need a law library. Why should they have one?
> Let 'em hire a lawyer.

In line with the type of thinking he had previously demonstrated, Porter was considering the sociologists or counselors
employed at the prison as a good place to cut prison expenses.
Porter said, "the sociologists have taken over the prison and
that's why we had the mess we had."

A group of 25 legislators toured the prison on Wednesday, April 30. The damages had been estimated to exceed
$2,000,000. The damage seemed to be less than they had antic-
ipated, but their attitude was "let the convicts suffer." Nearly 1,500 toilets were wrecked. The greenhouse was wrecked,
and Representative Phillips said, "Let them cut their flowers
from paper from now on." Their concern was the laundry,
since a Battle Creek firm was collecting $5,000 a week, ac-
cording to news reports, to have it done. That seemed to me
to be pretty high.

On Thursday evening, May 1, the guards' union, Local
1333, American Council of State, County and Municipal

Employees (AFL), called a meeting at the Otsego Hotel. They instructed their bargaining committee to draw up demands to be presented to corrections officials. Suggestions were (1) arming with modern weapons guards stationed at strategic points in and about the prison, (2) installation of turret cages from the roof in each cell-block and in the dining hall, (3) banning of counselors from areas where they interfered with custody procedures, (4) more guards, (5) better pay for guards, (6) a better retirement system, and (7) fringe benefits that were lost in a recent budget cut. Further, the current unofficial session of the legislature called as a result of the riot was attacked as a farce and "monkey business."

The legislature had met on Thursday, and the newspapers reported it as a comedy of errors. Attorney General Millard had indicated that nobody had the power to call a session, since the legislature had previously "recessed" until May 14 by joint resolution to prevent the Democratic governor from calling the legislature in extra session. Unanimous consent of all lawmakers had to be obtained before the present session could be legal. In a 40-minute speech, Williams estimated that it would cost from $1,250,000 to $1,500,000 to repair the prison. He noted that budget cuts had reduced the guard force from 460 to 412 men since 1948, and that further cuts would have to be made to meet the next budget. He defended the action we took in quelling the riot, since in the terms the state "yielded substantially nothing." Williams continued,

> I was advised by the state police commissioner and the corrections commissioner about 9:30 P.M. Wednesday that we could no longer temporize the situation. Both officials felt that unless the mutiny could be ended by persuasion that night, the prisoners would be completely out of hand, and the hostages would be slain. Both said that unless a surrender could be arranged the cell block would have to be stormed that night with the

probability that the hostages would be killed before state police could blast their way inside.

Preparations were made for the assault, and stretchers, ambulance and medical supplies were assembled.

Before actually abandoning the lives of the hostages it was decided to make one more effort to persuade the rebels to surrender. This last attempt succeeded. The leaders of the mutiny in 15-block made a written proposal almost identical with the 11 points they had previously issued to the press. They agreed to evacuate the cell block and release the hostages unharmed if prison officials would sign this document.

The State Police commissioner and the corrections commissioner urgently recommended that I authorize the acceptance of these terms. Both officials said that surrender of the convicts by agreement was the only alternative to the probable murder of the hostages during the night.

All of us were well aware that in following a policy of persuasion we ran a certain risk of appearing to accede to the rebels, and thus perhaps encouraging future mutinies.

On the other hand, if we sacrificed the guards' lives in a blood bath, we could hardly expect the future morale of prison security forces to be very high. The determining factor in our thinking was the lives of the guard hostages, whose doom would be sealed if we attacked the cell block. Any damage to discipline or morale which might result from a peaceful settlement could be repaired later. But if the guards were slain the loss to their families could never be repaired.

It must be borne in mind that the prisoners in command of cell block 15 were not rational men who could be moved by ordinary human reason. They were quite different persons from the prisoners who staged a similar outbreak in New Jersey recently. They were psychopathic individuals whose murderous impulses might have been exploded by any incident.

The newspapers reported that when the senators walked out of the capitol, they left two resolutions of Senator Charles S. Blondy on the table.

One would have paid the senate's respects to Dr. Vernon Fox, prison psychologist who received national attention for his congratulatory speech to the rioters.

It was the speech, now, for which I received national attention—not the handling of the riot! Senator Blondy said that I had gone far beyond the call of duty. The other resolution called for a five-man senate inquiry into the criminal code, prison administration, segregation of sex deviates, parole board, and the greater use by trial judges of probation.

Austin MacCormick arrived in the state and stayed at the warden's house. In one of our almost daily telephone conversations, the warden asked me to be available so that Mr. MacCormick could talk to me at his pleasure. I had always telephoned the warden or his administrative assistant, Johnny Spencer, whenever I went anywhere, so that was no change of policy.

By Sunday, May 4, I had been waiting impatiently for several days when the telephone rang. Mr. MacCormick wanted to see me at the warden's house. I went immediately. Mr. MacCormick finished his supper while we talked generally. After supper, Mr. MacCormick showed me a note written to me from Ward. The governor's investigating committee and Mr. MacCormick had visited the jails in which the riot leaders had been housed. The officials would not let the committee visit Ward in Pontiac, but Mr. MacCormick had managed to obtain a visit. Ward had told him that I had not voluntarily given the speech, but that he had written it for me, and then made me give it. The note was:

> You can feel free to tell Mr. MacCormick whether or not I wrote out the speech of congratulations you made and made you deliver it.

Remember what I said in front of Mr. Oakley up in front of my cell—that still goes—for one reason—it's the truth—I'm to blame.

I told Mr. MacCormick that it was not true that Ward had written the speech, that I had written it myself. Upon questioning, I admitted that Ward had told me some things that he wanted said and that I had jotted them down on the back of an envelope. MacCormick asked me if I could say that it had been dictated. I said that it probably had, but not in its entirety. It was dictated, in that Ward dictated that the speech be given with some of the ideas he presented, such as "no State Police will be in evidence" and "the inmates have won on every single point." It was not dictated in its entirety. Even so, Ward's "dictating" was not the *major* reason for the speech. I didn't think Ward's demands in this instance made any difference. I would have given the speech with or without Ward's "dictation" in order to dislodge the inmates from 15-block.

MacCormick telephoned Governor Williams and told him the situation. The governor apparently said that this gave a new light to the situation, but that he would wait for the official report from the fact-finding committee. When he hung up, MacCormick suggested that the news reporters be called. I objected. I had had enough of news reporters who reported statements without interpretation. I was afraid of further misinterpretation and lack of understanding. In a situation as volatile as this, I thought it dangerous. MacCormick said it would be the best for me and for the situation. He told me that the way the speech was put on the news wires made me appear as though, I "must have rocks in my head," as one of the deputy wardens at San Quentin had said. The fact that people did not realize what the situation really was made it imperative that this news be released at this time.

Resignedly, I told him to use his own judgment, but that I did not favor it. MacCormick picked up the telephone and read part of the note to a newsman and told him about what he had found. After Mr. MacCormick finished, he called me on the phone. Ken McCormick of the *Detroit Free Press* wanted to interview me. I did not want to be interviewed by anybody, particularly by McCormick. He told me that I owed it to the public to let them know all developments through the press. That did it. I promised to meet him in the parking lot in the rear of the State Police barracks.

When I went to the State Police barracks parking lot, there were Ken McCormick of the *Detroit Free Press* and Allen Schoenfield of the *Detroit News*. They repeated what Austin MacCormick had told them over the phone, and asked me to verify it. I told them that Ward had not written the speech, but that he had given me some of the ideas, which I had jotted down on the back of an envelope. Ward had told me not to tell anybody about his insisting that I make the speech. They asked me why I had kept it a secret. I told them that I had told the Optimists Club in Lansing that the speech was a "term of early surrender," which the papers accurately reported, but which was never referred to again. I had not revealed more because I thought that was all that was needed to convey the idea. I remarked, as I had previously remarked to friends, that the lives of eleven men were worth the career of one.

When the story went on the wires and appeared in the newspapers, it was dramatized considerably. The Jackson *Citizen-Patriot* carried frontpage headlines across the top of the sheet, "Ward Dictated Congratulatory Talk, Says Dr. Fox." That wasn't true, either! When Austin MacCormick had asked me if Ward had written it as he said, I had said, "No." When he had asked me if it could be said that Ward had dictated it, I said that probably it could—in that he gave me some ideas he wanted incorporated, demanded to check it before it went on the air, and dictated that it be given. He did not dictate the entire speech, however, and I never said he did.

The newspapers went further in their drama. They reported that I had had a "pact of secrecy" with Ward. I wouldn't betray my word to anybody, once given. Then it was reported that I broke down and wept! That was the ace tear-jerker! Even Austin MacCormick was reported to have said that, too, but I can't yet believe that of MacCormick. They were still trying to get public sympathy for me, I think, but as far as I was concerned, that was the most embarrassing report of the entire situation. In order to protect me, Ward had gone too far, saying that he wrote the speech. When I said that he didn't write it, but gave me some ideas he wanted incorporated, then Ward dictated the entire thing! When I failed to say that Ward had written it, then I was depicted to have honored the "pact of secrecy" above my duty to the state.

Reactions to news stories that "Ward dictated the speech" were varied. Warden Frisbie wanted to wait until more facts came in, and I was glad. Republican candidate John Martin came in with one of his shallow statements,

> I don't know that Ward's revelation can be entirely believed since we know that at least one of the prisoners' demands—that for a prison inmate council plan—has been one of Fox's pet ideas and was inserted in the prisoners' demands by Fox to accomplish his own ends.

How absurd can a politician get? It was free publicity, anyway.

Throughout the post-riot period, feelings and opinions and news reports went to extremes. Instead of unsensationally telling that he had given me some of the ideas for the speech, for instance, Ward said that he had written it. Instead of giving the proper interpretation as to the reasons for the speech, newsmen had said I was sorry. When searching for public sympathy, I was reported to have broken down and wept! Even when I spoke to my home-town friends of the Albion (Michigan) Exchange Club, their bulletin protected me beyond what I said, such as, "Vern didn't write the speech." The *Battle Creek Enquirer-News* reported the same speech exactly as I had given it!

An editorial in the *Detroit Free Press* referring to a television appearance, in which I said that the speech was designed as psychological warfare to "goad" the rioters out of 15-block, pointed out that Ward's dictating of the speech and the "pact of secrecy" did not support the "psychological warfare" thesis. The writer didn't agree with me, no matter "which Fox you believe." This particular editorial, in my opinion, was one of the most unethical and untruthful pieces of journalism to come out of the situation. It was as follows:

A strange epilogue has been appended to the tragic story of the Jackson Prison riots by Dr. Vernon Fox, deputy warden and psychologist.

He now contends that the speech in which he congratulated the rioting inmates and praised Earl Ward, the riot boss, as a "natural leader" was "dictated" by Ward.

In an emotional press conference, Dr. Fox, with tears running down his cheeks, told the strange tale only after he had been handed a note from Ward giving him permission to speak. Dr. Fox explained that he had been pledged to secrecy by Ward not to reveal Ward had written the congratulatory message or that he was "forced" to read it.

Released from his ridiculous bond with a psychopathic convict, Dr. Fox went on to tearfully tell how he had read the message to the inmates and sacrificed his career in order to save the lives of nine hostage guards.

Our puzzled governor said Dr. Fox's strange new story puts a "new light on the matter" of possible dismissal action against the psychologist.

Just a few hours before Dr. Fox's weird "confession," the psychologist had told a *Free Press* television audience that the congratulatory message was his own idea as part of his "psychological warfare" with the convicts.

It doesn't matter which Dr. Fox you believe. In whatever light that congratulatory message is read, it still remains one of the most shameful statements ever uttered by a public servant in Michigan.

It is just one more reason for firing Dr. Fox immediately.

The pattern was to depict me as a bundle of emotions. In reality, however, there were no "tears running down his cheeks" and no "tearfully" telling how he read the message to the inmates! I was frustrated because I was embarrassed that I would be depicted as having wept, and yet I could not adequately refute it because it was a minor issue. If the *Detroit Free Press* policy makers intended to embarrass me by it, I may relate to their satisfaction that their intent was accomplished. I think it very unethical of them to deviate from the truth for such a purpose, however.

I was amazed, too, that the *Detroit Free Press* would find too complex to handle the idea that there might have been two reasons for the speech operating simultaneously. It was apparently too difficult for them to understand that the speech (1) had to be made as a term of early surrender, and that it also (2) had to serve as psychological warfare to "goad" men out of the block who were not yet ready to come out. According to the writer, it had to be one or the other, and he didn't agree with either. He could safely do it that way, too, for the riot was over.

Republican State Chairman Owen J. Cleary attacked the "steak and ice cream" dinner from a political angle. He said,

> Of all the Jackson Day dinners sponsored by the Democrats, this one will live in Michigan history. The only thing missing in this abject surrender by the state was an orchestra and a square dance called by the governor. Apparently the criminals forgot to include them in their demands.

Cleary recalled that Williams promised in his 1948 campaign to take the penal system out of politics, but he appointed as commissioner of corrections a Democrat insurance agent who happened to be in his political corner. Politi-

cal favors have been handed out to parole violators and Detroit gamblers, Cleary charged. He reminded his audience
that the governor had even reached into the prison and
snatched a man convicted of goon-squad tactics during a
labor disturbance (Tom Flynn).

A coroner's jury on May 1 ruled that the killing of inmate
Darwin Millage during the riot was not criminal. Their report was in part as follows,

> Darwin W. Millage came to his death as the result
> of gunshot fired by an authorized unidentified officer
> employed by the state of Michigan in the line of duty
> protecting life and property on the premises of the State
> Prison of Southern Michigan.

I watched the newspaper accounts of the testimony before
the fact-finding committee. Some of it was not entirely accurate, and I wondered about it. I was sure that a competent
committee would search out the facts, however, and make a
good report.

One of the first findings of the committee was that a
24-year-old guard with less than two months' experience had
been assigned to 15-block. This guard, Thomas Elliott, had
worked at the prison five weeks in 1950 and had returned in
March, 1952, a month before the riot. Cells designated with
red cards are indicative that the occupant is a severe custodial risk of one nature or another, and is not to be permitted
out of his cell. Officer Elliott had opened a cell on the fourth
floor of 15-block which was designated with a red card when
Ray Young, the occupant of the cell, had requested him to
open it. Young had told the guard that he had a box he wanted
to give to another inmate in another cell. Young told Officer
Elliott that he was going to be released tomorrow, anyway.
Officer Elliott went into Ray Young's cell to get the box.
Young placed a knife on the person of Officer Elliott, took
Elliott's keys, and locked him in the cell.

Another version reported was that Elliott opened the cell,
turned to continue his tour of duty, and Young emerged

from the cell to place the knife on Ellott's person. Two reporters covering the same testimony reported different stories. At any rate, Ray Young proceeded to open all the cells on the tier, including that of Earl Ward. When all the inmates were out of their cells on one floor, it was merely a matter of time stealthily to get into position to capture the guard on the floor above and on the floor below, and then the guard on the base, or ground floor.

How an inexperienced guard had been assigned to the block was a matter of debate. Deputy Bacon was responsible for the custodial assignments, but he placed responsibility on Captain Tucker, who was the shift captain. Finally, it was learned that the assignment had been made by Lieutenant Louis Baldwin. Baldwin said he believed inexperienced guards were in less danger in the 15-block bastion than in an open cell-block. Lieutenant Baldwin said that Elliott was substitute for an absentee, and that with three other experienced guards, he would ordinarily have had no difficulty. Elliott insisted that he violated no rule when he opened the "red-card" cell, since those cells were permitted to be opened at meal time anyway, which was true. Warden Frisbie testified that those cells were to have been opened at meal time *only*, however.

Committee member Talbot Smith asked the warden whether he thought it was a mistake to broadcast the news to the other inmates. The warden said he believed it was the proper thing to do. It was better to let them have bona fide accounts than to risk garbled stories by "grapevine."

Frisbie's defense as far as he was concerned regarding my speech and some other phases of the riot was that he did not know what was going on. I thought that to be a poor defense for any administrator. At any rate, he told the committee that the inmate leaders were not easy to work with. During the testimony, Warden Frisbie told of an hour-long telephone conversation with Ward. Ward had "ranted illogically" and "laughed insanely" when he told how he had torn the barber shop to pieces and damaged the heavy steel door.

All telephone conversations emanating from 15-block had been recorded by the State Police.

Warden Frisbie took responsibility for permitting the inmates to go to the dining hall on Monday morning. Prisoners get surly when they aren't fed, so an additional custodial force was put on duty in the dining room. It would take all day to feed two meals to men in cell blocks.

The committee asked Elliott what might have happened had State Troopers stormed the block. Elliott replied that they would have tried to kill the hostages. Another news report was that Elliott had said, "I think they would have killed us all. They would believe they were going to die anyway and had nothing to lose. Some are in for life. If they killed us, it wouldn't cost them anything."

"But you were treated well while you were held hostage," Dodd commented, "What makes you think they would have tried to kill you?"

Elliott replied that he was certain that violence would befall the hostage guards if there had been such an attack on the block by troopers to free the hostages. In reply to the committee's efforts to determine how much training Elliott had received since coming to work at the prison, Elliott said he had been given a rule book in 1950. Guards learn as they go. Elliott had never seen any evidence of brutality, but "some guards like to be a little overbearing with a lead pencil, though," reporting minor infractions like getting out of place in meal lines, which might result in four or five days in solitary confinement. He hadn't known that the rubber hoses and other things the inmates found were even in 15-block.

The committee asked Elliott about the reported friction between counselors and the guards. Elliott said he didn't know what the counselors did or anything about them. He was asked what the guards talked about, and he replied, "They don't talk about much of anything."

The committee wanted to know from Warden Frisbie how Young could get possession of a knife in solitary confinement. Warden Frisbie said he would like to know the same thing. The custodial force is supposed to search each cell and person periodically and to prevent knives from coming in. Warden Frisbie and Elliott agreed that there was no inkling before the riot that there was impending violence. The reduced budget had forced the return of inmates from the Detroit House of Correction several months before the riot. Superintendent A. Blake Gillies of the Detroit institution agreed after the riot to take some of Jackson's trusties. Simultaneously, he asked Detroit jails to keep the prisoners with terms under 90 days in order to give him room for the state prisoners. Gillies wasn't worried about a riot, though he did not like the overcrowding at the Detroit institution.

On Saturday, May 4, the governor's fact-finding committee turned its attention to the counselor program. Three guards criticized the counselors. Officer Dzal, who resigned, said that the inmates were "getting sick of the counselors," because when they had legitimate difficulty, all they received from the counselors was "Well, how are you and how is your work going?" Dzal said that discipline was about the same then as it was when he first arrived at the prison. He said further,

> They've got too many counselors here. The new ones are getting too easy. If they'll keep their mouths shut and not tell the convicts anything, they'll get along better with the officers.

Officer Hinton said that the counselor system makes it more difficult to handle inmates, because the inmates asked "too frequently" for interviews with the counselors to tell them their troubles, real or imagined. Officer Carrier said that the counselor system keeps the inmates more "agitated and uneasy," and that their promises of things they can't fulfill makes unrest. Captain Tucker testified, "I think if given a chance to work in this institution, the counselors would give us a lot of help." However, the committee asked him if he would hire more counselors or more guards and the custodial captain favored the latter.

Captain Tucker said he believed that a special "shakedown squad" to search all cells would be helpful to the prison administration. Lieutenant Baldwin said that he would not let large groups of inmates out of their cells together to go to the recreation yard. Further, he suggested the establishment of armed guard posts in the yard, accessible only by a tunnel.

With some attention focused on the counselor system, a *Jackson Citizen-Patriot* reporter interviewed Deputy Bill Johnson with the theme that the "man-on-the-street" didn't know what a counselor was, though the program was now in the news. Johnson made the point that professional people perform the work of the counselor in some way in every modern prison and federal penitentiary. He pointed out that the work of the counselors paid off during and after the riot when records had to be checked and men had to be quieted. Counselors were the first to go into the cell-blocks to quiet the men and to bring them mail and newspapers. He indicated that custody uses the work of the counselors as much as the counselors benefit from custody. It was not a very good description of a counselor. His most obvious misstatement was that "Our counselors have the highest respect for Bacon and his long experience in prison work," which was diametrically opposed to fact. It was probably designed to improve relations between custody and the counselors which were worsening as a result of publicity.

The committee interviewed "Crazy Jack" Hyatt at the Clinton County Jail. Hyatt told them that the 15-block riot was planned, but that the riot in the yard was "mob hysteria." He said that the riot was a "shame." Hyatt said that he "imagined" that if State Police had attempted to rush the block, the hostages would have been killed. He told the committee that he had never been beaten up by anybody when he was in the mental ward because "they knew damned well they'd have to go when I got the chance."

James Hudson, 44-year-old colored inmate leader of the riot in the yard, was interviewed at Ithaca. Hudson said that he believed that officials tried to agitate racial hatred in the prison. Hudson and Hyatt were both reported to be critical of the counselor system.

On Monday morning, May 5, I was called to appear before the committee. I had been somewhat anxious to appear before the governor's fact-finding committee so that they would have my testimony on record under oath. Never having appeared before any sort of board like that and never having testified under oath, it was a new and interesting experience. With some naïvete, I had considered this board an impartial fact-finding committee that would weigh facts competently and arrive at valid conclusions. I trusted them implicitly. All I had to do would be to answer whatever questions they asked truthfully and completely, right down the line.

When I went into the Industries office at about ten o'clock in the morning, the three board members sat behind the tables arranged in a row. The witness chair was slightly to the left of their center, and the stenographer, Mrs. Marian Nichols, sat at a small table opposite the witness. There were newsmen distributed around the room in chairs against the walls. Some newsmen sat on a long table behind the witness chair. Lester Dodd, chairman of the committee, sat in the center. He appeared to be a friendly man, managing a smile whenever the witness looked at him. At Dodd's right, Chief of Police Rogers from Midland, Michigan, sat impassively. Rogers' smile appeared disinterested. Talbot Smith sat at Dodd's left.

Chairman Dodd asked me to tell in my own words what had occurred during the riot. I reviewed my experiences as accurately and completely as I could. Dodd would smile and nod on occasion. Rogers looked impassive and bored and smiled like Mortimer Snerd. Talbot Smith watched me with a sneer, as though I were Hairbreadth Harry about to foreclose on his mortgage. Chairman Dodd asked me if I had instructed Joe Dellinger to destroy the tape on which the speech was recorded. I had told him to go ahead and destroy it since there were plenty of copies, but on second thought, I had said that it might be better if the tape were not destroyed. Then he asked me if I thought that I were to be used as a scapegoat. I said I thought the people of Michigan were more reasonable than that. If he had asked me the same question fifteen minutes or a half-hour later, however, he would have received a different answer.

Before that morning session was over, I could visualize the ancient practice of Jewish antiquity in our modern day; that of bringing out the goat upon whose head were symbolically placed the sins of the people, after which he was suffered to escape into the wilderness. It was 12:30 P.M. when Smith began talking to me in his best courtroom snarl. He asked me why I didn't show the speech to the warden. I told him that it was a matter of time, and that the warden was in a press conference. I don't recall the entire exchange of conversation, but he ended by accusing me of dereliction of duty. I was furious! Here was a man who appeared as though he had been getting enough sleep telling another man who had worked solidly from Sunday through Thursday in a riot situation that he had been derelict in his duty! At one o'clock, the committee adjourned for lunch. They wanted to see me again after lunch. At their bidding, I telephoned Michigan State to tell them that I could not meet my two o'clock class. Dr. Zietz took the class.

It had become obvious to me by this time that the committee wanted a scapegoat and that I had been elected. The speech actually made little difference. It was the most obvious and tangible item then available. If the speech had not been there, then their attention would have centered on the "steak and ice cream" dinner. If neither the speech nor the steak and ice cream had been available, I think they would have attacked "negotiating with prisoners like a labor union." No matter what happened, I was convinced that they wanted a scapegoat and I was it. As a matter of fact, I began wondering if they were going to try to charge me with something in a court!

During the lunch period, I told some fellow employees that it had been suggested that I was guilty of dereliction of duty! They were flabbergasted. They assured me that the committee must be joking. I assured them that I thought by this time that the committee was not an impartial board, that they were thinking in political terms, and that they were not joking.

Reconvening at two o'clock, the committee began questioning me viciously and in a sarcastic manner. I was sorely disappointed and discouraged at watching the activity and questioning of what I had previously considered to be an impartial "fact-finding" committee. Trying to figure out why they were taking this approach was difficult. I thought that the governor's committee might be supporting the governor's stand, but nobody really knew what the governor's stand was. The Republican candidates had attacked him through my handling of the riot, and to avert that threat, the governor, too, had attacked me. He could beat them by joining them! Was this committee supporting or attacking him? I decided that it didn't matter. I was to be the scapegoat. That would protect the governor and simultaneously satisfy the Republican candidates' and editors' aggression, since they had identified me as symbolic of progressive penology which opposed the "get-tough" aggressive type of prison treatment.

Talbot Smith was still snarling. He asked me why I didn't tell the public that I had been forced to give the speech, if actually I had been forced. I repeated that I had been forced partially by circumstances and partially by Ward to give the speech. If Commissioner Leonard had not insisted on force, the speech would not have been necessary. Secondly, it was a term of early surrender, a fact which I had told the Lansing Optimists Club. I was asked to tell about the "pact of secrecy." I said that it was no formal "pact of secrecy"— that Ward had told me not to say anything to anybody about his insisting on a speech, and I had agreed not to tell anybody. When I was asked if I would have refused to tell the warden or commissioner, I replied that I would have told them had they asked me. There had been no time to do it otherwise. I had told them both several times during the week following the riot, however, that it had been a term of early surrender. Then, the committee told me, "You didn't consider the 'pact of secrecy' binding at all." They asked me why I didn't tell about the speech being a term of early surrender before now. I didn't reply adequately because I was sure the committee already knew that I had told the Optimists Club in Lansing the Monday following the riot that it was a term of early surrender! They weren't after facts now; I was sure of that!

Smith asked me why I made the talk, and I told him again that Ward had telephoned me twice in the morning, and in the second call, he told me that they would give up that day, but that I would have to make a talk or something to "take us off the hook with the boys." The committee began asking questions about details, and while I was answering them, I realized that they were confusing conversations over the telephone with those at the window of 15-block after I had returned to the prison. All those negotiations concerning the speech didn't take place over the telephone. Many people knew it, but I wasn't sure the committee did. Questions were coming so fast that I never had the opportunity to clarify the point, because the committee kept me going on other points. I'm sure now that the committee thought that most of those long arrangements were made over the telephone.

Talbot Smith asked me if it were not inconsistent for a man like Ward to try to hide the fact that he was in a position to dictate a speech to a deputy warden. I didn't try to interpret to him that what may seem logical to one person may seem to be inconsistent in the mind of another. Further, inconsistency in a psychopath is to be expected. I couldn't very well tell a man trained in law and not in the behavior sciences that it was inconsistent, because of the connotation he would have placed on the answer. He wanted me to appear

untruthful, and wasn't interested in a discussion of the dynamics of human behavior. I tried to get the idea across that
it didn't seem inconsistent to me. I'm sure that Smith wasn't
really convinced that he and Ward were thinking in the same
frame of reference, which meant that Smith's attack was being
directed elsewhere. He was building up a case against me by
implying that I was fabricating. Finally, I decided that
Smith wanted the question answered in his frame of reference, so I said it probably was inconsistent to him. It wasn't
inconsistent with Ward, though.

Much of the committee questioning and conversation was
not recorded. Frequently, they would talk with each other
and with newsmen, ask me questions, and then indicate to
Mrs. Nichols that we were "back on the record now."

They asked me why I hadn't volunteered the information
to the warden or the commissioner. I had already told them
several times that it was a term of early surrender. I told them
that I was exhausted and that the commissioner's attitude,
expressed by his statement that everybody had misunderstood, had been so final that I considered it useless to argue.
Smith to the attack retorted, "It's amazing to me that you
would accept such a statement as final." Smith was "amazed"
at a lot of things. They asked me if I had had any contact
with Ward after the riot. I told them about the Friday night
visit in 15-block in the presence of Officer Neil Oakley. They
questioned whether or not I had had other contacts, but I
assured them I had not.

They ridiculed my statement that I was exhausted. Apparently, they had no concept of the strain of 105 hours of
activity with an accumulated total of four hours of sleep. I
found that I could not recapture the tension and conflicted
atmosphere of the riot less than two weeks afterward, even
though I had been through it; and neither could they even
grasp the idea that mental and physical fatigue would influence behavior. As a matter of fact, they didn't seem to recognize the existence of fatigue. The newspapers reported of my

statement, "His only explanation was: 'I was tired and discouraged.' I said, 'What's the use? This is the end.'"

The committee asked me about the note Ward had given
Mr. Austin MacCormick. I told them about the first part. It
had said, "You can feel free to tell Mr. MacCormick whether
or not I wrote out the speech of congratulations you made
and made you deliver it." Ken McCormick of the *Detroit
Free Press* interrupted the proceedings to ask about the second part. I was sufficiently disillusioned and blocked by this
time to have forgotten the second part! Dodd wanted my lack
of memory in the record. He asked me about it "on the record," and I said on record that there was no second part. That
performance was very revealing to me as to how a witness
can completely "block" on a point. Fortunately, it was not
important. The committee, however, thought it was. They
telephoned California to get Austin MacCormick to read
the whole note. When the note was read completely, I recognized having read it before! The first part had been the most
important, and the only part that really affected me. The
second part was merely elaboration. That explained to me
my blocking. The committee probably thought, or wanted
to think, differently. At any rate, when they could not interpret the meaning of the second part, I informed them of
Neil Oakley, the Trembling Terror of 15-block, and his conversation with Ward. He had apparently failed to tell the
warden what Ward had told him to tell, despite the "yes sirs"
he gave so profusely to Ward.

The committee asked me what part of the speech Ward
had "dictated." They brought the tape and recorder into the
hearing room and played it, asking me to identify the parts
that were Ward's. By their tone, their expressions, and questions, I thought I could see that the meeting had degenerated
from an impartial fact-finding board to an inquisition designed to gain political ends. I became furious, tried to conceal it, and told them that I wrote the whole thing! That was
what they wanted. They asked me if the Ward note was a
"scheme concocted by MacCormick, Ward, this committee,

or anyone" to absolve me of "blame" for the speech. Ward's using the word "wrote" in the note had suggested to me that Ward was trying to do just that, but I couldn't accept such help. I indicated to the committee that Mr. MacCormick wouldn't do such a thing. I was sure that the committee didn't want to absolve me of anything, but would like to have made things appear worse. To see such a committee so blatantly prostitute the concept of impartial "fact-finding" could not help but disillusion me in regard to such committees.

Chairman Dodd was careful to interject that I had said that I was not being used as a scapegoat. I was quick to remind him that the committee had framed that statement. No matter who framed it, he wanted me to affirm that I had earlier in the meeting indicated that I did not expect to be used as a scapegoat. While I affirmed the factual information that I had answered their question in the negative earlier in the meeting, I recalled Shakespeare's line from *Hamlet* that he "doth protest too much." It had been obvious to me for some time that the committee had decided on my scapegoat role before the meeting had started.

Ken McCormick interrupted the proceedings again. He wanted to know what I had meant the night before when I had said that the lives of eleven men were worth the career of one. The committee laughed and incorporated it into the record. I explained in an embarrassed manner that I would do over again what I did to save the lives of eleven men, even though I might have to change careers. Dodd ridiculed me for playing the martyr, and said he didn't see that I was sacrificing anything. The committee adjourned. Dodd told me that they wanted to see me again later in the week, probably Friday, to discuss administrative procedures. I told him I would appreciate another opportunity to meet with the committee. News reports were that the committee was not satisfied with some of my answers and that they would call me back later in the week.

An interesting sidelight on Ken McCormick's slanting was its origin at a "Youth and Narcotics" workshop at Albion

(Michigan) College in January, 1952, and an epilogue in Florida in 1954. Mr. McCormick was one of several "interrogators" at that workshop where I had been privileged to be associated with such men as Dr. Alfred Lindesmith of Indiana University as one of the "experts" to be quizzed by the interrogators for the benefit of the audience in the area of narcotics control and therapy. When I was on the stand, Mr. McCormick brought up some irrelevant criticism of the prison and how it was administered. During the resulting altercation, the audience was with me, much to Mr. McCormick's embarrassment as I interpreted his reddened countenance. I think he was "getting even" with me during the riot publicity—as did several of my friends. At this time, a younger writer on the *Detroit Free Press*, Mr. Harold Tyler, was a close colleague and associate and learned much from Mr. McCormick. Two years later, during the summer of 1954 when I was scheduled to talk to a Florida Youth Workshop on a subject involving narcotics, Mr. Harold Tyler had become city editor of the *Tampa Morning Tribune*. It was coincidental that Mr. McCormick, I have been told, happened to be in Florida spending part of his vacation at the home of Mr. Tyler in Tampa just about the time the workshop program was distributed. My suspicion—based on conversation with mutual friends—is that the reporter covering the workshop had been given instructions, either directly or by inference, regarding his coverage of my talk. At any rate, quotations were taken from my talk and put together in such a way that an impression certainly different from that intended was printed in the newspaper. After a blistering attack by the *Tampa Morning Tribune*, which elicited alarm responses from a few local officials and politicians, President Doak S. Campbell of the Florida State University, on whose faculty I enjoyed some status, had a thorough investigation made, including interviewing persons who had been in the audience. The investigation revealed the true situation, little damage was done, and President Campbell received the plaudits of the local chapter of the American Association of University Professors.

As I left the committee, I realized that there was no possibility of operating a treatment program under this new "get-tough" policy, which the governor was imposing and the commissioner and warden were accepting without protest. I wondered briefly why the committee did not use the polygraph, which was readily available, to determine the truth from conflicting testimony, and then realized that the truth was less important to them than other considerations. I realized, too, that I would resign from the prison system. I wanted to resign right then, but didn't want to resign in times of crisis. My decision at that point was to ride out this difficulty, which might take a couple of months, resign in the summer, and join the faculty of some university in September, 1952. I had received overtures from several universities already, but those were dated before the riot. I didn't know what changes the riot and its political implications would make. I decided that if it came to a battle, I would whip the committee or anybody else in an impartial hearing before the Supreme Court, and after the smoke cleared away, I would resign and go to a university. In the waiting-out period, though, I told nobody of my decision. Some of my friends suspected it, however. Ferris Young, the academic school supervisor, told me about it with uncanny accuracy.

The *Jackson Citizen-Patriot* carried a front-page story headlined, "Probers Puzzled by Fox's Lost Chances," in which they wonder why I hadn't said before that Ward had forced me to make the speech. Apparently, they hadn't read the reports of my talk to the Lansing Optimists Club the Monday immediately following the riot, when I declared publicly that the speech was a term of early surrender.

Joe B. Dellinger, group therapist, testified before the committee late Monday afternoon. He told the committee about Bill Johnson's long antagonism toward me and any program I might try to promote. He explained that the majority of counselors and other workers in the department sided with me, preferring my policies to the custodial-type policies espoused by Bill Johnson. He told the committee about Johnson's saying that I was under the influence of Ward. I was depicted as liberal and willing to try new ideas, while Johnson was conservative and custodially minded.

"I stand with Dr. Fox all the way," Dellinger testified he told Johnson, when Johnson criticized him for taking the tape of the speech home to make sure it was not destroyed. Dellinger testified further that he went AWOL from the prison with the tape recorder to record interviews with the guard hostages, which were all favorable to me. He added that he went AWOL because Johnson would have prevented him from doing it had he asked permission. The committee did not ask for the tapes.

He explained to the committee his belief that the intent and content of my speech were being misconstrued by officials and the public and that he wanted to make sure that an accurate record of its content was kept for evidence.

Asked from whom he wanted to protect Dr. Fox, Dellinger said, "There's a man in my department who would very much like to replace him." He identified that man as Deputy Bill Johnson. He testified that "Johnson has been trying to get Fox's job almost since the counselor system was started three years ago." Johnson had told him that "Fox is no prison man and anybody can see it."

Dellinger told the committee that other than isolated cases that were quickly forgotten, there were no clashes between Custody and Individual Treatment. That was true, despite publicity. He reported that we had enjoyed a good working relationship with Custody until the time of the riot. He reported that he thought we had made great progress, but that more men were needed in the counseling program.

Assistant Deputy William H. Johnson testified that I was a poor prison man. In his eyes, anybody who is not custodially oriented is a poor prison man. I don't recall his believing that anyone but Bill Johnson was ever a good prison man. Johnson told the committee that Dellinger's charges were greatly exaggerated. He said that there were differences, but not to the extent that Dellinger had testified. He said that Fox was a very good case worker and handled individual cases very well. He pointed out that when men are needed for certain jobs, he himself saw to it that they went there whether they wanted to or not, while "Dr. Fox's theory is to give more leeway to individuals as to what they themselves want to do." He described friction between the custodial and treatment departments as largely an issue of salaries and misconceptions of the abilities of the counselor.

On Wednesday, May 7, I went to the Starr Commonwealth for Boys for a meeting of the Board of Trustees, notifying the prison officials where I would be if I were called for anything. On that day, the Flint Lions Club sent a plane to take me from Marshall, about eight miles from Starr Commonwealth, to Flint for a noon luncheon meeting, and returned me the same way so that little meeting time was lost. It was during this noon luncheon that I referred to the second verse of William Ernest Henley's "Invictus,"

> In the fell clutch of circumstance
> I have not winced nor cried aloud.
> Under the bludgeonings of chance
> My head is bloody, but unbowed.

And the newspapers echoed, "My head is bloody, but unbowed."

On that day, the committee interviewed some inmates. Ray Young said that an official friendly to the inmates had given him the knife. I was asked about the news report in Flint, and indicated that I found the story difficult to accept. Privately, I wondered to what lengths the committee was ready to go to trump up charges. I wouldn't have been surprised at anything. Nothing happened, however, except that the committee decided that Young was not telling the truth. Young went on to say that the riot was premature, that they had wanted to capture Assistant Deputy Warden Robert A. Northrup, but that they took advantage of the opening on

Sunday night. Asked what would have happened if State Police had stormed the block, Young snapped, "We'd have killed every copper that was up there!" Regarding the terms, Young said, "We tried to keep personal grievances out of it." Originally, the inmates had a list of demands "a mile long," which were narrowed down to the eleven that eventually were accepted.

Neil Oakley testified for himself, not for the union. Among other things, he said that he didn't think the guards had at any point asked for my dismissal, and that the report had been exaggerated. He further testified that he had "refused" my request to see Ward in 15-block, which was hardly the truth. He had said he was afraid, and I had told him that I wasn't anxious to interview him, and I left. The warden, however, apparently insisted that I see Ward. Oakley testified that when I walked into 15-block, a roar of welcome was set up for me, and that I had asked if they had heard the latest, referring to my being reassigned to work outside the walls. He said that when I went to Ward's cell, Ward demanded immediately, complete with obscenities, that Oakley join them. Oakley said he refused to come for about two minutes, but finally went to the gallery cage. Oakley testified that Ward whipped out a straight razor and ordered him to tell the warden that I had not written the speech. Oakley said that I remained inside another five or ten minutes. Under questioning, he told the committee that he saw no physical contact between Ward and me, though there had been "persistent" reports that I had repeatedly shaken hands with Ward and had my arm around his shoulder. Oakley testified that it would have been "almost" impossible because the detention cell doors are solid except for a narrow window slit.

The Reverend Father F. Leon Cahill, Catholic chaplain, testified that while he had sensed tension building up for a year-and-a-half, and while he heard many complaints against parole board tactics, he had not anticipated a riot. Asked about the counselor system, Fr. Cahill said that his experience was that counselor and custodial staffs were both easy to approach, and that he was unprepared for the revelations of rift between the two departments.

The union met again on Tuesday night, May 6, at the Otsego Hotel in Jackson. Guard Bernard Walicki said that, "Ward told me the day Dr. Fox was put on detached service that he had forced Fox to make that speech to inmates." Primary purpose of the meeting, however, was a 22-point list of resolutions designed to increase security at the prison, ranging from architectural changes to adequate training for new officers. One of the key resolutions was eliminated after an agreement with the warden had been reached, and Mr. Grosvenor, state representative for the union, reported that, "The counselors will be assigned a definite area of jurisdiction and they won't leave it." Guards interjected other suggestions by the dozen into the prepared list of resolutions. Modern weapons and fresh ammunition, a continuing training program, permitting the warden to run the prison without interference from Lansing, an improved retirement program, rise in salaries, specific plans to guide the custodial force in case of emergency, freedom of officers to testify at prison investigations without fear of reprisals, investigation to learn why paroles are not granted in cases where an inmate's good record warrants one, elevation of prison officials through custodial ranks, removal of 15-block outside the walls, and fewer cans and bottles available in the inmate store were a few of the demands. Other suggested demands included increasing the guard force in industrial plants, tighter security at the refrigeration plant because of potential "blow-up" gases, complaints that the prison "chain of command" is too cumbersome, and familiarizing the State Police with the physical lay-out of the prison.

The committee continued to meet throughout the week. The testimony ran the gamut: accurate, inaccurate, and misleading. When those classifications of information are collected, it is difficult to align the data in an accurate pattern.

Commissioner of Police Donald S. Leonard testified Thursday morning. He said that, "When Dr. Fox said we

were working toward a surrender too fast, I walked out of
Warden Julian N. Frisbie's office in disgust." He likened the
prison negotiations to a labor dispute, and said that he had not
favored signing the contract. He said that my negotiations
were "too long." When asked by Dodd whether he thought at
any time that 15-block should be rushed, he replied, "No."

I recalled the governor's speech to the legislature in which
such a plan had been suggested by Leonard and Brooks on
Wednesday night. Commissioner Leonard said that a deadline for the mutiny had been suggested but that none was
ever set. He said that an ultimatum of· one hour for the inmates in the beseiged block to surrender was never considered. He said, "I considered it proper from the start to go
along with the men in 15-block, but the time should have
been shortened." He favored the approach used, since it was
the only way to spare the guard's lives. When I read the newspapers, it was hard to believe that this man had testified in
such a fashion. It was so different from his actions during the
riot.

Commissioner Leonard had misled the committee, if the
newspaper accounts are correct. In answer to the questioning,
he said that he had not intended to "storm the block." That
was a play on words. He had proposed to blast it, but there
was nothing in the papers that indicated that this point had
ever been cleared up. I have witnesses who testify that they
heard him as early as Wednesday afternoon calling for "storming the block" and a "show of force." I don't know that the
committee even knew that he had moved hundreds of pounds
of TNT and other ammunition into the prison on Wednesday
night, April 23, for the purpose of blasting the block! This
manner of behavior before a fact-finding committee on the
part of a public official intensified my already well-developed
disrespect for Donald S. Leonard!

Attorney General Frank Millard's investigation got under way. He said that the investigation would not whitewash
anybody and that it was not to be political in any form. His
objectives were (1) to find out who committed crimes within

the prison and (2) to determine if there was misfeasance, malfeasance, or nonfeasance on the part of prison or state officials. Millard said, "Somebody has to be punished." Tape recordings made at the prison would be used, including those made by telephone calls from 15-block. The public, including newsmen, were barred.

Ken McCormick was reported to have spent considerable time with Mrs. Virginia Dunayski, the telephone operator. I was told he even took her to supper. It was the following day that she became a witness for the committee. She reported that she had monitored the telephone calls between Ward and me. She said that Ward had not said that I had to take him off the hook prior to the surrender. She said that I did not have to make the speech. I remember wondering how one operator could monitor one call in its entirety when she was occupied with five outside trunk lines kept busy by newsmen who waited in lines to make long-distance calls. Further, the State Police were recording all telephone calls emanating from 15-block. I knew that all the fact-finding committee had to do would be to play the recording and they would find the answer they wanted—or did they want the accurate information? The records of the phone calls emanating from 15-block to everyone else were available. The recordings of the telephone calls emanating from 15-block to my residence— the most important calls of all—were mysteriously missing! They were never made available to the committee. Did Donald S. Leonard destroy them? Were they never made? Where are they?

Earl Ward testified before the committee, and took full credit for writing the "congratulations" speech. He said he couldn't understand why I had withheld announcing it, although he had pledged me to secrecy. While he was unable to get a press conference after the riot, he had released me by his note to Austin MacCormick. Among other things, Ward said that the State Prison of Southern Michigan was the best state prison he had ever been in, and, "Any inmate who says it isn't is a liar. There's no gripe there." Immediately after his testimony, he was returned to the Howell Jail, complete with manacles and leg-irons.

During Warden Frisbie's testimony, he said that he had not heard Commissioner Brooks give me the one-hour ultimatum. I can believe that neither Frisbie nor Leonard heard it because of the confusion in the room and the fact that Brooks and I were in individual conversation at the end of the table. I do not think the warden or Leonard were inaccurate in this instance. They just did not hear it. There was no report that the committee had asked Commissioner Brooks the same question.

On Friday, Commissioner Brooks and Assistant Deputy Warden George Bacon were interviewed. Deputy Bacon said he thought custody should be paramount in all prison policy. In answer to questioning, he said that some of my decisions regarding inmates had made the job of custodial officers more difficult. I assume that he referred to having Alcoholics Anonymous and chess club meetings in the school on Saturdays, keeping the library open longer hours, and similar items. He opposed the transfer of trusty selection and work assignments to the treatment division. He said that the inmates felt that the parole board was resentencing them when they appeared before the board. Bacon said that the parole board should follow the judge's recommendations except when the public safety and health was concerned.

Repeating: there was no evidence in the news that Commissioner Brooks had been asked about the one-hour ultimatum he had given me on Thursday morning, April 24, about nine o'clock. Commissioner Brooks testified that he could not ascribe the riot to any particular cause. He said further, "No prisoner has ever had preferred treatment from me for that prisoner's own sake—only for the institution's sake." I reread the news report. While I could not prove Commissioner Brooks' intentions in days gone by, some of his preferred treatment was actually "preferred" treatment in my opinion, and the "good of the institution" was not concerned. I asked myself how men of the stature of Brooks and Leonard could blandly say such things under oath to a committee. True, I was only reading newspaper reports that could have been inaccurate.

I made mental notes of things that should be drawn to the attention of the committee as they appeared in the newspapers. Friday came and went, however, and the committee never called. Their investigation closed Friday noon. My impression was that this committee had obtained the information it wanted with the slant it wanted. Accuracy meant little, if the newspaper reports were correct.

After repeated attacks by prison people, the parole board asked Governor Williams for a competent, professional, and impartial investigation of the charges that the parole board policies had caused the riot at Jackson. The parole board charged that the riot stemmed from prison mismanagement rather than the "tough attitude" of the parole board.

Officer Neil Oakley resigned suddenly. Simultaneously, I noted that the letter written by inmate Embree who wanted to testify before the committee that Oakley had beat him was never made public. Friends reported that Oakley said he quit because the warden told him to change his story about Fox. I didn't believe that, because, from my point of view, the warden was more interested in saving himself than Fox! I believe that the warden came into possession of Embree's letter and advised Oakley to quit because otherwise he would have to turn the letter over to the "fact-finding" committee. I do not believe that the committee ever saw that letter.

On Monday, May 10, I talked at the University of Michigan's Natural Science Auditorium, sponsored by the Sociology Club. I reviewed what happened during the riot, just as I had reviewed it for the fact-finding committee. I indicated that the techniques I used were the only means available to save the lives of the hostages during the 93-hour mutiny. I answered many questions. The only one I attempted to evade was whether or not I had any feelings about the governor's fact-finding committee. I said "Yes," and went on to the next question. Subsequently, I said that while I did have feelings about it, I didn't consider it fair to make statements about it until after the committee had reported.

On Monday night, Ward created havoc in the jail at Howell. At the request of Sheriff Bassett, Commissioner Brooks agreed to request Ward's transfer to the Ionia State Hospital. Ward had shouted, cursed, smashed furniture in his cell, torn out the light, and tried to break up the sanitary facilities.

The State Administrative Board, meanwhile, refused to express itself in favor of hiring more guards, as the governor had requested, but turned the matter over to the Civil Service Commission for study. State Controller Robert Steadman reported that his office had set the losses during the riot at $1,091,548. He recommended that the laundry equipment be restored, but placed in the building formerly used for central stores.

One of the most significant occurrences was a telephone call from Dr. Ralph S. Banay, Secretary of the Medical Correctional Association. He invited me to speak at their luncheon meeting at the annual American Psychiatric Association meeting in Atlantic City on May 12. I thanked him for the invitation and accepted.

My wife and I headed toward Atlantic City. We arrived Wednesday morning, and went to the hotel. After talking with Dr. Banay and some very learned men in the psychiatric field, I was ushered into the room and seated. Dr. Banay pointed out some of the men present. I was awed in the presence of these men at whose literary feet I had studied and whose writings I had quoted, but whom I had never met. Men like Dr. Ben Karpman, Dr. J. L. Moreno, Dr. Wilson, Dr. Pescor, Dr. Davidoff, and many others of equal prominence sat around the tables. When I was introduced, I felt like apologizing for my presence. These men were very sympathetic, however, and they helped me to feel at ease. They were very friendly in the discussion afterward. Some suggested other jobs I might like to consider. After a friendly and pleasant luncheon and afternoon, we bade them good-by, and started toward New York City. Under the genial guidance of friends in Brooklyn, Mr. and Mrs. Jules Baer, we saw New York City's highlights.

The New York papers carried stories of the fact-finding committee's report. The warden was blamed for the big riot causing most of the damage, and it was implied that the committee didn't understand my speech. That looked better than I had anticipated. The publicity in the Eastern papers had been more objective than the Michigan publicity. Some of the papers had reported that I was the only person who had done anything during the riot. Dr. David Dressler, writing in the *New York Post*, pointed out that the counselor program was a good idea that was crippled before it started. Dr. Dressler said that as he went through the prison that, except for the counselors, "no one in the place really believes in a program of rehabilitation. When guards let down their hair, they spoke in crudest terms of prisoners, advocated beatings and solitary confinement." Guards call counselors' work "silly." He concluded that "Michigan is making habitual offenders in Jackson."

Returning to Michigan on Saturday evening, I read the collected week's local papers and was somewhat amazed by the difference in publicity from that in the New York papers. The committee had criticized the warden, but it had blasted me! It was as I had originally expected, but I had hoped that the New York papers had reported fully. Reviewing the report and the publicity, I think that perhaps the New York papers had reported more accurately, whereas the Michigan papers had embellished by emphasis the slant they desired.

The report said that the riot was not a riot of protest, but rather the result of an "atmosphere made highly explosive by violent internal tensions." This obviously referred to a remark I made in the early stages of the riot when Custody's 15-block bastion had been taken over, guards were accused of brutality, custodial deputy Bacon was called to be shown the hand weapons, and guards were held hostage—I had remarked that the riot was obviously a protest against Custody.

They reported that the causes of the riot "are fundamental of heterogeneous prison population and lack of adequate space for segregation." They witnessed no "creditable evidence" of sadistic brutality or brutal treatment. That term, "creditable evidence," seemed to me to be a convenient concept for that committee! The committee said that there were too few guards, and that the guards had been poorly trained and were "dangerously inexperienced." The most important factors leading to the riot according to the committee, were the prison's tremendous size, overcrowding, and lack of segregation.

The committee criticized the administration for not eliminating the conflict between Custody and Individual Treatment. They pointed to the "extreme disparity" between the pay of guards and the pay of counselors. They wanted the idea of capital punishment re-examined. The policies of the parole board were criticized by witnesses, but the committee did not take a position as to whether the charges were just. The warden was criticized for making the decision to feed the men in the dining room on Monday morning, thereby letting the men loose who did most of the damage.

The committee attacked me most bitterly, as I had expected ever since meeting with them. They said I made a valuable contribution to settling the riot, but then severely criticized me, and with emotion. They described my actions as "inexplicable." The committee was not satisfied with the "completely humiliating terms" of surrender. They said that those terms would not have been necessary had I taken a firmer attitude. They said that Ward at no time demanded that I make the talk, but that he had merely asked me to interpret Ward's surrender decision to the other inmates. They reported, "Giving Fox generous credit for the best motives in interpreting Ward's demands in the way he did, even assuming he thought he was making the broadcast 'with a gun at his head' (which assumption is not entirely borne out by the evidence), his subsequent actions cannot be justified nor satisfactorily explained." I do not know what the committee meant by "subsequent actions." They called the speech "a most extraordinary and to us amazing utterance," and discredited the idea that I was pledged to secrecy regarding Ward's part in making the broadcast.

The *Detroit Free Press*, and again I suspect the hand of Ken McCormick, followed with an editorial in which it absolved the "present state administration." Then the editorial went on:

> The glaring exception of this generality is to be found in the pointed fault found with current administrative personnel. Deputy Warden Vernon Fox was especially criticized for his "congratulatory" message.

The *Jackson Citizen-Patriot* also followed with an editorial. In part, its editorial was as follows:

> Dr. Fox has quite a following of persons who argue that he is being persecuted and that he actually is a hero. He is being kept busy with speaking engagements before audiences that give him respectful attention and rousing ovations. He is a capable, persuasive speaker.
>
> The governor's committee, after hearing days of testimony from Dr. Fox and other prison personnel and inmates, is not convinced that he is above reproach.
>
> * * * * *
>
> Dr. Fox had his chance to explain his conduct before this committee and apparently was far less convincing than he is when appearing before audiences which have only superficial knowledge of what happened at Southern Michigan prison during that hectic week of the riot.
>
> But we do recommend that those who are so certain that Dr. Fox is being mistreated, read the report of the governor's fact-finding committee.

Not because of the editorial, but because I didn't know how the committee's ideas got so jumbled in the newspapers, I decided to read the report if I could get a copy of it.

The report indicated that twenty-five witnesses were

heard and the committee had had access to all records of
the prison and the Michigan State Police. The board said
that they place no credence in the testimony of the "convict
leaders" unless substantiated by that of third persons, and
that no issue was resolved upon that testimony. The chrono-
logical story of the riot was reported quite accurately, but I
thought with too much emphasis on the Thursday morning
assertion by inmate Moore that the surrender was a double-
cross. It may have been quite accurate, however, in reporting the credence placed on it by Commissioners Brooks and
Leonard.

Sections of the report attempted to find causes of the riot.
Testimony of the prisoners indicated that the causes were:

1. Poor, insufficient, or contaminated food.
2. Inadequate, sanitary, or oppressive housing.
3. General or sadistic brutality practiced by prison officials upon inmates.
4. Callous or inhuman prison administration.

The committee discredited all the prisoners' reasons.

The reasons apparently were that the excessive size of
the prison, overcrowded conditions, and the heterogeneous
population without adequate segregation facilities created a
condition of constant tension. The antipathy against the parole board aggravated this tension. Lack of personnel caused
discontinuance of the guard training school. A properly
trained and efficient custodial staff would not have permitted at least three knives to be in possession of inmates locked
in 15-block. The working of the indeterminate sentence law
caused some prisoner unrest. The differences in philosophy
between the custodial departments and individual treatment
were considered to be a cause, though it was not once supported by the testimony from anyone, and several of us repeated that these "differences" were grossly exaggerated.

The first inaccuracy appeared on page 11 of the report,
when the "prison telephone operator [Mrs. Virginia Dunay-
ski] who monitored this conversation testified that this condition was not imposed." First, there were five trunk lines

into the prison, kept busy by lines of newsmen waiting to call their papers. The switchboard is operated by one girl at any given time, and the operator was kept busy by newsmen at all hours since the riot started almost four days before. No lone operator could possibly have monitored an entire telephone conversation. The second point I hesitate to make, because I have never administered an intelligence test to Mrs. Dunayski. Thirdly, the Michigan State Police made recordings of all telephone conversations emanating from 15-block. I again ask as I have asked before: where is that tape? That recording would have shown whether or not the condition had been imposed! Further, the specific arrangements and details did not go over the telephone wire, but were in face-to-face conversation at 15-block. Nevertheless, the recorded conversation would have taken care of the issue.

On page 12, the report said that no particular phraseology had been suggested by Ward, which was in part correct. Part of the omission was my fault, in that I had become angry in the hearing and stated that Ward had not presented any ideas and that I had written the entire thing! Actually, Ward had presented several ideas, such as "no State Police shall be in evidence."

On page 16, the report began to discuss different theories of penology held by Custody and by Individual Treatment. On page 17, the report continues, "While there has been no testimony to the effect that such differences were a contributing factor to the riots, the Board feels that, marked and positive as they were, they cannot fail to have manifested themselves to the prison population, thus contributing to the general unrest." The tone supported custody throughout, and on page 18, the committee called for a re-examination of capital punishment. After pointing out that my chief assistant, Deputy Bill Johnson, was also "custodially minded" (which was certainly true!), the committee said that there should "be some means for a summary elimination of offending personnel in cases in which disagreements have reached the point of such intense partisanship that the security of the institution may be jeopardized."

The committee reported that it was of the opinion that it was wise that no "hasty plan of forcible seizure of Block 15" was attempted when the riot started on Sunday night. It called the feeding of the inmates on Monday morning an unwise decision.

Pages 21 to 24, inclusive, were devoted to criticizing me. They indicated that "When his actions bring the authority of the state into disrepute and subject it to opprobrium and disparagement, such actions cannot be excused . . ." My reaction was that the board had failed to realize that the terms of surrender were progressive principles of penology prepared by a state official who then talked the inmates into accepting them, and saved the guard hostages at the same time. That did not seem to me to be disreputable and subjecting the state to opprobrium and disparagement!

The board said that they were not satisfied that "such completely humiliating terms would have been necessary had Deputy Fox taken a firmer attitude in his negotiations." Other officials had "assumed," the report continued, that the inmates would give up on Thursday, and Commissioner Leonard in particular "began to consider" other means of effecting the release of the hostages. This "beginning to consider" apparently referred to the hundreds of pounds of TNT that Leonard had piled in the administration building and that he wanted to use starting Wednesday afternoon.

The report said that although Warden Frisbie was available and had instructed me to clear all broadcasts with him, it was not done. My reply to that is that Warden Frisbie was in press conference when the speech was ready, and was not available, while time was running out. Secondly, while we agreed on Tuesday morning that I would check broadcasts with him, it was my suggestion and his agreement, rather than his order. Further, Commissioner Brooks assumed personal charge of the situation on Wednesday morning, set up offices in the parole board room, and told me to report directly to him. This action superseded the warden's authority in regard to the riot, particularly since this was an emergency situation in which I was given sole responsibility for 15-block, over which I had heretofore had absolutely no jurisdiction at any time. I think that most impartial hearing boards would have accounted for these considerations.

The report said that I may have thought I was making the broadcast "with a gun at his head," but, they added, "which assumption is not wholly borne out by the evidence." I have previously referred to the newspaper reports in which the committee's inept questioning and/or Commissioner Leonard's evasive answers suggested that there was no thought of storming the block. This was contrary to the facts, as I saw them, which included the moving in of TNT and Leonard's repeated and emotionalized demands for a show of force.

The committee set the pattern to be followed in criticizing the speech. They had made a major issue of the minor reason: whether or not Ward had demanded that I give the speech. They said Ward had merely asked me to "interpret" his surrender to the other inmates. The major reason for the speech—that of peacefully dislodging 169 reluctant and dangerous prisoners and eight hostages from their 15-block bastion by a specific deadline to prevent carnage—was never questioned.

The committee was disposed to "completely discredit any suggestion" that I was pledged to secrecy, and further, I was released from that pledge on Friday afternoon. The report said that it "is completely out of character for Ward to shrink from further proof of his complete subjugation of the constituted authorities." As I said previously, apparently inconsistent behavior from a man like Ward is to be expected. The committee accepted other reports of Ward's "insane, illogical rantings" and similar aberrations from the warden and others without question.

The committee said that after I was released from the "pledge," I had told nobody. Quite the contrary, I thought

I had told the world when news reports were released covering my talk to the Optimists Club in Lansing on the Monday following the riot. I told Warden Frisbie and Commissioner Brooks as well during that week that the speech was a term of early surrender. They had looked sympathetically at me and told me to keep quiet and they would handle everything. The two final paragraphs were, "His conduct as above set forth is to this board wholly inexplicable.

"We do not regard it as our function to attempt to harmonize Deputy Fox's actions with the duties and obligations of a public official."

And the goat was suffered to escape into the wilderness! The report said that all other officers of the prison and State Police demonstrated devotion to duty of the highest nature.

I decided that it was not the newspapers in this instance who had their facts jumbled! It had not been a trial. It was an inquisition. No scientific criminalistic device like the lie detector had even been suggested. This committee had reported feelings, emotions, accusations, and innuendo, some of which the committee itself reported were not based on findings in the testimony, distorted as some of it was. Testimony fitting the bias of the committee was accepted. Other testimony was ignored. I was not called back, as had been promised, to discuss administration and the refutation of false or biased charges. Truth had ceased to matter. For political reasons, the governor had to accept his committee's findings without reservation, regardless of his own knowledge of the facts. It gave him a point of origin from which to operate as long as feeling was divided; and its accuracy was not important.

After that report was issued, Senators Gilbert and Heath introduced a resolution into the senate as follows:

> Whereas, the people of the state of Michigan are shocked and outraged not only by the most serious riot which resulted in the physical plant of the State Prison of Southern Michigan, but by the inept and disgraceful

coddling of the prison population during and following the riot, and

Whereas, the report of the governor's committee concerning the facts regarding the riot and the causes thereof and press reports on the event clearly demonstrates that Dr. Vernon Fox is possessed of a total lack of and an absolute misconception of his duties to the state as deputy warden of the prison and is totally unfit to participate in any part or portion of the prison administration as indicated by his negotiations with the criminal population wherein he agreed, without the approval of his superiors, to the steak and ice cream dinner given the inmates of Cell Block No. 15 and his subsequent unauthorized broadcast to the prisoners, using such phrases as "Earl Ward, Jack Hyatt, Jarboe and all the others in charge are men of their word"—"Earl Ward is a natural leader"—"Their word has been good"—"This may presage a new era . . ."—"They have done a service"—"Congratulations to you men of 15-Block!"; now therefore be it.

Resolved that it is the consensus of the members of the Michigan State Senate that Commissioner Brooks forthwith fire, discharge and completely suspend said Dr. Vernon Fox from any and all duties as deputy warden and from every other duty in connection with prison administration, according Dr. Fox such recourse as he may have in the nature of a hearing before the Civil Service Commission in case he desires such proceeding.

The resolution was referred to the Committee on Senate Business and was never reported out.

The governor's "fact-finding" committee had taught me a lot about political fact-finding committees. Whereas I had previously considered them all to be fact-finding, interested only in facts, I discovered that they can be merely political tools by which governors and others transfer responsibility. I suspect that by proper handling, the committee could be manipulated to favor the witness, provided the witness is cognizant of the situation as it really is, with greater emphasis on political and other relationships than upon the facts under consideration. Dr. David Dressler, former executive director of the New York Parole Board and author of two books, *Probation and Parole* and *Parole Chief*, wrote to me, "Had you had some public relations advice, the situation would have swung the other way. You would have emerged as the hero of the day, let down at the end by the people for whom you were acting." This was exactly what had happened!

There were persistent reports that the disturbances in the prison were continuing. Warden Frisbie reported on May 13 that the situation "is absolutely under control." He said that they were making no deals with inmates, and that they are going to be tough with them now. The trouble-makers were going into 9-block, according to the warden, and "all they can do is yell, throw food trays to the floor and bang on their bars." He said that they were in the process of screening the inmates to find those who were trouble-makers and those who were not. He reported that 7-block had been granted dining-room privileges and limited yard privileges, and that 8-block would be next. Blocks 1 through 5 had already been granted those privileges. Soon then, only 9-block and 12-block would be restricted.

One of the papers reported that Brooks had said, "Fox is on his way out," and that I was currently in the East looking for other connections. That was not true. The warden telephoned Sunday morning to assure me that he had nothing to do with that, that he did not practice Communist tactics. I thanked the warden for his concern and hung up.

It was early Sunday afternoon when Commissioner Brooks telephoned. He wanted to meet me at the Hotel Hayes, in the lobby. I called to Laura, my wife, and asked her if she wanted to accompany me to my last conference with Commissioner Brooks. She came with me. We met Commissioner and Mrs. Brooks in the lobby. After brief introductory salutations, Commissioner Brooks suggested that I go with him to another section of the lobby. I complied and motioned Laura to come with us. Mrs. Brooks came, too. We sat down to talk.

He told me that there had been an unpleasant turn of events. The legislature wanted me off the payroll. I told him the facts regarding the speech, and that the legislators did not understand. Commissioner Brooks agreed that I was in the right, but did not agree that the legislators didn't understand. Rather, he said, they didn't *want* to understand. Commissioner Brooks said he had tried to explain the situation, maybe even transfer me to another state department or something, but the legislators were after a scapegoat for political reasons, and that I was the most handy scapegoat they could find. My past record meant nothing. All the Republicans were against me, since the Corrections Department was operated by a Democratic governor's appointee. The Democrats under leadership of Senator Blondy would stand up to be counted in my favor, but the Republicans were the majority party. Since I had no party affiliation at all, had never voted a straight ticket in my life, the alignment must have been on the basis of the party in power, rather than my political thinking. Commissioner Brooks said that the Democratic governor wanted to beat the Republican legislature to the punch.

I asked him if he meant that this was merely a political putsch in which neither justice nor the good of the state was to be considered. The answer was in the affirmative. I asked him if he was telling me either to resign or risk dismissal. He evaded that question by indicating that he was merely reporting a situation as he had been instructed to by the governor. At this time, I told him that it had been my decision to resign anyway, but that I intended to whip my opposition in the civil service hearing or in the State Supreme Court first, if necessary.

To explore his thinking, I asked him if I resigned, how long I would be on the payroll. He said he couldn't promise anything, but he'd do the best he could. I reminded him that he had permitted Sydney Moskowitz, a parole board member to take a questionable sick leave on full pay since December, that this was May—and how analogous was my case to that of Moskowitz? He said that Moskowitz would not be with the department long. I asked him about my overtime hours that had exceeded 1,600 in two years. He replied that anyone should be able to do his job in forty hours per week. I was furious. I thought of the hours I had put in on extra jobs, improving of program, Rorschach testing, and other duties, only to be told that I should be able to do my job in forty hours!

He asked me what I proposed to do. I told him that I didn't know. He asked me what my inclination was. I told him I was inclined to resign—but only after I had whipped the opposition. He said the governor wanted to know what I was going to do. I told him I'd let him know when I decided. The governor wanted to know today. The governor would have to wait!

I talked to many of my friends. Cliff Davis advised me to take it to civil service. I would win in a fair hearing. The warden had told me that I wouldn't get a fair hearing. Further, the warden and I agreed that the people who had misrepresented to the committee would also misrepresent to the Civil Service Commission. The Civil Service Commission would not buck the legislature and governor. I knew that from former Warden Ralph Benson's experience. I didn't propose to go through the experience that ruined Ralph Benson's health. That is why I wanted to go to the Supreme Court as rapidly as possible, beat them, and then resign.

Dr. Floyd Starr, Dr. Ernest B. Harper, Dr. Gustav Gilbert, Dr. Wilbur Brookover, and others all advised me to resign. Their point was that there was nothing to be gained in a political fight that was certain to get dirty. I didn't mind getting dirty. The situation was dirty already.

With so much advice to resign coming from men I had considered to be competent, I was left with doubt. I wanted badly to whip them and then resign. I didn't want to run away from what looked like a good brawl. They told me that there was nothing to be won, that any victory would be an empty one, and that the prudent thing would be to resign. The warden had told me the same thing, but his words had become meaningless to me, since he had already demonstrated, it seemed to me, that the only thing in which he was interested was in saving his own position. His actions after the riot had been just as limp as were his actions during the riot! I waited!

When I went to the office of the Department of Corrections in Lansing, my friends welcomed me. Harold "Kelly" Kachelski said that a lot of people are "getting on the bandwagon," meaning that they were lining up with the commissioner. Kelly thought that if I were all right a month ago, I must be all right now. I found that Gus Harrison had been vociferous in his criticism of me. I didn't recall having seen Gus at the riot or anywhere near it. Gilman gave me a sick smile.

I spoke at the Michigan State College Club on Tuesday noon, May 18. After the talk, Dr. Gilbert told me he thought I should let the public know about the political maneuvering. His advice was highly regarded. It was obvious that Governor Williams and Commissioner Brooks wanted to keep it secret. They wanted to appease my Republican and newspaper editor critics and at the same time not alienate my professional, academic, and public supporters. A newsman approached me asking about any pressure that was being brought to bear on me. He had heard such a rumor in the Department of Psychology at Michigan State, and he wanted to check. I told him that I had been given an ultimatum to resign or risk dismissal, and that they wanted the answer last Sunday. I had not decided yet. I wanted to fight it, but my advisers favored resignation, since that had been my ultimate intention anyway.

That afternoon, several of my advisers conferred, person-to-person and by telephone. Checking revealed that the senate would probably pass the resolution by the Republican majority, and it carried a rider eliminating the appropriation of my salary. Information from the governor's office was that G. Mennen Williams was personally sympathetic with my position, but that politically he had to act otherwise. I could not accept that position. I thought that Williams was a shrewd politician who was trying to placate both sides.

On Tuesday, May 20, I decided to resign, to remain on the payroll through June. I so notified Commissioner Brooks by telephone and prepared the following letter under date of May 20:

Dear Commissioner Brooks,

My handling of the riot at the State Prison of Southern Michigan between April 20 and April 24, 1952, was praised at the time, but was criticized when the immediate frustration was over. It is my firm conviction that the riot could have been handled in no other way without losing the lives of citizens of Michigan. My professional colleagues have been in enthusiastic agreement. However, criticism from others has made my tenure embarrassing to the governor.

Events in the past month have accentuated the wide disparity between the political and professional concepts of prison programs. It is obvious to me that for a long time to come in Michigan the expression of aggression has won the support of the political leaders who control the destiny of the Department of Corrections. After working conscientiously for an adequate rehabilitative program in Michigan's correctional system for ten years, I have seen the progress we had achieved rendered ineffective in the past month. Michigan is not ready for the rehabilitative program for which I stand. Consequently, I tender my resignation.

Commissioner Brooks denied that he had given me an ultimatum to resign or be fired. "I just don't work that way," he said. In part, his statement was as follows:

I simply talked the situation over with him, pointing out that he was going to be made a whipping boy for a long time if he stayed here. I pointed out that certain legislators had already made him a political issue by demanding that he be fired.

Furthermore, I pointed out that his utility to the system had been gravely impaired. Some of the guards have threatened to walk out if he came back and I wouldn't know where to assign him under the circumstances.

Dr. Fox is a capable man who has done pioneer work in rehabilitation of inmates and has earned a national reputation among penologists.

CHAPTER IX

Aftermath in Michigan

On the day I resigned, there were disturbances at the prison. State Police cars sped past my residence on their way to the prison, sirens screaming. Guards were called out. Inmates got word to me through trusties that the disturbance was because of my resignation. Personnel who called confirmed it. The newspapers reported the warden as saying that he was sure that the disturbance had nothing to do with my resignation. At any rate, water hoses were used to quell the riot.

On the same day, Sydney Moskowitz was removed from the parole board. Moskowitz had been an employee of the Department of Corrections for fifteen years. Starting as a psychologist, he had been parole eligibility examiner, assistant deputy warden, parole board member, and "jack-of-all-trades" or "trouble-shooter" with the department. Commissioner Brooks had previously told me that he had "outlived his usefulness." Cliff Davis, departmental personnel officer, told civil service that letters to him in Los Angeles had gone unanswered. I do not know what went on between Brooks and Moskowitz.

The *Jackson Citizen-Patriot*, ever ready to correct statements to fit its editorial policy, again "corrected" my statement. Their editorial following my resignation began as follows:

Dr. Vernon Fox confuses the issue in his resignation statement that he realizes "the state is now not ready for the rehabilitation program for which I stand."

Rehabilitation of prisoners at Southern Michigan Prison is not now, and never has been, the issue in the controversy over the psychologist.

The issues are the coddling of prisoners and an asinine statement to leaders of the riot.

The *Battle Creek Enquirer and News* carried a different version of the issues on its editorial page:

Under the circumstances, it was probably necessary that Dr. Vernon Fox be removed from association with Michigan's penal program. But his removal is Michigan's loss, and it need not have been necessary.

The basic conflict, within our penal system and outside it, between opposing theories of penology is responsible.

There are those who believe prison is for punishment, to hold a criminal in custody for the term of his sentence and then to return the criminal to freedom. There are others who believe prison is for punishment *and* rehabilitation, to take a person who has committed a crime and at the end of his sentence to return him to society as a useful citizen.

Dr. Fox, by becoming a controversial figure in this conflict, probably lost his usefulness in the prison system. But by the same token, he stimulated public concern with the state's penal problems and has caused some soul-searching by officials in positions of public responsibility.

For that, as well as for ending the riot at Jackson Prison without death or injury of any guard, Dr. Fox deserves better treatment than he has received from his state.

Corrections Commissioner Earnest C. Brooks made Dr. Fox's position clear when he told him "that he was going to be made a whipping boy for a long time to come if he stayed." "I wouldn't know where to assign him under the circumstances," Mr. Brooks admitted. "Dr. Fox is a capable man and has done pioneer work in the rehabilitation of inmates. He shouldn't have any trouble getting a job elsewhere."

Well, Dr. Fox has resigned, and removed himself from the state's problems as a point of controversy. But the problem remains. There is still tension in the prison at Jackson. It is likely to continue until there is more unanimity on policy within the penal system than there has been in recent years.

On the same day, my talk to the Albion Exchange Club, which I consider my "home-town" club, was reported accurately in the *Battle Creek Enquirer and News*, and appeared on the front page. The same talk was reported inaccurately in the club bulletin, apparently in another of the too-frequent efforts to afford me protection. I wasn't even mentioned by the *Albion Evening Recorder*, whose editor, Jack Bedient, had previously written a critical and uninformed editorial about me.

After my resignation, several resignations followed. Mr. William Richardson, considered by many custodial and treatment personnel as being the best music director the prison ever had, resigned when he found that Bill Johnson would be his immediate superior. He told me that Johnson had told him that all musicians were homosexual. Counselor Ed Green resigned and went into industry. Group Therapist Joe B. Dellinger resigned to become Chief of the Section on Alcohol Studies in the Bureau of Preventive Medicine of the State of Maryland. A few months later, the last vestige of the research program went with the resignation of Miss Joann Volakakis. Other of the trained and competent personnel began looking for other jobs. Many found them, including Director of Education Ferris C. Young, who went to the National Bank of Jackson as personnel director. Greg Miller completed his doctorate and joined the faculty at Michigan State.

There were also forced resignations and dismissals. Counselor Hilliard was dismissed for attempting to assist in the placement of a prisoner in a job, which is actually a parole function. The job of assistant recreation director was abolished so that the incumbent J. C. Williams, a Negro member of Michigan State's varsity football team for three years, was left without a position. Williams had conflicted with custody on several occasions. The speech correctionist was dismissed on charges of homosexuality, but individual treatment personnel have expressed doubt as to the validity of the charge brought by two custodial personnel. The remark was made that when confronted with such a charge, one can't win. Even if he wins in court, his reputation suffers.

Dr. Gustav Gilbert, associate professor of psychology at Michigan State, formerly psychologist at the Nuremberg trials and author of *Nuremberg Diary* and *Psychology of Dictatorship*, examined the riot leaders. He spent at least fourteen hours with Earl Ward. His diagnosis of Ward was psychopathic personality with homicidal tendencies. The final paragraph in his report on Ward was:

> The psychological examination shows that this man has both the intelligence (I.Q. 122) and the perverted emotions to be a dangerous criminal, in spite of his deceptively charming personality. Like the typical psychopath, he is in full possession of his senses and understands the difference between right and wrong, but holds social standards in utter contempt, preferring to act out and gratify his own impulses of aggression and seduction, and substituting his own peculiarly perverted code of "fair play." There can be no doubt that he would have killed the hostages in the Jackson Prison riot if Dr. Fox had not succeeded in appealing to this sense of "fair play" or if force had been used to quell the riot.

I am sure that the so-called "fact-finding" committee would not have been interested in such information.

I didn't know for sure what kind of work I wanted to go into at this time. I knew that I wanted to do something entirely different for a while. I was not sure that I wanted university work. In order to occupy my time and to get as wide a selection of possibilities for employment as possible, I wrote letters of application by the score. Warning my friends that they might as well prepare letters of recommendations with many carbons, I scattered my applications over the country. Some college presidents were afraid of the publicity I had had. Some industrialists had called it "a million dollars worth of advertising." I made trips to Detroit, Toledo, Cleveland, and other cities to keep busy through May and June while replies to my applications were being returned. Industrial placement in Jackson was available, but I didn't take advantage of it. There was the possibility of editing a book, but it did not look good to me. I was in New York City when the job arrived that I wanted. Ray E. Hibbs & Associates, management consultants, of Toledo, Ohio, had telegraphed an opportunity. I took it. I had always wanted some experience with a management consultant firm. This was that opportunity. I accepted that position on a temporary basis.

In the meantime in the Department of Corrections, Warden Frisbie told the legislative committee considering emergency appropriations that Commissioner Brooks had by-passed him and countermanded him. Further, Warden Frisbie testified that Deputy Bacon on occasion had actually reversed his orders. The members of the legislative committee commented that apparently some of the stories of Brooks' meddling in prison affairs were true. He told them that there was a running fight between those in charge of custody and those in charge of rehabilitation for power and authority at the prison. The warden said that there was no co-operation between the counselors and the parole board. He said that he needed more guards, since the proportion of guards to inmates made it necessary for the guards to get along with the inmates rather than the inmates getting along with the guards. Frisbie was apparently "playing politics" with the legislators. He had never before intimated that I was engaging in a running fight for power and authority. Rather, I had been engaging in a running fight to make Deputy Bacon let me run my own department! He knew that, too! I think he was trying to build up ego-defense for his leaving me out on the limb. Such behavior can be explained in terms of ego-protection, but cannot be justified in terms of ethics.

The prison was in poor shape. Prisoners had been received on May 19 for the first time after the riot. Governor Williams announced that Frisbie's appointment as warden would continue to be on a probationary basis. The warden announced plans for a new disciplinary block isolated from the rest of the prison, a "flying squadron" of armed guards, and installation of three posts for armed guards inside the walls. The legislative committee tentatively decided to spend only about $400,000 for restoration of the laundry. Engineer L. D. Johnson said the job could be done for approximately $120,000 to $200,000.

In testimony before legislators on May 22, Warden Frisbie had revealed that his instructions and orders had been reversed on occasion by Assistant Deputy Warden George Bacon. I remembered hearing about some of those occasions.

Seymour J. Gilman had just been appointed deputy warden by Commissioner Brooks without approval of Warden Frisbie. Gilman assumed his duties on June 1. George Bacon voiced his criticism of the appointment and of Gilman. He said that friction had existed for a year between Gilman and Warden Frisbie. He stated further that Gilman was only slightly acquainted with either counselor or custodial activities at the prison. "The present appointment of Mr. Gilman tends to make a dangerous situation more dangerous," he continued. Commenting on Warden Frisbie's testimony concerning the steel doors in 15-block as an example of his countermanding orders, Bacon said, "if any misunderstanding developed, it was through the warden's failure to

consult me on the extended plan when that plan affected facilities under my control." He said that there should be one
deputy warden, a custodial man. He was referring to George
Bacon.

As a result of Bacon's blast at the appointment of Gilman
as deputy warden, he was suspended for two weeks by a personnel disciplinary board. He returned to work on July 6.

My former secretary, Frankie DeNato, had remained at
the prison. He had been Gilman's secretary for a week, without duties, when Gilman called him in to put him to work.
Gilman talked for several minutes, telling him that when
he rang the bell, he wanted Frankie to jump, and explaining
other manners in which he wanted Frankie to react. When
he finished, Frankie said, "Now, I want to tell you something.
This is my last day." And Frankie went to the personnel office
and resigned.

Appearing before the Joint Appropriations Committee,
Dr. Heyns, warden at the Michigan Reformatory at Ionia,
testified in favor of the "model prison law" which was on
Michigan's statues from 1937 to 1947. When the commissioner serves at the pleasure of the governor, as does Commissioner Brooks, he is a political appointee, and it makes
the department "nervous." Dr. Heyns pointed out that Williams had campaigned on that point, but had done nothing
about it during the three years he had been in office.

The legislative committee finally decided to provide
$200,000 for the laundry as proposed by the prison engineer,
L. D. Johnson, rather than the $400,000 as proposed by Gov-
ernor Williams and his advisors. Johnson, by the way, was
reported to have been subsequently reprimanded by Commissioner Brooks at the warden's residence for "showing up"
the governor and his advisors by estimating at half their proposed figure.

Disturbances continued. On one occasion in May an inmate was shot and killed, but the newspapers referred only
briefly to the fact that a man had been shot. This assisted in
minimizing the difficulty as far as the news was concerned.

Frequently, however, additional State Troopers were needed. On July 6, a rather serious riot occurred. Another man was shot and killed, and this time the newspapers said so. It had started in a slow fashion at 5:30 in 9-block, an open cell-block. It broke out in high pitch as far as noise was concerned by about 7:30, when some inmates tore bars off their cells and took two guards as hostages, after dropping a sheet bearing a message that they wanted to see Warden Frisbie. State Police were called at 8:00, Deputy Gilman came at about 8:40, and Gilman acceded to some of the demands, after which the uprising was over at about 10:30. As a result of this riot, Frisbie was dismissed on July 10. William Bannan, deputy warden at the reformatory at Ionia, was made acting warden at Jackson. Bannan was surprised to find that reports of tension at Jackson had not been exaggerated.

On July 15, a shift of top personnel was announced by Commissioner Brooks in Lansing and by Warden Bannan in Jackson. Bacon was shifted to "special duties" outside the walls. He was subsequently made head of the trusty division. Assistant Deputy Warden in Charge of the Trusty Division George Kropp was transferred to Ionia as deputy warden at the reformatory. Assistant Deputy Warden Robert Northrup was placed in charge of the new guard training program. Assistant Deputy Warden Bill Johnson and Deputy Gilman were the only ones who remained at their posts. Inspector Charles Cahill was promoted to replace Bacon as Assistant Deputy Warden in Charge of Custody. My position was abolished for lack of a qualified candidate. Captain Harold Tucker was promoted to replace Robert Northrup as assistant deputy warden in the custody department. Captain Chester Powers was promoted to replace Cahill as custodial inspector. All these shifts were, of course, acting appointments, awaiting civil service approval. That would seem to me to be a minor matter, however, based on previous observations of civil service acting in the face of politics.

Magazine articles began to appear. With Bill Fay, I told the story of the speech in *Collier's* of July 12, 1952, in which

I said that under similar conditions, I would do the same thing again. I expected the politicians and the members of the fact-finding committee to disagree because I was writing the facts they did not want written—or had not found despite their availability. At Bill Fay's suggestion, I prepared a note to go with the article as follows:

> According to newspaper accounts of testimony given under oath which has been at variance with facts presented in this article, I anticipate a denial of some of the material in this article. I am anxious to submit to a polygraph test covering these facts, provided others I name will similarly submit and provided further that *all* results be made public.

I decided that to put it in the first run would appear to be too defensive on my part. I withheld it to await the hue and cry of the politicians. I heard none. One of my friends said Commissioner Brooks remarked that I was taking credit for what the State Police did, but I never saw such comment in print.

The September, 1952, issue of *Pic* carried an article by a former inmate who said that too many "little men" are trying to operate Jackson. He said that I had become a trusted friend and adviser to the inmates. He referred to me as "the one qualified administration representative" at Jackson. Paul McClung wrote an accurate article in the August, 1951, issue of *Front Page Detective* under the title, "I Swapped Steaks and Ice Cream for 180 Lives." Gordon Shelly, an inmate at the time of the riot, wrote for the November, 1951, issue of *Startling Detective* under the title, "Inside Story of the Michigan Prison Riots." He said that "the cons here had a word for Dr. Fox—regular." He called me liberal, farsighted, a top psychologist and sociologist, but "above all a humanitarian."

Attorney General Frank G. Millard released his report in two parts. On July 15, he reported that twenty-three inmates would be charged with kidnaping and morals charges as a result of the riot. There was no evidence to warrant charges against prison officials or guards. Three of the inmates were charged with kidnaping and sodomy, fourteen with kidnaping, and six with sodomy. The prosecutor of Jackson county, George Campbell, said that sentences would be added to the present sentences, rather than running concurrent with them, which was contrary to what happened later. Further charges of arson and malicious destruction of property would be made, according to Millard. In order to support those charges, the mail office had been instructed by Bill Johnson to keep letters for recording when inmates admitted misbehavior or reported viewing misbehavior during the riot.

The second part of Millard's report was made public on July 16. He charged that Brooks sometimes had by-passed the warden and dealt directly with others. The chain of command was violated by Brooks, according to the report. Brooks was further criticized for reversing decisions of the classification committee in dealing with assignments of individual inmates to institutions and jobs.

One part of the report surprised me. "Referring to the final 11 demands purporting to have been made by the mutineers in 15-block, we seriously question the authorship of numbers 2, 3, and 10." These demands were, essentially, (2) permit counselors free access to the disciplinary cell-block, (3) revise segregation procedures so that treatment personnel will have representation, and (10) an inmate council to be elected by the inmate body to discuss problems. It was absurd to question the authorship of the demands. I had written all the demands! "Authorship" was mine on all of them, but they all began with stringent demands which I had been able to reduce. Referring to the numbers above, demand (2) had begun with the request to fire the guards suspected of brutality in 15-block. Demand (3) had begun with complaints about the long months and months men were in segregation without being reviewed by the segregation board, and was just a neutral and ineffective term, with no assurance that the original complaint would be corrected.

Demand (10) had begun with their wanting to appoint an inmate council with power to review and veto rules and regulations pertaining to inmates!

The fact that this committee questioned the authorship of these three demands illustrates their inefficiency. I would have told them that I wrote all the demands, had they been sufficiently interested to question me. Everybody knew at the time of the riot that I had written the terms. I had dictated them to my secretary. Despite the fact that I was still living in prison housing on prison property and was available to testify, the attorney general's investigating committee never called nor questioned me! I told the editor of the *Toledo Blade* when he called for my reaction that I was amused at the report, that I had written all the demands, and that I was amazed that the attorney general had "rediscovered" three of them.

The report went on to indicate that the riot was caused by overcrowding, feeding inmates in the mess hall while a mutiny was on in 15-block, idleness, improper segregation, lack of properly trained guards, lack of adequate pay for the custodial force, lack of a well trained riot squad, lack of a uniform riot procedure, a letdown in discipline, friction between individual treatment and custody, failure of the commissioner to channel all orders through the warden, and other miscellaneous causes.

The first objective in the prison, they reported, should be Custody. Some way should be found, they said, for incorrigibles to be given hard labor. Liberalization of parole board policies should be made, they said. Uniform rules for all cell-blocks should be adopted. Above all, the counselors and all individual Treatment staff should be indoctrinated in custody. The report exhibited a reactionary and uninformed penal philosophy generally counter to progressive penology.

After the report, there was some question about whether Brooks would resign. I couldn't understand why, since Millard's report could hardly have been termed thorough or carefully prepared. Nevertheless, Lawrence Farrell, the governor's executive secretary, said that they could not let him resign. "He's a guy with a welfare heart. He just can't turn down a sob story. He'd give the shirt off his back to a fellow if he felt in his mind that he needed it." Further, his personal and financial position was such that he did not have to take abuse, and that he is on the job "only as a favor to the administration."

Millard then "investigated" the July 6 riot to see whether it had been staged in order to bring about the firing of Frisbie. He found no evidence that it had been staged.

In the meantime, my work with Ray E. Hibbs & Associates was very interesting. I passed up several academic opportunities, including a professorship in psychology, as well as several openings in industry and commerce. When the School of Social Welfare at the Florida State University offered an associate professorship, however, my family immediately pressed for relocation in Florida. My wife drove to Tallahassee to find housing. I had actually preferred to remain with Ray E. Hibbs because I thought his business offered more excitement than an academic career. Florida State University was a close second choice for me and a definite first choice with my family, so a compromise with my family was made. I reported to the Florida State University on September 1. The choice turned out to be a very rewarding one.

While I was in Toledo, the television show, "Inside Michigan," was interested in putting on a program about what was wrong at Jackson. Roger Cleary telephoned to tell me that Attorney General Frank Millard and former State Police Commissioner Donald S. Leonard were participants, and that I was the logical third participant if I would appear. I told him that I would like to appear, and that it would be a clambake! He laughed, agreed that he suspected that it would be with that trio, and we hung up. A few days later, he called and said that an error had been made, that someone else had already invited Commissioner Brooks, and that I would be invited some other time. That didn't sound true to me. I thought that Donald S. Leonard and Frank Millard were afraid of me. After coming to Florida State University in September, I wrote Roger Cleary the following to find out:

> When I was in Toledo you telephoned me regarding a TV program on what was wrong in Jackson. You wanted me to participate with Attorney General Millard and Commissioner of Police Donald S. Leonard. I recall thinking that such a program would be of value, but doubted that Millard and Leonard had enough facts to face me in a public appearance.
>
> Subsequently, my doubts were confirmed when you telephoned me that "an error had been made." Commissioner Brooks would take my place, and I would go on in a later program. The later program was never arranged, which is as I had expected.
>
> My reconstruction of what happened is that you had set up what would have been a good program, but that Millard and Leonard had too much to lose by public debate with me. Consequently, they wanted someone like Commissioner Brooks who would be more suave and without as many facts. It is my guess that Millard and Leonard felt more comfortable on the program with Commissioner Brooks.
>
> Would you please confirm or deny my thinking on this matter. I intend to use it in an academic manner in the study of public opinion and political maneuver.
>
> Your cooperation will be greatly appreciated.

Weeks passed without reply. In December, I received an attractive Christmas greeting card from Mr. Cleary. Inside the card was written, "You do a wonderful job of analysis—I hope you have a very wonderful year at the University. Sincerest good wishes. Roger."

The first two inmates to be arraigned for kidnaping were Ray Young and Anthony Mazzone. They appeared before Jackson's Municipal Judge Hatch on July 16. Earl Ward, "Crazy Jack" Hyatt and James Hudson were arraigned on

August 4. Ward was most belligerent. He interrupted proceedings repeatedly with strongly worded protests. He wanted to know if there was such a thing as second-hand kidnaping, since he took the guards as they were handed over to him. He demanded to know who his lawyer would be, how much he would be paid, and protested that he might get a divorce lawyer. He charged that he had been held incommunicado since the riot. He shouted angrily at Judge Hatch a profane name after a dramatic exchange of ideas and after the judge had risen and left the bench. Hyatt was more docile, but snarled about Michigan justice when told that the lower court could not hire a lawyer for him nor subpoena witnesses. Hudson said that he would answer no questions, that he had been held incommunicado, and hadn't had a bath in three months.

James Hudson again appeared in circuit court on kidnaping charges on September 30. He was attired in a blue denim prison jacket with a Communist party emblem, a picture of Joseph Stalin, and a Communist red star attached to the front.

Ray Young, the inmate who captured the first guard to start the riot in 15-block, was convicted of kidnaping in early October, 1952. He was sentenced to 15 to 30 years. The sentence was to run concurrently with the term he was already serving. Young was the first of the inmates charged with kidnaping during the April riot to be tried.

On September 19, another by-pass by Commissioner Brooks hit headlines. Attorney General Frank Millard revealed that on August 13 Commissioner Brooks had transferred Pete Mahoney to Camp Brighton, thirty miles from the scene of his last crime. Mahoney, one-time associate of members of the famed Purple Gang in Detroit, had been convicted of conspiracy to murder the late Senator Warren Hooper, but the conviction had been reversed by the Supreme Court. He was currently serving 25 to 50 years for the hold-up of the Aristocrat Club, a Pontiac gambling house, in 1944. While his police record dated back to 1924, this was the first offense for which he had been imprisoned. The orders for transfer of Mahoney were transmitted from Brooks to the classification committee by Robert Schumacher. The classification committee's notes said the transfer was made "on orders from Commissioner Brooks." Millard charged that "when Governor Williams says that there is no scandal in his prison administration, he doesn't know what he is talking about."

The *Citizen-Patriot* reported that Brooks censured Warden Frisbie for coming to the prison once or twice a week to pick up his mail. Bannan said that during these visits he was "agitating the employees." Governor Williams wanted to know why this ex-employee was "still hanging around." The *Citizen-Patriot* editorial page attacked the governor and defended Frisbie. It also said that I was "one of Brooks' boys" and that I did many things that were approved by Brooks, but were unknown by the warden or done without his approval which, of course, is a false statement.

A joint committee of the Michigan State Medical Society and the Michigan State Hospital Association investigated the medical facilities at the prison for the first time since 1947. In 1947, they had reported shocking mistreatment and lack of care for sick inmates. While in their report of September 22, they lauded the prison for excellent improvement of medical facilities and service since 1947, they deplored the "pitiful" condition with respect to overcrowding and lack of segregation of sex deviates and psychotics. More and smaller prisons were advocated. They said that had there been no overcrowding and had there been proper segregation, there probably would have been no riot in April. The report said that there were 1,500 sex deviates and 200 psychotics in the prison, and that segregation was fundamental but impossible. "Serious thought," the report continued, "should be given to the classification of prisoners as to moral character."

On October 3, President John Smith of the Sparks-Withington Co. in Jackson announced the hiring of General Julian N. Frisbie as coordinator of defense production. The announcement followed a charge from Governor Williams that Frisbie "has obviously been promised a return to the state payroll in some capacity." Frisbie denied that any such promise had been made by Fred Alger, who had emerged from the primaries as the Republican candidate for governor, nor by anyone else. Rather, he indicated that he intended to stay in private employment.

On October 4, another of Commissioner Brooks' injudicious favors appeared in headlines. Walter "Mickey" Maguire was transferred to Camp Brighton on January 25 on orders of Commissioner Brooks. On Friday afternoon, October 3, he stole an automobile and escaped. Maguire had been serving a life term as a habitual criminal, having been sentenced to correctional institutions eight times. The letter which gave the commissioner's orders was signed by S. J. Gilman, and addressed to Assistant Deputy Wardens Vernon Fox, George Bacon, and George Kropp. Maguire had been a favorite of Brooks' for some time.

The prison situation was mentioned in the political campaigns, but it did not play as important a role, according to my observation, as many persons had predicted, nor as many persons said it actually did. Correctional institutions are not important in the governmental hierarchy in the eyes of the voting public. Chuck-holes in the highways are much more real to the public than what goes on behind the walls of some faraway prison.

Actually, the prison had degenerated considerably under the new administration. The individual treatment program had degenerated from an active and enthusiastic group to a program just going through the motions. One man pointed out that the counselors had become a disgruntled bunch of men. They had been left out of a recent pay raise. They began giving up prerogatives we had gained for them, such as approving correspondence and special purpose mail, which is but one of the ways the program is integrated with the practicalities of everyday living at the prison. The counselors were becoming merely mass producers of social histories and progress reports for the parole board.

Deputy Bacon started feuding with Deputy Cahill, according to my information. A regulation he had won while inside the walls became unsatisfactory to him now that he was outside the walls. He insisted on handling it in his own way. Applications for additional hobbycraft activities were delayed days, weeks, and months inside, without action. While it was destructive to morale, Bill Johnson made no attempt to do anything about it. He said "To hell with them, put the blame on Custody."

One of my correspondents wrote, "If you thought there was lack of co-operation when you were here you should see things, now."

Another correspondent told about giving a custodial officer a ride home who bragged that the officers now could reach right through the bars of the cells and strike inmates. When they beat an inmate now, he had no recourse. Sergeant Spooner, the bragging officer, said, "We have a warden now who'll back us up!"

Many of the persons at the State Prison of Southern Michigan have written to tell me they wished I were yet with the program. None told the others, so I am sure that the writing was independent. As a matter of fact, some of them destroyed my letters to them so that Bill Johnson and others would not find out their sentiments, or that they even contacted me. Two excerpts from examples of such letters are:

(1) "You will never know just how much my association with you meant to me. . . . The institution is not the same nor will it ever be in my estimation."

(2) "I suppose you already know most of the events that have taken place since your—exit? Well—as I said frequently (please believe me) during the confusion after the riot, and often since—in fact, only yesterday, while loafing at the coffee counter I repeated to K——, G——, and B—— that when you left,

our department suffered its greatest blow!! Some of
your enemies, yes—even L. E. S. now admits that
we're *doomed*, since our department can be likened
to a once mighty, thriving and seemingly indestruct-
ible oak tree—girdled by the jealous, vindictive
neighbors, merely because their own yard lacked
shade!! You nor were any of us given credit for our
performance in restoring the prison to normal—instead, we were relegated to the role of a whipping
boy—as you well know. Without you to speak for us
we soon lost all of the hard-fought-for ground we had
gained. Once again custody reigns supreme!! Gone
are many of the programs which you introduced—
and what few remain are of superficial value—merely being tolerated by those in power.

All of our group, including myself, are still subject to ridicule and criticism by nearly all the other
prison workers—even down to the very inadequate
clerks in Inmate Accounting office (still a sore spot
with the inmates). To make a long story short—wish
you were here to cope with our many, many problems, and so do many of the others.

These are representative of many similar written opinions
expressed in my correspondence with persons still connected
with the prison.

One of my professional correspondents wrote, "Bannan is
worthless." Others said that he took over the prison "like a
mouse" and that his "harsh disciplinarian" attitude referred
to his decisions supporting custody rather than his personal
attributes. Some considered him to be an emotionally insecure person who permitted brutality as a compensatory device. Regarding Cahill, one statement was that now he was
a deputy, he wanted to spend his time talking about his
younger days when he broke somebody's jaw in a fight. Bacon's feuding with Cahill, who assumed his job as "inside
deputy" was mentioned frequently.

Frisbie agreed to appear on television over WJIM-TV,

Lansing, Michigan, to answer the question, "What Caused the Riots at the Prison?" Advance notices were that he would blame Commissioner Brooks and his policies that resulted in some 300 youthful inmates being retained at the State Prison of Southern Michigan, rather than going to the Michigan Reformatory at Ionia. Frisbie denied that he had been offered a state job in case Fred Alger were elected governor, and denied that he was being paid in any way. His time was donated as a public service.

On the program, Frisbie charged that a Democratic blunder which allowed sex perverts to prey on 300 teen-age boys inside the prison was the main cause of the costly April rioting. He said that the prison became a "cesspool of depravity" after Commissioner Brooks had ordered that no inmates 21 years of age or younger be transferred to the Michigan Reformatory at Ionia who had an IQ under 85 (the IQ limit had actually been placed at 75). Brooks' decision had forced the prison to turn 300 teen-age boys loose among 4,000 older felons. "Many of the kids were 15 or 16. Many of the felons were sexual perverts," he said. Continuing, "You might as well have herded those kids into a slaughtering pen like so many cattle." General Frisbie related that from that day on prison discipline began to crack up. Fierce jealousies flared up among the hardened old-timers with twisted minds. We had fist fights, knifings, and other forms of violence to contend with. The prison was a powder keg, and the situation got worse every day." Regarding Brooks, Frisbie said that he was a good business man, politician, a vote-getter, but absolutely not fitted for his job. Frisbie reported that Brooks gave orders to his wardens, over-rode the orders of his wardens inside the institutions, and refused to accept the recommendations of his wardens. With one exception, he offered no explanation. In that one exception, he said his orders came from the "big boss." He reported that the prison staff fought bitterly the decision to keep the teen-agers with low intelligence in Jackson, but the decision stood. Frisbie charged that favoritism to certain convicts, including Earl Ward and

"Crazy Jack" Hyatt, had undermined the warden's discipline. The commissioner refused to send Ward, for instance, back to Marquette. Frequently the classification committee recommendations were overridden by the commissioner without explanation.

Frisbie reviewed an incident involving a legislator. "One sure way to break down a warden's authority is to break down his disciplinary measures. For instance, I sent three inmates to solitary for 10 days because they had arranged a picnic with their wives in the prison parole office contrary to all regulations. They had connived with a member of the legislature in the deal. But when I sent them to solitary, the commissioner countermanded my orders. It's easy to see what the other inmates—the men without pull—were thinking about when the prison grapevine brought them news of irregularities like that."

Regarding the appointment of Gilman as deputy warden, Frisbie said, "A man whom I would not have recommended for the post was made a deputy warden of the prison on orders from Governor Williams."

He referred to another incident in the offices of the prison paper, the *Spectator*, which I had been reviewing, "censoring" if you choose, for good taste and policy. Frisbie said that Commissioner Brooks "called me up to the office of the newspaper. The staff (of inmates) had been assembled. He delivered an address, telling the convict editors and reporters . . . that they were to have full and free expression of opinion; that the policies of the paper were up to them. I could see from the look on the faces of the staff that my authority . . . was fast slipping."

He said he did not resign his job because his 30 years in the Marine Corps had taught him that you get your orders from the superior officer whether you like him or not. "You don't run out because the job is unpleasant, unjust or dangerous." He noted that there was a wide disparity between military discipline and political control.

Frisbie reported that he had been severely censured by the governor for telling a legislative committee the riot-torn laundry could be fixed up for $250,000, when the governor had reported $405,000 was needed. Frisbie reported that the job was actually being done for about $175,000. He reported, "Because I saved some money, I was upbraided by the commissioner and his underlings, and at my own dinner table, too. They said I shouldn't worry about such things—it wasn't my money anyway."

Frisbie said that the reduction of guards was not entirely the fault of the legislature. Over his objection, Commissioner Brooks had transferred 21 guards outside the walls of the prison, without replacement, and had also pigeon-holed a plan Frisbie had submitted for handling riots.

At the close of the telecast, Frisbie was asked about the steak and ice cream dinner. "I don't know the story behind the steak and ice cream," he replied, "I had no knowledge of it until we were committed. It was apparently arranged by somebody with a lot of authority, but I don't know who it was. It was just another case of taking prison management out of the warden's hands." Actually, I had arranged the "steak and ice-cream" dinner on Tuesday, but only *after* conference with the warden.

Commissioner Brooks made his bitter reply to Frisbie's telecast through Governor Williams' office on Sunday night, October 5. He said that Frisbie was fired because he disregarded orders, and accused him of lying in the "Republican-sponsored" telecast. Brooks said that Frisbie was a "disgruntled ex-employee who was removed because he failed to do his job. Every important point in his television broadcast is at variance with facts or with his own testimony as to the facts." Brooks continued:

> If the conditions described by him actually existed at Southern Michigan Prison, why didn't he reveal them to the governor, the attorney general, the fact-finding commission or the newspapers? Why did he wait until now to tell his story?
>
> His claim that he didn't know about the steak and ice

cream dinner is false. I have in my possession a transcript of his sworn testimony that he knew of and approved the steak and ice cream dinner early in the morning of Tuesday, April 22, three days before it came out in the papers.

His charge that his recommendations on transfers were over-ridden contradicts his sworn testimony to the governor's fact-finding commission that his recommendations were generally followed.

His statement that he had never been asked the real cause of the riot is false. He was asked that question repeatedly, and I have a copy of his testimony under oath. He said in that testimony that the basic cause was a heterogeneous prison population and overcrowding. Under repeated questions he never mentioned the homosexual factor which he now says was the real cause of the riot.

When he said he was warden in name only and lacked authority, he must have forgotten that he testified under oath that he had the final decision on every move during the entire period of the riot.

When he accuses me of responsibility for the shortage of guards he contradicts his own sworn testimony. He testified under oath that the Legislature did not give him enough guards three years ago and had been reducing his guard forces ever since.

His charge that we restricted transfers of young prisoners to Ionia Reformatory in order to make "an institution of higher learning" is a lie. We restricted transfers because there was no room in Ionia for all the young prisoners who should have been taken out of Jackson.

That was the fault of the legislature which has rejected our requests for funds to build additional space at Ionia to house those kids. Since we could not move all of them to Ionia we decided to take those who had the best chances of rehabilitation—with preference given to the youngest ones. This decision was made in full consultation with Warden Heyns of Ionia.

He was removed because he could not restore order at the prison. One of the reasons for his failure was the fact that he would not go into parts of the prison where there was personal danger. He always sent someone else to do the dangerous job. Both officers and inmates soon lose respect for a warden who is afraid of his job.

His disregard of order was a direct cause of the second riot July 6. More than a hundred inmates had been locked up in Cell Block 9 on suspicion of having taken part in the rioting. Many were there because they were fingered for reasons of personal spite or revenge by other inmates.

Frisbie was instructed to screen those inmates and get the innocent ones out of the block as soon as possible. Instead, he left them there for nearly 60 days. They sent word to him asking his personal assurance that their cases would soon be heard. He refused to approach the cell block.

When they finally began to tear up the block, it was Deputy Warden Gilman, not Frisbie, who went into the cell block and restored order at the risk of his own life.

At the proper time I will cite chapter and verse from his own testimony to show that Frisbie is not telling the public the truth.

Frisbie's reply was, "I expected a general denial of my charges, and have no further comment."

Republican gubernatorial candidate Fred M. Alger, Jr., attacked Governor Williams for mixing politics and penology. He dared him to fire his corrections commissioner to end unrest at Jackson. Alger said that Williams is serving notice by retaining Brooks that "Michigan has no place in its administration for top-bracket executives who won't sacrifice professional honor to the demands of backroom politics." He recalled that Frisbie, a retired general, decorated for bravery with the Marine Corps, "winds up being called a liar and a coward by a political appointee of Governor Williams." He charged that Governor Williams had quarantined Michigan for men of ability who might be summoned to the service of the state. He noted that the prison atmosphere was filled with tension, and that men connected with the prison are powerless to do anything about it because the corrections administration is faulty at the top. He pointed out that neither the one-man commissioner nor the commission control of corrections will work so long as politics dictates appointments.

Dr. Garrett Heyns, warden of the Michigan Reformatory, denied that young offenders of low intelligence were automatically barred from Ionia. "Any boy who was in danger from homosexuals at Southern Michigan could have been transferred to Ionia," he said, "Warden Frisbie had only to ask us to take him." Heyns said the order simply gave priority to those boys who were free of venereal disease and epilepsy and who had an IQ high enough to give them some chance of benefitting from the schools at Ionia. He said that many exceptions were made to the rule.

Governor Williams had a weekly television show from Detroit which had been devoted to stories of how the Democrats had "built Michigan." Brooks was to take the governor's place on Sunday, October 12, because of the strong accusations that he and his irregular administrative practices had been essentially the cause of the riot. Williams said that, "We're going to spike those charges flatter than a pancake. The charges are a pack of lies and the ravings of a disgruntled employee. Reasons for the riots are overcrowding, the large size of the prison and the lack of guards. The Republican legislature can be blamed for the lack of guards." Lester P. Dodd, chairman of the "fact-finding" committee, reported to Governor Williams five points in which Frisbie's speech was at variance with the sworn testimony. On the program, Commissioner Brooks said that Frisbie told "lies that were put in his mouth. He spoke what was written for him at Alger's campaign headquarters." In the script originally prepared for the show, Brooks had said that Frisbie lost his nerve during the riot, but he changed that part for the broadcast. He said:

> The week of anxiety while those guards were held hostage in 15-block did something to him. Matters that required his personal attention in dangerous spots were not taken care of. The second riot on July 6 was a direct result of his failure to carry out orders.

He insisted that the "real culprit" behind the Frisbie broadcast was Alger.

Fred M. Alger, Jr., replied that Frisbie had donated his time. He said that Frisbie was being penalized for his frankness by means of abuse and vituperation by the Democratic administration whose fumbling he exposed. He continued that anyone familiar with the history of the United States Marine Corps would know that Frisbie was not a coward and a liar as he was branded by Commissioner Brooks.

Frisbie's reply was:

> The attitude of the corrections commissioner seeks to imply that my statement concerning prison affairs and waste of public monies was made for political reasons. Actually, it must be as clear to him as it is to the people of Michigan that my sole purpose was to present some of the things that had been left unpublished.
>
> I had a complete realization that I was taking a calculated risk in exposing myself to political sniping, which I was not familiar with, but I was willing to take such a risk.
>
> This sort of personal attack on my courage and gullibility makes me a little weary. I am doubtful if the many veterans of Michigan, Marine or otherwise, will greatly appreciate such tactics.
>
> I have no intention of becoming embroiled in further controversy. What I have said stands.

Governor Williams said on October 13:

I made up my mind that if this ex-warden's story
contained any truth, I would correct the situation and
punish those responsible for it, even if it meant loss of
this election. My investigation is now complete. I have
established beyond a reasonable doubt that the story . . .
in all its essential points is a foul fabrication.

He had previously said that if Brooks had been responsible for
the riot, he would not still be corrections commissioner. He said
that his own fact-finding committee did not find Brooks to
blame in their probe of riot causes.

At the meeting of the American Prison Association on
October 6 in Atlantic City, the National Wardens Association blamed riots on lack of trained guards, and an insufficient number of prison personnel. Warden Roy Best of Colorado and Warden Garrett Heyns of Michigan reported that
prison riots and the pantie raids in American colleges followed a pattern that reflected the tantrums of unruly boys.
Other causes of riots they mentioned were political interference, divided authority, too many prison investigators, and
a desire on the part of the prisoners for publicity.

Throughout October, the prison situation continued to
be an issue in the political campaigns, but I think it was a
relatively minor issue. Democratic Governor Williams had
side-stepped much of the attack through my resignation, a
"get-tough" policy, and firing Warden Frisbie from an impossible position in which he was to restore order under the
"get-tough" policy dictated by the governor—a feat that I
maintained could not be done by anybody. He had expressed
the aggression the Republicans wanted to express. The only
issue left was whether or not Commissioner Brooks should be
retained. Republican gubernatorial candidate Alger promised to remove the corrections commissioner and replace him
with someone who understands penology. He promised, as
candidates had promised many times before, to "take the
prison out of politics."

Alger said about G. Mennen Williams, "He will sell out

the people of Michigan, he has already sold out his party, the Democratic party, to the CIO. I am now told that he is telling the CIO to ditch Stevenson and (Senator) Moody because he is worried about his own re-election. I don't know how true it is, but I'm ready to believe it about Williams. The only thing he cares about is Governor Williams, and where he is going politically."

Newsmen found that a round-robin statement was being circulated among the inmates in late October, a couple of weeks before election, to get the inmate body of the State Prison of Southern Michigan to sign a denial of recent reports of prison unrest. Prison rumor was that the plan originated in Lansing. It was reported that some 400 inmates had signed the mimeographed forms, which read as follows:

> We, the undersigned inmates of the State Prison of Southern Michigan, brand as an untruth the Republican candidates' statements that this prison is a "tinder box ready to burst into a rebellion" and that the homosexual situation is out of control. Such misstatement of facts is highly dangerous to the excellent morale of the entire inmate body, as well as misleading to the public. Furthermore, it puts into the hearts and minds of inmates' parents, wives, children and friends worry and fear about the inmates' safety and welfare. We consider such tactics uncalled for and inhumane. The prison is now back to normal operation, such as existed before the April mutiny, and there is no evidence, visible or otherwise, that this is not so. It is the desire of the undersigned that the public be so informed through the medium of the press and radio.

Such a "petition" or statement had never before been circulated among inmates. I suspected that Brooks had been in contact with one of his inmate friends, and that this plan had begun with his instigation or knowledge to reinforce his position as commissioner of corrections in time for the elections on November 4.

Commissioner Brooks, however, said that his department had had "nothing to do with preparing" the statement. He said that some prisoners had told him the week before that they were circulating the statement, and that he had "tried to discourage it" because he feared it would not be "properly understood" by the public. I suspected that the commissioner could have stopped any petition he wanted by telling the warden to stop it—provided, of course, he *wanted* to stop it. Warden Bannan said he had known nothing of the petition until it appeared on his desk with the request that it be sent to the press. He expressed surprise at also reading the story of it in the papers in which the exact wording was given!

A letter written by an inmate accusing the corrections commissioner of inspiring the petition, according to Governor Williams, was smuggled out of the prison and taken to the Republican party headquarters. He charged that the Republicans were using inmates in the institution for political purposes. Such tactics, he said, brought on new tensions within the prison after things had quieted down since last April. As a result, one inmate had to be moved to another institution for fear of his life.

Williams won the election by a close margin. He had won the previous election by about 1,500 votes, but this election was won by a more comfortable but still close margin of several thousand votes.

Dr. Frank E. Hartung of Wayne University presented a paper to the Michigan Sociological Society at Ann Arbor. News reports were that he listed the following reasons for the riot:

1. Indiscriminate herding of radically different types of inmates
2. Abuse of the counselor system
3. Destruction of a semi-official, informal kind of self-government
4. The nature of the maximum custody prison.

I wrote to Frank to request his paper or notes or comments about it. He did not reply for several months. Then he wrote and told me he had lost the paper.

Gilman had become unpopular at the prison. Custodial personnel did not like his braggadocio. Inmates had obtained the same impression of him as had Ward. On Thursday, November 6, Gilman announced that he would return to his job as assistant to the commissioner in Lansing. Gilman said that there had been an understanding with Brooks when he came to the prison in June that he could return to his old job when conditions in the prison became normal. In part, Gilman's statement read:

> My ability to organize and command hundreds of inmates convinced Mr. Brooks that I should come to Jackson and contribute towards settling the place back to normal. This I believe I have done to the best of my ability.
>
> I would like to point out that the second riot of July 6 was handled by myself and that in an hour and 20 minutes I had settled a bad situation which was out of hand with hostages already held when I was called into the prison at 8:40 P.M. that Sunday night. I also would like to point out that I did not create the 9-block situation but inherited it as a backwash of the April riot.
>
> Since being here, many steps were taken to restore a normal situation to the institution and I believe I played a major role in these steps.
>
> Warden Bannan is a very capable penal administrator and I am sure that he will have a very successful administration.
>
> I leave with no malice or ill-feelings against anyone.

The laundry was placed in operation during the second week in November. It was the first major service, other than the kitchen, to be restored. The laundry was placed in the building from which the old central stores had been removed. In the meantime, citizens in and around Jackson were contributing old books to re-stock the library and money to rebuild the chapel. A check for $1,189.59 was presented to Warden Bannan for use in rebuilding the chapel. Old books were collected and donated to the library.

The "Little Hoover" Committee and a special unit chosen by Governor Williams to study riot causes met on November 14 to discuss their report. While the meeting was held secretly, news reports predicted a "showdown fight" in the 1953 legislature on how the Michigan prisons should be operated. The issue was said to be whether the five-man commission plan or the single commissioner should operate the Department of Corrections. Prentiss M. Brown, formerly United States Senator (Democrat) for Michigan, had been appointed chairman of the group. Brown said that Austin MacCormick would have his recommendations ready early in December.

Robert S. Hannum of the Osborne Association issued a statement that the basic cause of riots is the "punish 'em" attitude of the public that allows mistreatment to continue. To reform prisons, Hannum listed eight objectives:

1. Remove prison administration from politics and put it on a civil service basis.
2. The inmate should be clearly informed of all laws and rules which affect him.
3. Guards should be punished for brutality.
4. Idleness should be replaced by work which has meaning and which teaches usable skills.
5. Food should be improved with better quality and quantity.
6. Psychopaths, incorrigibles, homosexuals, and others not normal should be segregated.
7. Prisons should be modernized.
8. It should be made easier for a man to get a parole hearing.

Hannum concluded, "Perhaps the public will come to realize that crime is costing them more than $40,000,000 every day of their lives. Is there a taxpayer who thinks that's good business?"

Late Tuesday afternoon, November 18, there was a disturbance in the yard again. More than 2,000 inmates milled about in the yard, but officials estimated that there were only 80 active rioters. No guards were held hostage. Only five inmates were hurt, one hit on the head with a flying plate. Prison officials estimated that the damage would not exceed $2,000. The disturbance started in the dining hall when an inmate shouted, "This spaghetti's rotten!" Inmates had been grumbling about the food for several days. Someone else yelled, "There's salt in the coffee." The 600 men in the dining room became active, some swept back through the kitchen and bakery, seizing what they could to eat. Outside, the 1,600 men waiting to be fed went out of control of the guards charged with the line. The group in the laundry set fire to piles of clothing. Another group went to 2-block and 1-block where they seized the brake levers to prevent the inmates there from being locked in. The barbershops there were ransacked, razors taken, and furniture smashed. No hostages were wanted. As a matter of fact, guards were pushed out of the way. A *Jackson Citizen-Patriot* editorial said it might have been because the riot was not well organized, but emphasized the position the editor preferred that the rioters remembered the severe penalties for kidnaping meted out after the April riot.

During this riot, the counselors were forced to carry guns. This did not improve their morale any, for the sight of a counselor, chaplain, school teacher, psychologist, physician or similar "helping" person with a gun would militate against his effective working in his specialty. Certainly they did not add to the strength of the prison force with their lack of training or practice with firearms and their reluctance to use them. My correspondents complained bitterly about this. Had I been there, I would have objected strenuously to such action. I wager Bill Johnson favored it.

Warden Bannan was in northern Michigan, deer hunting. Assistant Deputy Cahill set into operation the plan for handling riots as worked out by former Warden Frisbie after the April riot, and "completed" by Warden Bannan. Officers from the trusty 16-block came inside to guard the powerhouse. It called for an armed squad to go through trouble spots immediately while other armed guards take places on the roof to control the prison yard. This "flying squadron" went to the kitchen and chased out the group that was there, then to the dining room, and then to the laundry. They circled the central store, went past the hospital, and through the south side. Then they attacked 1-block and 2-block. Going through 5-block, 4-block, and 3-block, the squad arrived at 2-block. It took a cell-to-cell drive to get the inmates locked up. When the squad entered 1-block, men on the fourth gallery began throwing pipes, chairs, bars, furniture, and similar missiles down on the guards. The guards retreated, entered l-block by the back door, and opened fire with a tommy gun and smaller weapons. By six o'clock, all inmates were in cells. The intermittent rain also aided in quieting the crowd, in that many inmates preferred the dryness of a cell-block to the soggy yard.

Other preparations included calling the National Guard at Jackson, but the riot was quelled before all were notified. One hundred and twenty State Troopers were called. Newsmen were not permitted inside the prison, but gained their information by interview. This again, apparently, was based on the consensus among the Department of Corrections and prison administrative staff that the corps of newsmen had added to the confusion in the April riot.

This quick action by custody was the way I wished the riot in April could have been handled. It would have saved much damage. Assistant Deputy Bacon had no guards trained for the purpose, however. Even when he knew the situation was tense, the extra guards he placed in the kitchen for feeding that Monday morning were neither trained nor armed, I could almost sense the security of that armed squad going around the yard and recalled two scenes that I hope

never to see reenacted. The first was my going out into the
yard during the April riot, unarmed and alone, attempting
to take men from the fringe of the riot and bring them inside. The second was seeing Assistant Deputy George Bacon
walk through an empty yard on Monday evening, flanked by
six armed State Troopers. Quick action by custody last April
would have made unnecessary both of these scenes.

Beef stew was served on Wednesday, feeding being accomplished by bringing one cell-block at a time to the dining
hall. The last three blocks were served steaks, which the
newspapers were careful to describe as "only sizable cuts of
an inexpensive grade of beef," but which my friends at the
prison say were choice cuts in comparison with the "steaks"
served the prisoners at the end of the riot in April. One of
them had eaten one of the steaks and said that "they were de-
licious T-bones."

Nine men were placed in detention as a result of this
riot. There were no charges of inciting a riot or destruction
of property. There seemed only to be an evaluation by Ward-
en Bannan that time was the main factor. If the riot plan can
go into effect speedily enough, it will not give the rioters time
to organize. Bannan called the riot "routine." He said that a
dining hall fracas can happen any time in any prison, and if
it had not been for the April riot, this one would hardly have
been noticed. He said, "When I was at Ionia, I once was
picking pea soup out of my ears for a week and the dining
hall uprising never even got into the papers."

An interview with Bannan regarding riot causes was reported in the December 19, 1952, issue of *U. S. News &
World Report*. Bannan said that the "psychological counselor" has come into the prison faster than the prison population can take it. He said that we don't have discipline in
the home and school any more—"all these new methods have
been tried, and in the prisons they are now backfiring." He
said that many problems arise "because of the newfangled
ideas of raising children." He concluded with, "I'd like to
sum it all up with one little bit of psychology: The more

trips to the woodshed, the fewer trips to the penitentiary." And that is the man selected for probably the most responsible wardenship in the nation!

Dr. Donald Powell Wilson and Dr. Harry Elmer Barnes wrote an article published in *Life* of November 24, 1952, under the title, "A Riot Is an Unnecessary Evil." In that article, they discussed prison problems in terms of brutality, overcrowding, idleness, dangerously low budgets, politics, and poor pay for personnel.

On Wednesday, November 19, five of the April riot leaders were transferred from county jails to the Branch Prison at Marquette. They were James Hudson, Russell Jarboe, John Crockard, Alfred Lovett, and James Styles. This left only three in county jails of the 13 men originally so placed. They included Ward, in the Oakland County jail at Pontiac, Hyatt in the Clinton County Jail at St. Johns, and a third man in the Washtenaw County Jail at Ann Arbor for his own protection, but his name was withheld.

The guards' union, Local 1333, State County and Municipal Employees, AFL, hastily called a special meeting after the riot. They drafted further demands for the safety and protection of guards. Robert Grosvenor announced the demands as follows:

1. Construction of an entrance from the prison roof to a balcony overlooking the dining room where an armed guard could be posted.
2. Provision of entrances from the roof to each cell block so armed guards might reach catwalks and guard cages in the tops of the blocks.
3. Construction of an iron gate across an exit from the prison kitchen leading to the officers' dining room.
4. Increasing the guard force to required strength.
5. Installation of adequate toilet facilities on wall posts occupied by guards.

Similar demands had been made previously, but no action had been taken. Besides the above demands specific to the prison situation, the union requested a three per cent cost of living rise in salary. Warden Bannan reported no progress on a previous union request for a special fund for injury compensation.

Governor Williams announced that he had investigated the reported beatings of two prisoners as a result of the new "get-tough" policy at the prison. He said that one prisoner suffered a broken wrist and that another was severely beaten about the head "several weeks ago" in 15-block. Williams said that Warden Bannan had been having a rough time with inmates in 15-block, and "it appears that guards were sent into the cell block in an effort to quiet the prisoners and that resistance developed, which resulted in guards using fists and clubs." Self-defense was claimed by the guards. The incident occurred on November 30.

Dr. Russell Finch, the medical director for the Department of Corrections, resigned in protest against the new "get-tough" policy. Commissioner Brooks told newsmen that Dr. Finch did not oppose prison policies, but that he was "very much upset" over recent beatings of inmates. Brooks said, "He has resigned previously and I persuaded him to stay on. I hope I can persuade him to stay once again." Brooks said that the beatings were necessary to head off another riot. Paul Weber, press secretary to Governor Williams, said that the beatings had no relation to Dr. Finch's resignation.

In early December, Assistant Deputies Cahill and Bacon were made deputy wardens at the same salary level as the wardens at Ionia and Marquette. This fulfilled for Bacon a long-standing ambition and fulfillment of a promise made by Brooks.

Commissioner Brooks said on December 19 that in the absence of Warden Bannan, when some men in 15-block were shouting, a deputy took some guards to their cells. They ordered the "trouble-makers" out of their cells into the corridor, where they "were given a severe reprimand about obeying block rules." Brooks said that quiet was restored only after several inmates had been removed by force. In the melee, four were injured.

Dr. Finch compared the size and number of the guards to the size and number of the inmates involved, and decided that self-defense by the guards against a 120-pound youngster whose limbs were broken was somewhat difficult for him to accept. Dr. Finch charged that brutality existed at the prison under the "get-tough" policy. He reported an incident in which an inmate lost an eye as a result of a direct close-range hit by a tear gas gun blast. "A policy of brutality has no place in a civilized and Christian community," Dr. Finch said. Continuing, "It is high time that we have officials with more adequate knowledge of modern penology who would replace the archaic ideas and practices now used at Southern Michigan prison." Dr. Finch's resignation stemmed directly from the beatings of November 30, but at least two other incidents were reported to have occurred. Dr. Finch said that in his opinion Brooks distorted the true facts when reporting the situation. Dr. Finch charged further that state law provides that no corporal punishment be administered without the prison physician in attendance. This law, he said, has not been complied with. He pointed out that the Branch Prison at Marquette had been overcrowded since 1922, and there were no riots there—nor brutality.

Newsmen learned through undisclosed sources that a Negro had been severely beaten on October 23.

Dr. Finch's charges were met with denial from Governor Williams, Commissioner Brooks, and Warden Bannan. Brooks made a long statement on formal corporal punishment and denied that it existed in Jackson. When guards have to defend themselves from attack, however, he did not consider the resulting violence as corporal punishment. The warden said his information was more reliable than Dr. Finch's information. Warden Bannan also said,

> I can say nothing about Dr. Finch's medical ability and I regard him not only for his medical ability, but

for his personal integrity. However, I do feel that in fairness to the corrections department, my employees and the inmates of this institution, I must support my administration.

This institution is populated with nearly 6,000 inmates—95 per cent of them want to do their time, pay their debt to society and return to the free world. It is not fair to this large percentage of inmates to have a few troublemakers take over.

I would be wanting in my duty to the state if they were not subdued.

Bannan's official comment, however, was "No comment." Editorials in the *Jackson Citizen-Patriot* supported the "get-tough" administration.

A petition asking for Dr. Finch's return was circulated among the inmates by the inmates, and reportedly had 2,000 signatures in a short time. Warden Bannan halted it. Dr. David B. Sher, a member of the prison medical staff, was appointed medical director.

The cost to the taxpayers of the state of Michigan of restoring the prison to "normal" as a result of the April riot was placed at one and a half million dollars. Because only the essential services were replaced, the actual damage was not computed. The actual cost will undoubtedly never be known.

When the legislature convened in January, Senator Greene introduced a bill to restore the five-man corrections commission. Representatives Whinery, Bolt, and Borgman introduced a similar bill into the house of representatives. It was noted that Governor Williams had campaigned during his first term as a friend of the commission system, but since his election has shown some reluctance to lose the right to appoint a commissioner. Representative Adrian DeBoom suggested a new medium-security prison to house 600 men with "rehabilitation and vocational programs." He also wanted a school for prison guards at East Lansing, conducted by the State Police. Simultaneously, pay raises were considered by the civil service department for persons below the executive classes "who have supervisory and custodial authority over inmate or population groups involving responsibility for disciplinary actions concerning inmate behavior." "Guards" would have been a much simpler way of saying it.

In the meantime, the situation at the prison had become less and less efficient and progressive. It had become brutal and reactionary. The rehabilitative services were present in name only, and hardly received lip service. One of my correspondents described it as "a circus of ineptitude." Deputy Bill Johnson had long since cleared out my files and burned them. He destroyed valuable records and information on the program which cannot be replaced. He called it "efficient organization." On one occasion, he went into the Research and Selection office and took all the worksheets of a research project I had started on escapes from prison, with the comment that he did not want that data to appear as published material under my name in some professional magazine. The implication was, of course, that one of my friends would have sent it to me had I asked for it. It is my information further that all the research project statements I had formulated for anyone who desired to select one were also destroyed.

Ward went on trial for kidnaping in Circuit Judge Harry D. Boardman's court on January 19. Ward's defense was that he was coerced to participate in the riot by the other inmates, and that he protected the lives of the guards and maintained order. He said that Hyatt and Young had told him to join them, and that he started to take leadership to restore some semblance of order before affairs got out of hand. He admitted some beatings because men had been caught in acts of perversion and that some of them were trying to thwart the surrender of 15-block on Thursday afternoon.

In the courtroom, Ward verbally abused the judge. He slugged Sheriff G. H. Austin at the county jail. Lee Osborn of Rives Junction, acting as jury foreman, announced in the courtroom that Ward was guilty as charged. Judge Boardman sentenced him to 20 to 30 years to run concurrently with his present sentence. Computing his "good time" and subtracting it from the sentence, Ward will be eligible for parole on April 27, 1964. His eligible release date on his original sentence was January 4, 1963, which means that as a result of the riot, Ward's eligibility for a parole hearing was extended one year, three months, and twenty-three days. Ward was transferred to the Branch Prison at Marquette immediately after the trial.

The House of Representatives Prison Committee called Warden Bannan on Thursday, February 13, for an interview concerning the charges of brutality made by Dr. Finch. Bannan brought with him sworn statements by the officers involved and the chaplains to support his assertion that he did not order the beatings and did not condone corporal punishment. He denied that the injured inmates had not been accorded immediate medical treatment. Bannan said that Dr. Finch intended to resign anyway, and used the beatings as an excuse. He then recalled that during the April riot the inmates "accused Dr. Finch's medical department of inhuman practices." He said that Dr. Finch had resented his objection to "taking too many inmates to Ann Arbor" for treatment because it was too costly. Representative Borgman moved that Bannan be voted a "clean bill of health," but Chairman Pears set the motion aside, to take official action at another date.

Several legislators were interested in taking action regarding the prison situation. Revision of the good time law was of primary importance. Bannan reported that every time the legislature took interest in the prison, "inmates feel they are being favored." He said that the proposed revision of the good time law would release 600 men from the prisons. Representative DeBoom filed legislation to set standards for inmates who were being transferred to prison camps. He said that it would make certain that inmates doing time for sex offenses would not be permitted to go to the camps. Bannan made several proposals for legislation. He suggested that the State Prison of Southern Michigan never house more than 5,237 inmates, the construction of an extensive set of catwalks, guard towers, assault-proof arsenal, guard platform inside the dining hall, a ward for tuberculous patients, construction of facilities for the 200 more criminal insane at the Ionia State Hospital, moving the disciplinary block outside the walls, using 15-block for housing inmates who work in the kitchen and dining room, concurred with other corrections officials in placing a limit of 4,000 inmates inside the walls (there are 4,827 cells inside the walls), and additional housing of the medium-security type.

His proposed disciplinary block would be a self-sufficient unit housing 100 men. There would be twenty maximum punishment cells with double doors, no artificial light, and with two-inch water hoses available for use by guards in subduing inmates. It would be a one-story building surrounded by a high fence topped with high voltage wires and be under immediate supervision of four new guard towers.

Dr. Donald Powell Wilson, author of *My Six Convicts*, lectured in Detroit on February 13. During an interview, he expressed the opinion that the State Prison of Southern Michigan was archaic. He said that the authorities apparently did not want to see the prison run properly, that the only efficient administrator they ever had was fired shortly after he started. Commissioner Brooks commented that he was probably referring to the late Commissioner Joseph W. Sanford, and added, "I think I'm a pretty good man, myself." Warden Bannan said, "I believe Wilson meant Vernon Fox and not Joseph Sanford when he referred to the firing of an administrator."

Some of the improvements which had been worked on prior to the riot were continued. Fred Bates, the state supervisor of probation, had worked out a plan whereby the presentence investigations prepared by the probation officers could be used as social histories at the prison. The plan went into effect in February, 1953, about a year after its proposal. The orientation of new inmates had been a continuing problem which had been revised several times. None of the revisions had been entirely satisfactory. Warden Bannan established another orientation plan whereby the warden, individual treatment representative, record clerk, a counselor, and the business manager of the prison talked to new inmates in panel form. Subjects covered included classification, transfers, records, parole and discharge procedures, medical and mental programs, inmate store, inmate accounts, academic and vocational school programs, recreation, religious services, work in the industrial plants, custody procedures, mail, visitors, and group therapy services. Television, for which I had voted in committee on several occasions, was obtained for the mental ward.

The special committee to study the Michigan Department of Corrections, headed by Prentiss Brown, with Austin Mac-Cormick as the member under whose supervision the report was prepared, presented their report to the governor on February 12. The committee was made up of Glenn Allen, Jr., mayor of Kalamazoo; Roscoe O. Bonisteel, regent of the University of Michigan; Joseph A. Brown, attorney; Paul G. Goebel, mayor of Grand Rapids; Frank N. Isbey, president of the Detroit Fruit Auction Co.; Alexander G. Ruthven, president emeritus, University of Michigan; Nate S. Shapero, president of Cunningham's Drug Stores, Inc., and Richard A. Ware, Secretary of the Citizen's Research Council of Michigan. They were assisted by Austin H. MacCormick, executive secretary of the Osborne Association; Donald Clemmer, Commissioner of Corrections for the District of Columbia; John Barker Waite, professor emeritus of the University of Michigan and professor of the Hastings College of Law, University of California; and Randolph Wise, Commissioner of Public Welfare, Philadelphia. The committee reported that the following factors caused the riot:

1. The excessive size of the prison and the combination of overcrowding and idleness.
2. The heterogeneous nature of the inmate population.
3. Administrative weaknesses in the department of corrections at the prison.
4. The personnel situation at the prison.

5. The penal and parole laws.

The first major recommendation was the immediate construction of a new and smaller prison in Michigan. This prison would house 1,200 to 1,500 men. The second recommendation was that facilities be provided for greater emphasis upon individual treatment of prisoners including more diverse and expanded counseling work and educational programs. The third major recommendation was the retention of the single commissioner type of administration of the department of corrections. The last of the major recommendations was that the four-member parole board be enlarged and divorced from direct control of the commissioner of corrections. The committee suggested that the governor be allowed to make appointments to the parole board. The parole board would be responsible for the administration of parole supervision over inmates who had been released.

Following the letter of transmittal, which included the above brief statement of riot causes and the major recommendations, was a section on recommendations. This section was divided into two parts which were the recommendations made by the research staff and approved by the committee and the recommendations made by the committee.

The recommendations made by the research staff were voluminous. Regarding administration, it was recommended that the state of Michigan retain the single commissioner form of control, with certain modifications of the present administrative structure. These modifications were that the governor could remove a commissioner only after due notice with reasons and a public hearing if the commission wants it; permitting the governor to appoint parole board members from a civil service list; increasing the parole board from four to five members; making parole supervision a responsibility of the parole board; establishing a bi-partisan Corrections Council; separation of the Division of Prisons and Industries into two divisions; establishment of a Youth Division to concentrate on programs for youthful offenders over 17; and placement under civil service of the division heads so that all personnel except the commissioner would be under civil service.

There were 21 recommendations regarding institutional facilities, primarily aimed at the construction of a new medium-security correctional institution for 1,200 to 1,500 men, the acquisition of the Detroit House of Correction for women prisoners, the remodeling of facilities at Marquette so that all cell-blocks would have plumbing and other improvements, that facilities be used at Jackson to stress the medical and geriatrics programs, and that 6-block be designed as a reception center as a separate administrative unit. It is interesting to note that the first of the "prisoners' humiliating demands" appeared in less refined manner as one of the committee's recommendations, when they recommended abandoning 15-block as the disciplinary unit not only because of its location, but because "its dungeon-like cells fall far below modern standards for such buildings."

Eight recommendations with respect to personnel suggested that all custodial and professional services be kept filled with highly qualified personnel. The "scandalous lack of even a single psychiatrist on the staff of Jackson Prison" was mentioned. The committee wanted the position of deputy warden at Jackson filled at all times, a recommendation which made me wonder if they were aware of the history of the position. A recommendation was made that the counselors' caseloads be reduced to a "realistic level" and that counselors be relieved of some of their responsibilities "which can better be carried by other personnel." This indicated to me the lack of understanding of the practical difficulties in getting professional services integrated into the total prison program. They wanted "a careful program of indoctrination and interpretation" to give the custodial staff a better understanding of classification and counseling. They suggested that the educational staffs be built so that a large percentage of the inmates could go to school.

The seven recommendations regarding inmate population aimed primarily at better classification, segregation, and treatment of "reformatory type" inmates, insane inmates, misdemeanants, criminal sexual psychopaths, and other special groups. Re-examination of the criminal sexual psychopath law was suggested. With attention to the subject of the televised debate between Frisbie and Brooks during the political campaign in which Frisbie was called a liar, the committee recommended "that the policy of not transferring Jackson prisoners in the reformatory age group to Ionia Reformatory if they have low mentality or are suffering from epilepsy, even though their seizures are being kept under control by medication, be reversed. . . ."

With regard to discipline, the recommendations were that a firm but fair discipline be maintained without resorting to brutality or laxity, that the rules forbidding corporal punishment be rigidly enforced, and that 15-block be abandoned as the disciplinary unit at the earliest possible date.

The recommendations concerning parole and probation were left to the reports by the representative of the National Parole and Probation Association in the body of the report.

The committee approved the recommendations of the research staff, and presented eight recommendations of its own. These were that a statewide survey of probation be made by the National Probation and Parole Association, that any survey of probation include consideration of the Wisconsin plan in which the judge might withdraw a first offender from the reception center after sixty to ninety days provided the classification committee recommended probation, that a program be developed for district or regional jails, that orientation of prisoners to parole programs should be made more effective, that the camp program not be used solely as a means of reducing "inside" population, that the "good-time" statutes be reviewed and judges be better informed on parole, that the advice and assistance of business and labor unions be secured to assist in planning courses and to assist in finding employment for inmates, and that the Department of Mental Health be placed in a position to provide more beds to relieve the Department of Corrections from furnishing facilities for the insane.

Following the recommendations came the body of the report, which covered 111 pages of description, tables, and opinions. The introduction gave a general background of the series of riots of which the Michigan riot was but one. Two paragraphs are of significance.

> The most striking thing about the 1951-52 riots is that they have occurred in some of the worst prisons in the country and in some of the best, in the oldest prison and the newest, in the largest prison and some of the smallest, and in every section of the country. While it is possible to discover basic causal and contributory factors in each of the riots, it is difficult to explain the fact that there have been more in the past 18 months than in the preceding 18 years, that they have spread over such a wide geographical area, and have occurred in such a variety of institutions. Even the most careful study of each disturbance does not reveal a single factor or set of factors that can be considered the basic cause of the entire series.

* * * * *

> While the Ohio Penitentiary riot apparently involved as many prisoners as the Jackson Prison affair and resulted in greater damage to property, the latter must be accorded the dubious distinction of being, in many ways, the most dangerous prison riot in American history. Never, for example, have hostages been in more danger for a long period than those held in Cell Block 15 by the homicidal psychopaths who were the leaders of the riot there. Never has it been necessary to mobilize so large a force of State Police for what amounted to combat duty inside the walls of a prison. A force of approximately 275 officers and troopers of the State Police was mobilized at the time of the riots at Jackson Prison in April, and they were not withdrawn from the institution until August. It was possible to withdraw the last of the troopers then only be-

cause the prison officials had organized their own riot squads and because assistance could be furnished quickly from the State Police barracks near the prison. Never has a large prison population been, so long after a riot, in a state of ferment where violence may break out again at any moment.

After the introduction, this information was divided into sections as follows:

I. Excessive Size of Jackson Prison, Overcrowding Accentuated by Idleness, and Description of Other Institutions

II. Heterogeneous Nature of the Inmate Population of Jackson

III. Personnel Problems in the Prison System

IV. The Michigan Parole Board

V. Administrative Structure of the Prison and Parole Systems

The material presented in this section is primarily descriptive, with a few opinions interjected.

The section on the Michigan Parole Board was of more interest to me than much of the institutional material. I thought that there were more erroneous statements in that section than in other sections. An example referred to the parole board as "the primary cause" of the riot. Actually, the parole board was not even mentioned in the early negotiations at 15-block. When I was surrounded by these men in the yard Monday afternoon, the men shouted to abolish the parole board, but it was not mentioned by the men in 15-block. The first time I heard any comment that the parole board might even be a factor was verbally from Commissioner Brooks on Monday morning, when I replied that I had not heard of it. When it was first presented to me as a term on Tuesday, however, it had been built up quite strongly, and presented difficulty. The eventual term was that the warden would write a letter to the parole board, which remained quite impotent. I had observed later that I was the only institutional official who had not attacked the parole board in hearings and, further, had defended it in speeches and on television appearances. Yet, the report on Michigan parole prepared by Randolph Wise said that it is significant that the parole board was not attacked early, that Commissioner Brooks did not refer to parole administration as the cause of the disturbance, but that I had said that "the parole board item presented the most difficulty." The paragraph ended with, "In no other official account of the disturbance is so much emphasis placed on the board as the primary cause of the rioting." I had never said or written that the parole board was a primary, secondary, tertiary, or any cause of the rioting! This is only one of many instances in which words, attitudes, statements, and actions had been attributed to me by taking material out of context, by inference, or by outright fabrication!

The report charged that the board "is cynical, cryptic, sarcastic, and dictatorial in its dealings with inmates"; that the inmate must plead guilty to the charge for which he was sentenced; that the board lives in isolation as far as inmates and institutional personnel are concerned (which I sometimes think is a good idea!); that the board does not spend enough time in hearings; that the board takes no initiative to interpret parole to inmates; that the even number of the board tends to militate against inmates when decisions cannot be reached at the hearing; that "certain members assume the role of pseudo psychiatrists" during hearings; that few decisions can be made conclusive at the time of hearing; that " 'flops' appear to be determined on the basis of tradition rather than on the basis of individualized study"; that the board has lacked stability of composition during the past three years; and that the "executive session" delays decisions unnecessarily. The report stated, however, that all inmates who obviously deserve parole are given a parole. It failed to mention that figures readily available show that Michigan paroles with significantly greater liberality than the national average.

The eleven recommendations were aimed at correcting the charges. Further study of probation and periodic studies of parole were recommended. The recommendation to increase the board from four to five members was made. One recommendation, that seemed to indicate that Mr. Wise had not investigated thoroughly, was that a report should be compiled which the board should have at the time of the hearing and which would include a statement of the inmate's offense, parole plans, attitudes toward the future, and other related information. Ever since I went to Jackson in 1942, and for several years before, the parole board had had such a report at the time of its hearings. It had been called a "Pre-Parole Progress Report," and included all the information for which Mr. Wise asked.

The information presented in the section on Administrative Structure of the Prison and Parole Systems expressed opinions that are open to debate. There was the statement that a major defect at the time of the April rioting was that three of the four top administrative positions in the Department of Corrections were vacant. There was no Director of Prisons and Industries nor Director of the Division of Pardons, Paroles, and Probation. Civil service employees, however, the report did not point out, had assumed the functions of these jobs. Assistant to the Commissioner Gilman worked with the prison program, Ed Haight was manager of industries, Gus Harrison handled parole functions in his position as State Supervisor of Paroles, and Fred Bates handled probation. The jobs had once been filled, but there were not enough duties assigned to keep the incumbents busy. Emery Jacques and Seymour Gilman had at different times been in the office of Director of the Division of Prisons and Industries, and neither could even appear to be busy. Dr. Ralph Hall Ferris, during his later and ailing years, handled what duties there were to the position of Director of the Division of Pardons, Paroles, and Probation by coming to work half-days. As far as the position of chairman of the parole board was concerned, there actually was no vacancy. All positions on the board were filled. One had not been designated as chairman of the board. I didn't think that constituted a "serious defect."

The report emphasized, as all the other reports had emphasized, the differences between philosophies of Custody and of Individual Treatment. Deputy Bacon was aware of the need for treatment but emphasized custody. I was aware of the need for custody but emphasized treatment. Many were the problems we solved between us. Only in a few instances did we have to go to the warden or commissioner to settle a difference. We entertained each other in our homes, bowled together, "flipped for the Cokes," and engaged in other similar social activity. Deputy Bacon and I have said independently that the differences between our departments have been grossly exaggerated, probably because it was an obvious and almost expected difference in a period when people were looking for causes for riots. Despite the fact that no testimony was available from anyone that this difference in philosophy even contributed, it has been listed as a cause of the riot!

The vacant position of deputy warden at the prison was listed as an administrative weakness. Actually, most persons at the prison and outside the prison thought that the prison was top-heavy in administration. The position referred to as "deputy warden" was never a functional one, and was created to provide a place for Ralph Benson when he was reinstated by civil service to his status and compensation. Simultaneously, the warden's position had been raised to sort of a "super-warden" in order that Julian N. Frisbie would remain as warden despite Benson's reinstatement. Benson didn't work at the prison, but was generally on other assignments. Being incapacitated, he was unable to do much anyway. Benson had died shortly before the riot, and the position had not been abolished. I was quite surprised to learn from this report that failure to fill the position was "an administrative weakness."

Apparently referring to Commissioner Brooks, the report said,

> Persons who are eminently qualified in other respects can learn "the prison business" on the job, but the system they head is bound to suffer while they're learning. The

state cannot afford, either on the basis of current expenditures or the cost of future crime, to have anything but the most competent personnel in the correctional system from top to bottom, and the prisons and the correctional system must be taken out of politics once and for all.

The parole board attacked the report of the citizens' committee as a "shoddy performance" and branded some of the findings as "silly." From the erudite phraseology of the parole board's rejoinder, I am convinced that it was written in whole or in part by A. Ross Pascoe, whom I consider to be one of the ablest release men in the country. In part, the reply was:

> The parole board had fervently hoped that there could be no justification for any dissatisfaction to the extent of the search into parole, much less a letter of open protest at the conclusion of the committee's work.
> That there is a deep feeling of disappointment and resentment on our part is occasioned by the shoddy performance of the investigators assigned to examine the parole activity and by the lack of time given to it.
>
> * * * * *
>
> We cannot in honor and good conscience accept the committee's findings that parole was a factor causing the disturbance at Southern Michigan Prison nor concede the truth of the faults laid to the parole board in the survey of MacCormick and Wise.
> It is our considered opinion that this survey is a sad reflection on the National Probation and Parole Association and those who participate in its submittal.

The board noted that Governor Williams had assured that Austin MacCormick had agreed to give the parole board the fullest opportunity to be heard, but Mr. MacCormick reported that he was too busy to handle that phase of the inquiry. As a result, "no more than 20 hours" was spent with parole officials by Randolph Wise, a welfare commissioner with four years of probation and parole experience as consultant for the National Probation and Parole Association. Wise spent as much as three hours talking to a long-term habitual criminal at the prison, which is a period longer than he spent with any parole official. The parole board said that, while all official reports and Commissioner Brooks had accused the parole board of contributing to the riot, nobody had listed any supporting evidence. It denied that inmates appearing before the board had to plead guilty to the charge for which they had been sentenced. The parole board pointed out that the 1947 law gave the single commissioner of corrections administrative powers formerly handled by the parole board, and that it also took from the board the previous ability to interpret action.

A four-member parole board, concerning itself with 6,000 to 8,000 interviews with inmates, interviews with lawyers, relatives and friends, with the pardon and commutation function, etc., is exactly as free to do "interpretive" work as the old woman who lived in a shoe.

Replying to the charge that inmates were kept waiting by the parole board, the report said,

In a situation where they have probably been in jail nine months before sentence, or sometimes held in 15-block three days before a trial board hearing (by prison officials for a rules infraction), we are accused of "inconveniencing" the inmates by keeping them waiting.

The board denied that all decisions were later checked by a reviewing member. Approximately 70 per cent of the decisions were made at the time of hearing. It compared that action with the federal parole board which does not render decisions for several months after hearings. The board defended the executive session, which was used 158 times in 6,000 cases, and which delayed decisions for discussion by the full board. The inmate was given the opportunity of being passed over in doubtful cases or of reserving the chance of parole on a four-member talkout. The board reported that it would be easier on parole board members not to use the executive session at all, but that in eliminating it, the board would be rejecting one of the most important aspects of their treatment of the human beings who make up the prison population. The parole board offered statistics to show that Michigan has the most liberal and equitable parole policies in the United States, has fewer parole violators, and the most liberal good time laws.

The comment of Randolph Wise in Philadelphia was, "I stand by my findings." Austin MacCormick said, "The parole board's reply to our findings is interesting but not necessarily true." Governor Williams said of his citizens' committee report, "I feel it was a good report in all ways."

It was on March 4 that Warden Bannan announced that he had discovered the cause of the riot. The news about Tower Furniture's huge furniture sale leaked out, Bannan said, and the prisoners thought by destroying the present furniture the warden would have to take advantage of Tower's low prices!

During debate on a bill to force the parole board to hear passed-over inmates every 12 months, the board was accused of prejudice against attorneys. Representative Lesinski of Detroit, sponsor of the bill, said, "If the board finds that an inmate is represented by an attorney, the prisoner is flopped over the next seven or eight times. This bill will give prisoners some hope and initiative." The bill was defeated 73 to 50.

Governor Williams called a meeting of corrections officials and wardens to discuss what action should be taken on the citizens' committee report. They decided to ask for the new institution as recommended. Further, the governor would ask for funds to hire directors of the division of pardons, paroles, and probation, and the division of prisons and industries. Further, the governor would ask for funds for "extra" counselors, classification men, teachers, and vocational instructors. The group also recommended that the parole board be expanded from four to five members. It was decided at this time to use 15-block for kitchen help and to make a disciplinary block of the now existing 1-block. Gun galleries would be installed in all cell blocks, the mess hall, and gymnasium, and a fence was suggested to be built around the industries section of the prison. The group decided not to take over the Detroit House of Correction, but to ask for a women's prison. Six-block at Jackson would be made into a reception unit, if possible. If this were not possible, then the requested new institution would be designed to handle that function. Governor Williams said that the problems of psychotic prisoners and the criminal sexual psychopaths were for the mental health commission to solve.

Because of the drastic changes suggested by the committee's report, the legislature invited Austin MacCormick to appear before a joint meeting to discuss the reforms he recommended. The cost of the proposed changes was estimated at $20,000,-000. The estimated cost of the new prison had been reported by the corrections commissioner at $15,000,000. Representative John Kruse wanted the institution located at Manistee, and announced his intention of introducing a resolution into the house to that effect.

In the meantime, "Crazy Jack" Hyatt was declared sane and able to stand trial, according to Dr. O. R. Yoder, superintendent of the Ypsilanti State Hospital. John Crockard and Russell Jarboe were also declared sane and able to stand trial. Tried about the same time as Hyatt were Anthony Mazzone and Virgil Alden, all on charges of kidnaping. All were found guilty and sentenced. Hyatt was sentenced to 15 to 23 years, Mazzone was sentenced to 4 to 10 years, and Alden was sentenced to 2 to 4 years, all to be served concurrently with their original sentences. The newspaper articles were captioned, "Pen Rioters Escape Extra Confinement."

Before the legislature on March 4, Austin MacCormick warned that another riot would hit the system if the public did not solve the "prison mess." He called Governor Williams' "get-tough" policy a mistake. He hoped that some day Michigan would get a career penologist to administer the prison system. He said that administration was secondary at the time and that last April's riot would have "exploded under the best management in the country." In essence, MacCormick repeated the findings he wrote in the citizens' committee report. MacCormick said that he had changed his mind about the commission form of administration. He had long recommended the commission form, and had termed Michigan's 1937 corrections law a model for the country. However, he believed at this time that a "straight line of authority is best," thereby supporting the single commissioner type of administration. MacCormick said that parole board policies had created "considerable bitterness" against the board, and that they were "perhaps major contributing factors" in the riot.

No sooner had the cost of the proposed reforms been estimated when editorials appeared expressing opinions about it. It was pointed out that a legislature faced with a probable $90,000,000 deficit should proceed cautiously in spending money. The *Detroit Free Press*, for instance, carried an editorial on March 7 in which it was pointed out that the difficulty lay in finding the money to make "these constructive and needed changes." The final sentence was, "It should impress upon the lawmakers and the governor the need for correcting Michigan's fiscal imbalance as the first essential step in any program of improvements." The editorials attacked the estimated cost of the proposed new prison. Senator Porter of Blissfield was quoted frequently as saying the estimates were way out of line. The cost would be something like $12,500 per cell, which is the same as some of the country's most modern hotels.

A special state senate investigating committee headed by Senator Harry F. Hittle said that many sentences authorized by law were excessive and in no way related to the seriousness of the offense committed. Further, "good-time" laws need considerable alteration to make them effective. For instance, the forfeiture of all earned "good time" by parole violators was not proper administration of justice. The Hittle report stated further that courts should prescribe a sentence in such a manner that the parole board would not re-sentence a prisoner. The committee wanted to allow wardens greater latitude in recommending parole and special good-time allowances. More jobs for prisoners inside the walls to reduce idleness was another recommendation. Further, the parole laws should be revised so that the length of time a person remained on parole bore a direct relation to the time served in prison. The committee wanted to send persons convicted of minor crimes, including contempt of court, to county jails, rather than to the prison. The Hittle report wanted parole officers to be required to help inmates get jobs, because there were many who could not get out because they could not find jobs (this had been a function of the parole officers since 1937).

Representatives Betz and Warner introduced a bill to provide for capital punishment in Michigan. It would fix death by electrocution at the State Prison of Southern Michigan for first-degree murders.

Bills were introduced by the Hittle committee to fix one standard of good-time allowances for inmates, regardless of their past records, allow the judges to set the maximum sentences for a crime, provided it did not exceed the present statutory maximum, and permit prison wardens to take away good-time allowances if inmates did not behave properly. The good-time standard would allow five days off for each month up to two years, six days a month for the third and fourth years, and seven days a month for the fifth and sixth years. Graduated increases would reach 20 days per month after 20 years. In addition, wardens could award "special good time" of 2½ days per month. Estimates were that the law would affect 1,500 men in the prison system, and that it would make from 400 to 600 men immediately eligible for release.

Representative Stanley Novak introduced a bill to provide a $1,000 life insurance policy for all state law-enforcement officers, including State Police and prison guards. Included was a provision to appropriate $7,500 to pay premiums.

Governor Williams asked the House and Senate Appropriations Committees to pledge cash for the establishment of a psychiatric unit at the prison at Jackson. He noted that the legislature had in a previous session approved the establishment of the unit but had provided no money. Senator Porter replied that he was in no position to make pledges for the legislature.

Senate action on the corrections department's budget began with argument. While the pay raises were intended only for guards, it appeared that all personnel had been considered for increases. Senator Porter said that the request for 190 new employees for the Department of Corrections would be the first point of attack. The civil service requirement that pay raises ordered for one prison must be extended to all others having employees in that job classification also perturbed the senators. Confusion over the designation of "custodial personnel" who were to get the raise led to the mix-up, since civil service officials had rules that the definition set up covered anyone who came into contact with inmates. Persons in medical services, engineering, business administration, and many other functions also were qualified for raises under the definition.

Governor Williams called a meeting of state and local law-enforcement officers, in which he asked for an increased use of probation. He told them that overcrowding in the prisons made greater use of probation urgent.

In a special message to the legislature, Governor Williams asked for $14,250,000 to build the new prison at Ionia, new or remodeled cell-blocks at Marquette and Jackson, a study to determine whether a women's prison should be constructed, more gun galleries at Jackson, and more employees. He asked for a fifth member on the parole board, a youth division for the Department of Corrections, and a camp for probationers. He repeated his request for a psychiatric unit at Jackson.

The National Broadcasting System presented a series of one-hour programs at 9:00 P.M. Friday nights, entitled, "The Challenge of Our Prisons." Michigan's riot was broadcast on March 6 and 13, and the story of Earl Ward was broadcast on March 20. The programs were built on tape recorded by Walter McGraw of McGraw Associates, New York. Although I would probably have changed a few items because the actual facts were clear in my mind, McGraw did an exceptionally

good job of putting together conflicting testimony and opinion
with a minimum of error. The broadcasts assisted me in viewing
the total situation. It was the first time I knew the reason
given for the agreement being ignored after frequent promises
that it would be honored. Governor Williams stated on this
broadcast that the way the terms were framed made it impossible to carry them out. This, of course, is not true. Brooks
and Frisbie read them when they signed them, and they were
the ones who would implement the agreement with action.

I had been presented in an unfavorable light on several
occasions by shifts of emphasis unwarranted by the facts and
by relating irrelevant facts to situations to imply blame. For instance, my reason for the speech was not given. Further, while
I was in charge, I did not know who assigned the inexperienced
guard to 15-block. Actually, even though I was in charge for
the week-end, I had been told not to bother Custody and that
any custodial decisions would be within the jurisdiction of
Deputy Bacon. The inference was, however, that I was inefficient. Another example was when newsman Boyd Simmons
said that toward the end of the riot, I was defending the inmates—that they had won me over instead of my winning
them over. Actually, this was the period when the strain and
fatigue had reduced co-operation among the official staff
to the extent that we emerged as individuals, and I had found
myself defending the inmates in order to prevent Commissioner Leonard from blasting the cell-block.

Gilman said that on Monday morning during the riot, I
had "sidled up" to 15-block and begun agreeing with Ward,
and that he was thereby ousted from his position as chief negotiator. While this was not true, Gilman probably needed
the interpretation for ego defense. I recognized partially, too,
what "Kelly" had meant when he had said a month after the
riot that a lot of people were "getting on the bandwagon."

Ward said on the programs that he had been double-crossed
by the governor. He said further that if he had it to do over
again, he certainly would, and "the next time it will be bloody."
He also said that I was "diabolically clever" and not to be

trusted, indicating that he believed that I was not bargaining in good faith which, of course, is not true. I have repeated and I repeat again that there was not a term signed that I did and do not want myself!

The programs ended with my comment that it is inconsistent to maintain a parole board and at the same time to maintain a punishment program.

On April 1, a bill was solemnly read by Senate Secretary Chase to advocate a 100 per cent tax on dividends of the Mennen Co. due Governor G. Mennen Williams so that he could build a plush prison "for the everlasting comfort of those who may run afoul of the law, and where steak and ice cream dinners may be served." Any money left after the construction would be spent for a 1,000 man committee composed of Democrats to study the "need, site, and type of architecture on a women's villa, because the Michigan legislators are fed up with the annual bickerings with the city of Detroit over the state's payments for use of the Detroit House of Correction." The villa would have outside rooms, bathrooms in green and white (Williams' campaign colors) and "easy-on-the-body mattresses" with electric blankets.

Hittle's bills to force wardens to release men after serving three times the minimum sentence and to revise the goodtime allowances were labeled in the newspapers as a "bill to release convicts." Judges Simpson of Jackson and Sweet of Kalamazoo testified before a senate judiciary committee and said that the release of such a bill would give too much power to the wardens while taking it away from the parole board. Newspapers reported that legislators were "outraged at disclosure that several hundred burglars, hoodlums, racketeers, and petty criminals may immediately walk out of Michigan prisons." Senator Gilbert wanted the "beneficiaries" identified before further action was taken. He said he was "impressed" by possibilities of new riots if the senate failed to take favorable action on these bills. He said that the bills were a struggle for power between the wardens and the parole boards. He said, "I am impressed the wardens are sometimes prone to seek the early discharge of malcontents" to ease custodial problems. Gilbert continued that it was time "to stop shedding tears over men in prison who are trying to run the state legislature." Hittle denied that his bills were to appease inmates, but that they were attempts to individualize justice.

News reports were that the parole board members, protected by civil service from legislative reprisals, were trying to retain their powers over inmates. A motion for a public hearing was voted down. Hittle pointed out that his bills were not criticized by any top penologists. After bitter debate, the senate voted 15 to 15 on the bill to grant standard good-time allowances. Since bills need 17 votes to pass, it went back to committee for burial. With it went the measure to fix maximum sentences at three times the minimum if the trial judge did not fix the maximum less than the statutory maximum. Little attention was given the bill to force wardens to release men after three times the minimum term had been served. Hittle said he would press no further during the current session for his reform bills.

The senate on April 16 reversed its action concerning the good-time allowances. Amended so that the approximately 600 men would not be released without parole board review, the uniform good-time bill was passed by the senate. Then it was discovered that fewer than one hundred men were immediately affected. The senate passed the bill to send to county jails all prisoners sentenced to one year or less. Simultaneously, the house of representatives approved and sent to the senate the bill to render sex offenders ineligible for placement in corrections camps.

Senator Perry Greene of Grand Rapids introduced a bill to put a six-man commission in charge of Michigan's prison system. The commission would be bipartisan, with three Democrats and three Republicans appointed by the governor with the advice and consent of the senate. The director of corrections would be appointed by the governor from a list of candidates submitted by the commission. After confirmation, the director would serve at the pleasure of the commission, but could be removed only after civil service hearing. The director would be responsible for prisons, industries, and probation, as well as criminal statistics and administrative services. The parole board would be expanded to five members and would be divorced from political and departmental influences, responsible only to the commission. The senate passed the bill and sent it to the house of representatives. Before a house committee, A. Ross Pascoe said that the assistant director of pardons and paroles, as envisaged in the Greene Bill, should be appointed by the parole board rather than by the commission. Debate centered around that issue.

At the prison, a camp was constructed across Cooper Street from the main gate of the prison for 125 prospective parolees. Men were to be sent to the camp after they had been favorably received by the parole board. While at the camp, they would work half-days and attend classes designed to prepare them for return to civilian life. This was to be administered by the state parole office, but the prison staff would be responsible for feeding, housing, and other services. Civilian clothing would be worn. Kenneth Shea, parole officer at Ann Arbor, was selected to operate the school.

The riot's anniversary passed without event, according to Warden Bannan. Newspapers ran brief stories about the present status. The *Detroit News*, for instance, ran a story under the headline, "Scars of Jackson Prison Riot Disappear after a Year of Discipline." The most distinctive reminder of the riot were the new gun turrets, according to the writer. The *Detroit Free Press* ran three pages of pictures in the Sunday magazine section under the title, "Jackson—a Year after the Riot." One of the pictures showed a reporter taking notes of a conversation between Ward and Assistant to the Commissioner Seymour Gilman, and the caption under the photo reads, "*Free Press* reporter Ken McCormick, who covered riot story last year, listens in on conversation between prison official and Revolt Leader Earl Ward. A hostage is in the background."

Thirty miles away, the University of Michigan canceled its curriculum in correctional administration because of the state of corrections in Michigan. Dr. Lowell J. Carr "flunked the state of Michigan for its efforts in the field of penology." Dr. Carr made four points in this regard,

1. Michigan is parasitic on the brains of the rest of the country in prison work.
2. The state haltingly makes use of techniques discovered in more enlightened areas in the field and is laggard in picking up demonstrated techniques of prison operation.
3. Michigan does not seem interested in finding the best practices in convict treatment.
4. Apparently neither the governor nor the legislature is interested in a scientific approach to the problem rather than a political one.

Dr. Carr continued, "Nothing much has been accomplished since the riot. The investigation of causes was not nearly extensive enough. They've settled for a superficial explanation." He pointed out that research has shown that 25 to 35 per cent of Michigan's approximately 9,000 inmates do not need to be shut up. On the average, 98 per cent of the prisoners remain in prison less than five calendar years. He considered the bill in the senate to send to county jails men sentenced for less than a year a pathetic evasion of the problem.

On May 6, ninety prisoners assigned to maintenance work staged a sit-down strike at the prison in a demand for increased pay. The wages in the prison ranged from 5 to 20 cents per day. Some inmates had received unauthorized increases from foremen or inmate clerks. When these were cut off, rumors were that all proposed increases were doomed. They refused to go back to work until Warden Bannan heard their demand. Warden Bannan told them that their compensation depended entirely upon budgetary action of the legislature.

Legislators planned to question Brooks about the sit-down strike, but Brooks did not appear before the house ways and means committee. Warden Bannan appeared instead, and he was not asked about the strikes. He was informed that $130,000 was earmarked in the budget for inmate pay as compared to last year's $100,000. This meant, of course, that the old minimum of 10 cents per day for inmate work could be restored. Bannan had recommended a maximum of 35 cents per day, rather than the current 20. Depending upon the manner of distribution, the new appropriation could meet Bannan's desires.

Commissioner Brooks distributed a form letter designed to prevent the passage of the commission form of administration of the corrections department. He said that it would cost $75,000 to $90,000 to make the transition. House Republicans said it would be closer to $30,000, but Representative Hoxie said that it would be well worth the money if good administration could be obtained. Representative DeBoom said he praised Mr. Brooks whenever he spoke of him saying, "He is one of the best insurance men I know." Republicans recalled that while Williams campaigned for a return to the model law before his entry into the governor's office, he had been quite silent about it since he appointed his own corrections commissioner.

The uniform good-time bill passed the legislature and was sent to the governor for signature. The bill permitting the judges to set maximum sentences was killed in committee. The bill preventing sex offenders from going to camps was passed. The bill which created the six-man corrections commission also passed the legislature after an unsuccessful effort by house Democrats to defeat it, and it was sent to the governor. Editorials pointed out Williams' position. If he signed the bill, then he would have accomplished the fulfillment of an early campaign promise. If he signs it, however, "he throws down the corrections commissioner who had had the governor's unwavering support." If he should veto it, one paper reported "the Republicans could have a practical field day." He had until June 26 to decide.

Governor Williams almost immediately signed into law the bill providing that all persons sentenced to terms of one year would serve in the county jails or in the Detroit House of Correction. He signed into law a bill to transfer incorrigible boys 16 years or older from Boys Vocational School to facilities of the Department of Corrections, other than prison. He signed the uniform good time allowance law. He continued to hold the bill creating the corrections commission.

At the trials of rioters, Russell Jarboe was sentenced to 7 to 10 years for kidnaping, and was then transferred to the Ionia State Hospital for the Criminal Insane. Alfred Lovitt had also been found insane. John Crockard was given a 15 to 30 year term for kidnaping. The last man to be sentenced for kidnaping was Kenneth Moore, sentenced May 13 to 15 to 25 years. All sentences were to run concurrently. Some of the charges against rioters were dropped, but most of the accused men were convicted.

The Federal Bureau of Investigation sent agents to Michigan's prisons during the latter part of May. No reason was given Warden Bannan or Commissioner Brooks, and Governor Williams had nothing to say. Speculation was that the government might have been interested in possible violation of federal civil rights statutes by either prison guards or civilian employees through mistreatment of inmates. The *Detroit News* said that it was also a probe to determine whether Communists were to blame for instigating riots in the prison at Jackson and elsewhere, a hypothesis suggested by United States Senator Homer Ferguson. The agents talked to Dr. Finch in Lansing. The inmates who were injured in the November 30 beatings were named for the first time as being Jack Russell, 23; Robert Fisher, 24; Harrison Wilson, 48; and Tom Gisevan, 27. A fifth man, Luther McCoy, 23, had been injured similarly on December 7. The house committee on prisons had previously cleared Warden Bannan of blame for these incidents by what they called "a clean bill of health." The F.B.I. subsequently said that inmates had not been deprived of civil rights.

Politics was considered to be a principal riot cause by Dr. Garrett Heyns and Warden Bannan at a meeting of the Central States Corrections Association at Louisville, Kentucky. Bannan said that too much interference from people who want to come in and put new ideas into action overnight is a principal cause of riots. Warden Jesse Buchanan of Kentucky State Penitentiary said that politics had nothing to do with riots at his institution last summer. That may have been politic!

The American Prison Association issued a booklet on the causes of riots. Entitled, *A Statement Concerning Causes, Preventive Measures, and Methods of Controlling Prison Riots & Disturbances,* the booklet reviewed many of the articles and reports concerning prison riots. Immediate causes were separated from basic causes, on the premise that the immediate causes are merely symptoms. The basic causes were given as follows:

1. Inadequate financial support and official and public indifference.
2. Substandard personnel.
3. Enforced idleness.
4. Lack of professional leadership and professional programs.
5. Excessive size and overcrowding of institutions.
6. Political domination and motivation of management.
7. Unwise sentencing and parole practices.

I considered to be their primary conclusion the statement, "The underlying causes of poor prison administration all stem from a lack of public understanding of the problem and from a consequent reluctance to provide adequate financial support and to keep politics out of management."

A feature story in the *Detroit Free Press* by Ken McCormick reviewed the Jackson riot in terms of the causes given by the American Prison Association's booklet. He concluded with a statement from A. Blake Gillies, retired superintendent of the Detroit House of Correction, "If it was up to me, I'd let the Army use the monstrosity for bomb experiments and then build four new prisons that would each house no more than 1,500 convicts."

A series of four articles concerning the prison and the

riot appeared in June, 1953, in *The Saturday Evening Post,* written by John Bartlow Martin, and this material was subsequently included in a book entitled *Break Down the Walls.* Surprising to me, the articles were a poor bit of reporting and interpretation, substandard, I thought, to appear in this particular magazine. Exceptional cases were presented as representative, the facts reported accurately were reported without explanation and out of context so that the implied meaning was inaccurate, emphasis was shifted without justification, and interpretations indicated that the writer was not acquainted with prison administration. My impression was that he had used the prison previously as a source of writing materials, and he wanted to adopt a slant so that the prison would remain for him a source of information which he would like further to exploit. I considered refutation when the series appeared, but the inaccuracies were so general, including what I consider to be some fabrication, that it would be difficult to correct them. Needless to say, they contributed nothing to penology.

After remaining silent on the bill to return Michigan corrections to the commission form of administration, Governor Williams finally signed the measure before the June 26 deadline. He announced that Commissioner Brooks had indicated that he did not want to be considered as a candidate for the position of director of corrections under the new law. Williams said, however, that he would ask Brooks to accept appointment as one of the commission members. The new administrative structure of the Department of Corrections was to become effective on October 2, 1953. Governor Williams appointed his legal advisor, Philip A. Hart, as a "special deputy" to reorganize the corrections department in accordance with the new law. Hart appointed committees to study various phases of it, particularly the women's prison and the new youth division.

Governor Williams' office "let it be rumored" that James V. Bennett, director of the United States Bureau of Prisons, might be induced to come to Michigan. The rumor was that

United States Attorney General Herbert Brownell would eventually get rid of Bennett, in line with a policy to eliminate personnel who played a major role in the Roosevelt and Truman administrations. It was noted that his reputation as a penologist would give Michigan corrections a top man and might affect the riot publicity. Whether or not there was any basis for these rumors was not known. The governor did not formally announce it, but "those close to" the governor let it be rumored. Whether or not there was some basis for it, the release of the rumor was a shrewd political maneuver. The mere mention of the possibility of Williams' administration bringing a top penologist to Michigan was unexpected good news and would help to affect the opinion that Williams continued to play politics in the prison system—even though the release itself was shrewd politics.

Warden Bannan announced on June 24 that "I have the Southern Michigan Prison under control." Further, he said, "The prison is the quietest it has been in six years. I don't take full credit for getting the prison back in shape—only for getting back the line of command. I have no fear that the place will blow up. It took a long time to get back a line of command from guard to sergeant, lieutenant to captain, deputy to warden, but today that line of command is established." What he was saying was that *custody* was operating the prison without any "interfering" treatment philosophy.

All persons closely connected with the handling of the riot have been eliminated from the Department of Corrections. I resigned a month after the riot. Warden Frisbie was summarily dismissed within three months after the riot. Commissioner Brooks' job was abolished by legislative action which installed the commission form of administration in the Department of Corrections. Only those who took no effective or active part in the riot remained.

A conclusion from the general review of other prison riots in earlier chapters and the more detailed review of the Michigan riot and its aftermath in this and the last chapter is that in terms of political action, the true situation within the prison is of only passing importance. More important is that *some* explanation for the riots has to be given to the general public, whose aggression is always aroused when "convicts" dare to rebel. This explanation has to bear sufficient credence to gain the support of editors and others who shape public opinion by the selective releasing of information. The explanation also has to protect the individuals or groups at the highest echelon, politically, who may be most affected by the decision of public opinion.

In such instances, after the explanation has crystallized, a process by which the most generally acceptable explanation takes shape and emerges from the early confusion of news reports, then action of some sort has to occur. Because aggression on the part of inmates arouses aggression on the part of the public; finding an outlet for the aggression of both groups is necessary, though generally incompatible. In the case of the inmates, a "get-tough" policy is generally invoked by public declaration. This satisfies the public and frustrates the inmates further. Consequently, disturbances continue in the prison and the administration is viewed as strong men who refuse to "mollycoddle" prisoners. In the case of the public, some individual or group who can be considered expendable by the persons who need to be protected must be found. This individual or group must be identified as being close enough to the situation so that he can logically accept blame for it as far as the aroused public is concerned. The emergence of the explanation pattern occurs when this individual or group has been identified. By this time, the true situation within the prison walls has been forgotten. Action taken to expel this individual or group from the situation completes the "scapegoat" process, and tends to alleviate the intensity of public feeling by accomplishing a goal directed by the aroused aggression.

After the scapegoat has been eliminated from the scene, there comes the period of "reconstructive" action. This "reconstruction" need not be actually beneficial, but rather a change of some sort which can be made to appear constructive.

As a matter of fact, the change can be contradictory to the recommendations of the "experts" called in to help find the explanation. In Michigan, for instance, Austin MacCormick and many other experts said the "get-tough" policy was a mistake, but that did not alter the "get-tough" policy because that policy was designed for public consumption rather than for the treatment of human beings. Austin MacCormick and the Citizens Research Council recommended retention of the single commissioner type of administration. The legislature, however, paid little heed and made a change which could have been embarrassing to the governor, but the governor astutely sidestepped and the commission form was adopted. Which form of administration was the better was of less concern than that some change had to be made.

After the changes are made, the public interest becomes diffused in the current war, the current labor troubles, and what is happening to surplus potatoes or Senator McCarthy. Apathy regarding the prison system returns to normalcy without much real thought being given to what the prison program is doing to the human beings confined there. In the meantime, the rehabilitation program has been gutted. It remains on the scene in terms of personnel being present, figures in the budget requests, and window-dressing, but its effectiveness is ruined by ridicule, lowered morale, reduced prerogatives and freedom of movement, and withdrawn support on the part of new wardens. Public opinion has been placated, but the prison program has been set back a decade.

The most dangerous riot in American prison history exemplified all these processes more vividly than any of the other riots. What occurred in the riot itself became clouded by explanations, "subsequent actions," and investigating committees with axes to grind. The fact that due to the action of one man, the most dangerous riot in American prison history was settled on terms that appeared to be torn from a textbook of progressive penology and with the loss of but one prisoner's life, and the loss of no lives at all in the 15-block bastion where twelve officers were once held hostage by dangerous men—that fact had no bearing on subsequent public relations and political action. It meant little or nothing. Of greater importance was the handling of public opinion to maintain the political status quo.

Michigan corrections continues its turbulent course. Michigan went past the effective date of its new corrections law without a director. No competent man of national reputation could be induced to accept such a position in Michigan. Gus Harrison, an obscure but smiling member of the parole division, who many colleagues said "backed into" his position as state supervisor of paroles, also "backed into" the directorship of corrections. Almost immediately he was censured by Governor Williams for failure to act fast enough, and the turbulence continued.

Michigan corrections has shifted its emphasis, as was well stated by Warden Bannan in a speech to Jackson's Kiwanis Club,

> One of the nicest sights I have ever seen was a psychologist out in the yard with a shotgun telling an inmate he would let him have a blast of buckshot if he didn't get in line.

CHAPTER X

Riot Causes

Since the beginning of prisons and since the beginnings of prison riots which, as far as can be determined, were almost simultaneous, the search for causes has continued unabated. After a new riot or series of riots, new causes are advanced, or the old causes in a new setting. In each case, the proposed causes are at first widely variant but as reporters and investigators and writers become more prolific, the "causes" become crystallized. Sometimes the end result does not exactly match the situation and persons on the scene are surprised at the "causes." For example, in the Michigan riot, a primary "cause" which crystallized was the extreme rift between the divisions of Custody and Individual Treatment. Father Cahill, the Catholic chaplain who had worked with both divisions for years, expressed surprise at such a revelation. Deputy Bacon and I admitted that there were differences of opinion on a few points, but that there was agreement on the vast majority of points, and that the "rift" had been grossly exaggerated.

The idea of a rift was a convenient and plausible "intellectual discovery," however, and easy to promote. Consequently, most writers, not to be left with the minority, agreed that the extreme rift between these two divisions in the prison administration not only existed, but was a primary cause of the riot. In turn, such reporting and writing caused an extreme rift between the two divisions to which everyone could point for confirmation. "Causes" of riots seem to be more closely associated with the numbers and prestige of the writers and their productions than with the total situation as it actually exists.

The causes of the riot in Michigan were given as many and varied situations, most of them to some extent real. Governor Williams blamed it on the legislature for its budget cutting and short-sighted economy. The legislature said it was the administrative policies of Governor Williams' appointee, Commissioner of Corrections, Earnest C. Brooks. The excessively large size of the institution was cited unanimously, a "discovery" that everyone had discovered long before the riot. Lack of facilities for the segregation of inmates was cited as a cause. James V. Bennett, Director of the United States Bureau of Prisons, thought that the true cause of the Michigan riot was in the past history of politics in prison and the legislature's policy of saving money by keeping pay below that of other Northern prisons and jamming 6,400 men in a single institution.

After several months of blaming and counterblaming, the opinion seemed to be that responsibility for the riot "was widely distributed among prison officials, the governor, and the state legislature, as well as the people of Michigan who had seen a succession of prison scandals and investigations occur during the past decade without demanding more than superficial corrective measures."[1] After nearly a year of verbiage flowing toward causes of the riot, the "causes" seemed to crystallize. Consensus seemed to be that the riot was due to a combination of causes: (1) the excessive size of the State Prison of Southern Michigan, (2) the heterogeneous population, (3) the overcrowding and consequent lack of segregation, (4) understaffing, and (5) inadequate training programs for guard personnel.

Causes of prison riots other than Michigan's are equally difficult to determine and I suspect that the "causes" similarly became crystallized through volume of writing. Several writers and committees have concerned themselves with riot causes in general. Academic criminologists, newspaper report-

---

[1] Presthus, R. Vance; *The Jackson Prison Riot: A Study in Administration and Politics*, third draft of unpublished manuscript, Michigan State College, 1953, p. 46.

ers, prison men, and inmates and ex-inmates have made their contributions. Dr. Kinsey reported in 1955 that some riots are caused by tensions arising in normal prisoners from sexual frustrations.

Summarizing these generalizations is difficult, except to note that opinions as to the causes of riots differ according to the vantage point from which the author is viewing the riots. The academic criminologists seem to emphasize more than others the results of (1) idleness, (2) dangerously low budgets, and (3) poor pay for personnel.

Newspaper reporters tended to emphasize (1) politics from outside the prison and (2) slack administration within the prison.

Prison men emphasized (1) overcrowding, (2) political interference with prison operation, and (3) the "agitating" influence of the press and radio which helped to promote the "epidemic" of rioting.

The inmates and ex-inmates tended to stress (1) "too many little men in big jobs" in prisons, (2) persons treated as a mob tend to think as a mob, and (3) public opinion too apathetic to care about corrections.

Professor Frank Flynn of Chicago referred to the "dehumanizing programs" in prison, such as mass treatment, mass feeding, mass discipline, idleness, despotic and tyrannical rule, and limited contacts with the outside.[2] Ex-inmate "Jack Clair" emphasized the apathy of the general public, which he called "GP," and the large number of incompetent men in prison work.[3]

The Committee on Riots of the American Prison Association issued a pamphlet on *Prison Riots and Disturbances,* in which the "basic" causes for riots were differentiated from the "immediate causes."[4] They listed as basic causes, (1) in-

---

[2] Flynn, Frank T.; "Behind the Prison Riots," *The Social Service Review,* March, 1953, Vol. XXVII, No. 1, pp. 73–86.

[3] Clair, Jack; "The Story Behind Prison Rioting," *Pic,* Sept., 1952, Vol. 23, No. 4, pp. 12–15, 80.

[4] Committee on Riots; *Prison Disturbances and Riots,* May, 1953, American Prison Association.

adequate financial support and official and public indifference, (2) substandard personnel, (3) enforced idleness, (4) lack of professional leadership and professional programs, (5) excessive size and overcrowding of institutions, (6) political domination and motivation of management, and (7) unwise sentencing and parole practices. "The immediate causes given out for a prison riot are usually only symptoms of more basic causes," the Committee on Riots reported.[5] These may be bad food, brutality, inept management, lax discipline, and similar factors.

From the mass of literature on the causes of prison riots, a pattern emerges. This emergence is on the same basis as has been the previous emergence of "causes" of single riots—the volume of agreement in the writing. Most generalizing writers tend to agree that riots are caused by (1) overcrowding, (2) idleness, (3) dangerously low budgets, (4) political interference in prison management, (5) public opinion against rehabilitative methods or treatment, which has been interpreted as "sentimental" or "coddling," (6) employment of men in responsible prison positions who have neither the ability nor the professional qualifications for the job, (7) unwise or inconsistent sentencing and parole procedure, and (8) poor segregation.

After reviewing these causes, I find myself wondering why riots have been reported from California, New Jersey, Michigan, New York, and the United States Bureau of Prisons; and why they have not been reported from Mississippi, Oklahoma, and South Carolina.

Causes of any phenomena, social or otherwise, but particularly social phenomena like riots, are difficult to find. Most students of any phenomenon set up criteria for determining and identifying a "cause." It is not conclusive that because one activity occurs just before another activity occurs that the first *caused* the second. Even when the first activity occurs every time just before the second activity occurs, it cannot be defi-

---

[5] Ibid., p. 7.

nitely concluded that a causal relationship exists. The connection between cause and effect must be demonstrated. A swelling of the abdomen of a woman and the subsequent birth of a baby does not mean that the swelling of the abdomen caused the birth, although the former precedes the latter every time. The cause of the birth, many would agree, was the conception that occurred several months before—generally, but not always, nowadays—during sexual union of two persons of opposite sexes. Perhaps the terms "antecedent" and "consequence" could be more correctly applied to this and other phenomena which are related to each other.

One of the basic criteria which all natural and social scientists hold to be necessary for a cause is that it be universal in its application. If a factor can be called a *cause*, then this factor must be present everywhere the phenomenon under observation occurs. On the other hand, everywhere that factor is present, the phenomenon under observation must occur. If such is not the case, then the factor cannot be called a *cause*.

In the application of this criterion to all of the "causes" thus far listed with rioting in prison, it is difficult to find a *cause* which was present at all prison riots. On the other hand, I know of many prisons which have conditions as listed among these "causes," but which have never reported a riot. I am acquainted with prisons with more overcrowding problems, more idleness, lower budgets, as much political interference, operating in the same or more conservative public opinion milieu, employing poorer trained personnel, serving worse food, and have poorer segregation than the riot-struck prisons of Michigan, New York, California, Illinois, New Jersey, and Ohio. Yet these prisons have never reported a riot.

Further examination of the "causes" listed for riots and their application to prisons in which riots have occurred and those in which riots have not occurred reveal that not one factor thus far listed can be considered to be a "cause." No constellation of factors thus far listed has occurred in every riot or has caused a riot everywhere it has occurred. It is obvious that the "investigators" have been satisfied with super-

ficial reasons sufficient to placate public opinion. Dr. Lowell
J. Carr of the University of Michigan shares this opinion and
made such a statement when the University of Michigan dis-
continued its curriculum in corrections.

All the riots seem to have elements of protest in them,
though in many cases that protest has not been verbalized.
Most of the verbalized protests have been in respect to food
and similar tangible items. Much of the protest, too, has been
against restrictive and rigid regulations or policies. Specific
protests of this nature have been against the warden's denying
visits or mail to everyone for a period of two weeks because
he had been hissed at by the inmates. The riots have been
protests against something, rather than struggles for something,
though few positive demands may be made to correct the issues
under protest.

A few riots have occurred under prison administrations
that have provided no constructive means for the inmates to
express aggression. Many psychologists, psychoanalysts, and
psychiatrists have suggested that conflicts within the personality generate frustration which may be resolved by aggression.
The frustration-aggression hypothesis holds that aggression
may always be traced to frustration. One of the most illustra-
tive demonstrations of the use of aggression in human behavior
is incorporated in the Szondi projective technique for evaluating personality. Persons who are not able to discharge their aggressions steadily experience a paroxysmal accumulation of
energy which must be released periodically. The epileptic
convulsion may be an extreme demonstration of this periodic
release of energy. Psychiatrists have pointed out that in the
treatment by electric shock or other types of shock (in which
convulsion must be produced to be effective), the patient
becomes quite co-operative, relaxed, and docile, although prior
to the treatment the patient may have been irritable and
hostile. Most of us express our aggression steadily by short
emotional outbursts at home, football games or boxing match-
es, ill-concealed insults and sarcasm, and a myriad similar
techniques. In the prison situation, the steady release of ag-

gression through inmate counselors, law libraries, music, athletic competition, manuscript writing, art, carvings, and other means release accumulations of energy that need expression. This principle would explain the universal interest in boxing in prisons.

In searching for the balances between expression and suppression in terms of custodial control, it is desired that the relations between the administrator and the inmates should be such that expression is permitted and that the accumulation of energy within the group does not turn to violent expression. Means should be provided whereby a steady and even expression of hostility may be afforded the inmate. In prisons where riots have been reported, this freedom of expression has not been fully recognized.

It is noted that the same principle regarding the accumulation of aggression and its expression in socially approved channels may be applied to any group behavior whether it be public reaction to a riot or frustration as a result of differences in ideology. Group aggression needs to find expression in socially accepted channels. It may be channeled into a police action in Korea, the finding of a scapegoat, or the activity of a politically appointed fact-finding committee.

Riots do not occur in minimum-security institutions. In these institutions, custodial control of inmate activity is lessened. Further, there is freedom of action and movement, so that aggression can be steadily released in normal channels. Social intercourse between people is more nearly normal in these wall-less institutions than in most walled institutions. Because of the absence of restraining devices, too, the program must be better in order to keep the inmates interested. The program becomes its own custody, its own discipline. Consequently, the minds and thinking of the inmates are more likely to be occupied in constructive channels.

A strong administration which is attuned to the rehabilitation objectives and is able to communicate that philosophy to the inmate body can achieve its primary objective peacefully. Many inmates in prison are "starved" for some sort of

help. I have had many beg for psychotherapy when the staff
was so heavily laden with volume of work that there was no
possibility of taking advantage of the inmate's readiness to
accept the help we wanted so much to provide.

It has been observed that prison riots occur in institutions
which have strong administrations. California, for instance,
has a strong administration. It has what could be considered
a "treatment" approach. On the other hand, a riot occurred
in New Mexico where there is no "treatment" program because the deputy warden was "too tough." Riots have occurred
in New Jersey, Michigan, Illinois, and Ohio, where the administrations have been sufficiently strong in numbers to
exert custodial control over the prisoners. On the other hand,
in many prisons where the administration was not strong and
where insufficient money was provided in the budgets to hire
adequate numbers of custodial officers and other personnel,
there have been no riots.

When an insufficient number of personnel is provided by
the legislature, some of the routine work necessary to operate
the institution must be performed by inmate help under some
sort of supervision by guards. As a matter of fact, it is usually
by way of inmate help that the limits of progressive programs
are extended. For instance, when classification sections are
begun, inmate clerks and typists are usually called upon to do
work which is confidential in nature, in order to get the work
done. Group intelligence and aptitude tests are frequently
given and scored by inmates under supervision of a civilian
psychologist or educational director.

The personnel in prison who select these inmate workers
prefer the capable inmates. In many prisons, these capable
inmates are used for almost all clerical functions, to open
gates with keys, to keep the accounts, to operate the recreation
program, publish the prison paper, and to operate the inmate
store or canteen. In some prisons, inmates are used as guides
for visitors. In some cases, where supervision is lax, the inmates
who operate the inmate store or canteen may retain all the
profits of the store except that necessary to replenish the stock.

In some prisons, preferred cell changes and preferred job assignments may be acquired by the inmate with an item of barter or personal service which is given in exchange for preferred treatment to the inmate clerk who works in the position which enables him, by default or neglect on the part of his civilian supervisor, to control cell or job changes.

Where these capable inmates have special privileges or positions which enable them to exploit other less fortunate persons or enjoy prestige reward, these capable inmates have an interest in maintaining the status quo. This provides social control and gives stability to the inmate body to which prison men refer when they say that "lifers stabilize the prison." It is an admission that the administration is not completely in control. Because of his investment in the existing social order and the interest he has in maintaining his position in it, the capable inmate will act to preserve the peace and maintain the present order within the prison. Few riots are reported from these prisons.

In prisons where the administration is sufficiently strong to control cell and job changes and all other phases of routine administration and to enforce a high level of discipline without the assistance of inmates, the capable inmates do not have these special privileges and advantageous positions which enable them to exploit other inmates or control them. As a consequence, these capable inmates are not so much interested in maintaining the status quo. From these prisons, such as New Jersey, Michigan, New York, and Illinois, prison riots are reported. The control from within the inmate body and the stability which capable inmates with an interest in the status quo provide are not present.

I am not prepared to assert that strong administrations cause riots and weak administrations avoid them. A strong administration with a philosophy attuned to the rehabilitation of men, and sufficiently adequate communication so that the inmate body knows it, can be the most effective in achieving its primary objectives, and do it peacefully. It is apparent, however, that force begets force. If the administration is strong, then it can afford to avoid a direct show of force. The nature of the relations between the strong administration and the inmate body in the prison is crucial in operating a prison. If the administration is strong and the inmate body feels that it is being oppressed, then a potential riot is generated.

Riots have occurred in prisons with strong administrations when these administrations assert their strength in oppressive ways to the neglect of the treatment of the men they serve. Such riots have occurred in Colorado and New Mexico.

Riots have occurred when strong administrations set themselves apart and ignore the inmates. "Transitory" administrations during political changes leave the inmates with a feeling that the "job" or "political plum" is what is important to the leaders, rather than the men themselves. The inmates in a prison and the administration of the prison generally think widely apart in terms of social values and objectives in penology. With little basis for communication, verbal negotiation breaks down before it starts on a formal basis, and physical violence results. For example, witness the riot in the coal mine at the Kansas State Penitentiary in 1915.

A strong administration which does not let the inmate body know what it is doing and why it is doing it may have riots. For instance, the Sing Sing riots during the disagreements between Warden Thomas Mott Osborne and Superintendent of Prisons Riley were immediately caused by transfers of men from Sing Sing to other prisons. The lists were made by Riley in Albany, based on no logic or reasoning that could be detected at Sing Sing. Nobody ever found out on what basis Riley selected the men for transfers.

A strong administration can avoid riots by excessive custodial procedures, in which case the prisoners are regimented severely, all decisions made for them, and corporal punishment used. Riots have not been reported from some of these institutions. Of course, the pent-up hostility may be released against society when the prisoner is released. The success of the chain gang in the reformation of prisoners has never been publicized.

When inmates riot, it means that there remains in the inmate body sufficient morale and motivation for self-improvement to take action, but they are unable to organize and channel that action constructively.

Riots do not occur when inmate morale is exceptionally good, nor do they occur when inmate morale is very bad, but they may occur when inmate morale is good enough to sense possible success in actively demonstrating against undesirable treatment. Most of the "causes" of riots as listed by writers, like overcrowding, idleness, and the like, are factors which impair morale. It might be noted here that the news broadcasts of riots in other prisons that were sufficiently successful to embarrass the administrations may influence the inmate morale toward rioting, given other conditions creating the need for releasing aggression.

Revolution comes when oppressed peoples become sufficiently enlightened and able to strike back. Such was the theme of the American Revolution, the French Revolution, and that against czarist Russia. Such has been the theme in the history of prison riots. Such social changes occur when a few capable people get an idea and believe that they have a chance of putting it into effect. This is true as well in prison riots. We have been unable to find a prison riot in which the leaders were not capable, in which there was not a "progressive idea," even if it were only in getting rid of the old, and in which the leaders saw no chance of winning. In many of these riots, there was no attempt to escape, so that was not the purpose of rioting. In prisons where there are no capable inmates, no ideas and no chance of winning, no riots have been reported. As Walter McGraw so capably put it in a series of broadcasts for NBC in 1953, "Inmates can be clubbed into submission, but they are not reformed in the process."

Riots may occur sooner when two or more philosophies or policies are in conflict. In the first place, division of administration creates a morale problem. In the second place, the presence of a philosophy which the inmates favor gives them hope that aggressive action may assist in swinging the administration in the favored direction.

There has not been a riot, to my knowledge, reported from a prison in which the administration may properly be considered "weak." All the riots have been reported from prisons with administrations strong enough to be effective inside the walls. A weak administration that permits the capable inmates to operate many phases of the prison avoids riots through that control exerted by these capable inmates who have a vested interest in the status quo.

Riots may be considered to be the "growing pains of penal progress." They occur when rival philosophies of penal treatment are being exercised in competition. The inmates develop a feeling of resentment toward one and favor toward the other, and more frequently than not, the professional psychologist, sociologist, social worker, and progressive criminologist, with the inmates, favor the "progressive" philosophy, while the custodial personnel from the "old school" favor more restrictive methods. Riots have been considered a spontaneous manifestation of the aggression generated by frustration caused by seeming lack of movement in the favored direction. Hence, many riots may be interpreted as protests against restrictive methods.

If a prison has no riots, one can suspect that either the administration is both strong and adequate, which can partially be determined by the recidivism rates of its parolees or dischargees, or else insufficient progress is being made. Constructive action to avoid riots and still maintain a strong administration would involve considerable implementation in the majority of American prisons.

"Causes" are not really the most important phase of prison rioting from the administrative point of view. The public relations phase, which I neglected in the Michigan riot, determines to a great extent the direction of the modifications of program that are bound to come after a riot. One of the most convenient political strategems following riots has been the fact-finding committee or board of inquiry, usually appointed by the governor or other high state official. The purpose is secondarily to get the truth of what happened, but primarily to give the governor some point of origin from which he can take political action. By the time several weeks roll by, the actual truth of what happened and the "causes" cease to matter, and "Where do we go from here?" becomes paramount.

Based on the review of many riots and of several prisons which have never had riots, I would suggest several hypotheses for further exploration.

1. Rebellion and riots cannot begin in the absence of a real problem.
2. Riots can always be interpreted as a protest against restriction or punishment, rather than a struggle for something.
3. A prison administration which provides the inmates no means of expressing aggression in a constructive way must look for that aggression to be expressed destructively.
4. Riots do not occur in minimum-security institutions where there is no custodial oppression, where there is room for freedom of action and movement, and where the program must be sufficiently interesting and constructive to occupy the thinking of the inmate body.
5. A strong administration which is attuned to the rehabilitation objectives, and is able to communicate that philosophy to the inmate body, can achieve its primary objectives peacefully.
6. A strong administration which asserts its strength to the neglect of the men it purports to serve may have riots.
7. A strong administration which sets itself apart from the inmate body it serves with no form of communication, either by using capable inmates in key inmate jobs or in some type of participation in administration by way of an advisory council, may have riots.
8. A strong administration which does not let the inmate

body know what it is doing and why it is doing it may have riots.

9. A strong administration can avoid riots by excessive custodial procedures, in which case the prisoners are severely regimented and virtually clubbed into submission, and the hostility is held inward, only to be released on society when the prisoners are paroled or discharged from prison.

10. When prisoners riot, it means that there remains in the inmate body sufficient morale and motivation for self-improvement to take action, but they are unable to organize and channel that action constructively.

11. Riots do not occur when inmate morale is exceptionally good, nor do they occur when inmate morale is very bad, but they may occur when inmate morale is good enough to sense possible success in actively demonstrating against undesirable factors. Most of the "causes" of riots as listed by writers, like overcrowding, idleness, and the like, are factors which impair morale.

12. A weak administration that permits the capable inmates to operate many phases of the prison will avoid riots through the control exerted by these capable inmates who have an interest in the status quo.

13. Riots may be called the "growing pains of progress" in prisons because they occur when rival philosophies of penal treatment are being exercised in competition, without being integrated, and the inmates develop a feeling of resentment toward one and favor toward the other. The riot is a manifestation of the aggression generated by frustration caused by lack of sufficient movement in the favored direction.

14. If a prison has no riots, one can suspect that either the administration is both strong and adequate, or else insufficient progress is being made.

15. The most important phase of prison rioting from the administrative standpoint is not what caused it, but how it has been interpreted to the public. Governors'

"fact-finding committees" have been successfully used in most major riots as political strategems.

While it is desirable to have a peaceful prison, it is more important to have an effective one. Effectiveness is predicated on both strength and understanding. An effective prison without riots can be built—one with a strong administration which, like a strong father, can use its strength in an understanding and judicious manner, helping and permitting emotionally immature personalities to mature. It takes a treatment orientation, though, to understand and use the dynamics of human behavior and the processes of therapy for the betterment of society. The treatment approach must prevail to be effective. Treatment and custody should compatibly intertwine—but custody can't come first.